AN INTELLIGENCE SUMMARY

ENEMY ON LUZON

Published by Books Express Publishing
Copyright © Books Express, 2011
ISBN 978-1-780391-98-4

Books Express publications are available from all good retail and online booksellers. For publishing proposals and direct ordering please contact us at: info@books-express.com

**GENERAL HEADQUARTERS
UNITED STATES ARMY FORCES, PACIFIC**
MILITARY INTELLIGENCE SECTION, GENERAL STAFF

PREFACE

The Sixth Army and its component Corps and Divisions have written a brilliant record in the Campaigns of the South West Pacific.

The intelligence factor in these Campaigns, its application in combat, with all its phases, and the use of the product of G. H. Q. intelligence agencies have established a skillful pattern of intelligence in the field of which the Assistant Chief of Staff, G-2 Sixth Army, can well be proud.

C. A. Willoughby
Major General, G.S.C.,
Asst. Chief of Staff, G-2

RESTRICTED

HEADQUARTERS SIXTH ARMY
Office of the Assistant Chief of Staff, G-2
APO 442

1 December 1945

This publication is intended to present a historical review of outstanding intelligence developments in Sixth Army during the Luzon operation.

The campaign on Luzon presented situations and problems unique in the Southwest Pacific war against the Japanese. For the first time battle was joined on a large land mass which gave both sides the capability of large-scale maneuver. For the first time also, the enemy had an armored division to employ. He brought a number of new weapons to light. His tendency to form conglomerate combat organizations and to intermingle units was indulged to an unprecedented extent. Cave and tunnel warfare constituted an important part of the Japanese defense of the island. These and similar developments in their intelligence implications are discussed in this publication.

The enemy's dogged defense of a large city, that of Manila, was also unique in Southwest Pacific operations; inasmuch, however, as the account of that defense was fully described in another publication, "The Battle of Manila", a report by XIV Corps published by this office, it is not being included in this survey.

H. V. WHITE,
Colonel, G. S. C.,
AC of S, G-2.

RESTRICTED

TABLE OF CONTENTS

CHAPTER	TITLE	PAGE
Chapter I	A SHORT HISTORY OF THE LUZON CAMPAIGN	1-20
Chapter II	ENEMY TACTICS EMPLOYED	21-70
Chapter III	COUNTERINTELLIGENCE PROCEDURES	71-86
Chapter IV	SPECIAL RECONNAISSANCE OPERATIONS	87-118
Chapter V	PHOTOGRAPHIC AND TOPOGRAPHIC INTELLIGENCE	119-128
Chapter VI	TRANSLATION AND INTERROGATION	129-136
Chapter VII	PSYCHOLOGICAL WARFARE METHODS	137-140
Chapter VIII	ENEMY ORDER OF BATTLE	141-191
Chapter IX	TECHNICAL INTELLIGENCE DATA	192-219
Chapter X	ENEMY MATERIEL CAPTURED OR DESTROYED	220-230

Note: For Map of Luzon
Refer to Back of
Book.

CHAPTER I

A SHORT HISTORY OF THE LUZON CAMPAIGN

INTRODUCTION:

As American forces moved west across the Pacific in 1944, General Yamashita, forced to consider plans for the defense of Luzon, was faced with two alternatives—he could choose a decisive battle in the Central Plain in which case an unfavorable turn of events would mean the end of all organized resistance on Luzon, or he could sacrifice Manila, the Central Plain, and the airfield centers and withdraw to the mountains to fight a long delaying action. A captured Japanese 26th Division estimate of the situation, which obviously reflected the opinion of higher headquarters, revealed that the Japs recognized their inability to halt an advance through the Central Plain because of our overwhelming superior power, particularly in respect to armor. The estimate, dated September 1944, was published when the 26th Division was stationed in the Lingayen Gulf area and at a time when the enemy fleet was relatively intact, when the Japanese still had a considerable air force in the Philippines, and before the heavy losses of the Leyte campaign had been incurred. Therefore, even when the Japanese were relatively strong on land, sea, and in the air, they had decided that they could not afford a decisive battle on the Central Plain, and that withdrawal into the mountains to fight a long delaying action was the better plan.

Prior to November 1944 Japanese combat troops on Luzon were disposed in the following areas: the 103rd division was in Northern Luzon, the 26th Division garrisoning the Lingayen area, the 58th Independent Mixed Brigade along the coast between San Fernando, La Union, and Damortis, the 2nd Armored Division in the Cabanatuan—

Sibul Springs area, the 8th Division in Batangas, and the 105th Division in Southeastern Luzon and the Bicol. By the end of December the bulk of the 26th Division (of which one regiment minus one battalion remained on the east coast of Luzon), and the 1st Division, which touched Luzon briefly, had been sent to Leyte; by that time also the 10th Division, the 19th Division (minus the equivalent of one infantry regiment) and the 23rd Division had arrived on Luzon.

Meanwhile, plans had been made for withdrawal to the mountains of Northern Luzon via Highway #5, to the mountains east of Manila, and to the hills west of Ft Stotsenburg. This withdrawal which began in early December was accelerated by our Mindoro landing. On 8 January, two days after our preliminary bombardment began, the 14th Area Army, highest Japanese ground forces Headquarters on the island, issued an order speeding the withdrawal. This order included the disposition of troops for defense. Five battalions of the 105th Division with as much artillery and as many engineers as possible were to move from Tayabas Province to Cabanatuan, protect Highway #5, and relieve the 2nd Armored Division so that the latter could move to Tarlac to stop our advance on Clark Field. At the same time the 10th Division, newly landed, was to concentrate in the Tayug area and protect the Highway #5 withdrawal route. The 23rd Division with the 57th IMB attached was to defend the Pozorrubio---Rosario area and the coast north to San Fernando (La Union). The 19th Division, strung out along Highway #9 between Bauang and Baguio, was to be prepared to reinforce or relieve the 23rd Division and the 58th IMB.

Not only were all major Japanese combat units except the 23rd Division and the 58th IMB on the move when our troops landed, but the landing area, the south shore of Lingayen Gulf, was undefended since the Japanese considered a landing there impossible. The enemy's orderly and planned redeployment of troops was, therefore, disrupted by our rapid and unopposed advance as well as by the merciless pounding of the escape routes from the air. Because of these factors and because the major portion of the redeployment began late, the bulk of the 10th and 105th Divisions failed to arrive along Highway #5 on time. The 2nd Armored Division was, therefore, employed to screen the Highway #5 withdrawal. This, naturally, left the road to Clark Field wide open, and our troops moved into the area against practically no opposition. A hastily formed force of approximately 27,000 Japanese, composed of miscellaneous air corps personnel, service troops, the major part of the 1st Raiding Group, and a few other combat troops, all under the command of Lt Gen Tsukada, withdrew into previously prepared positions in the hills west of Ft Stotsenburg to deny us the use of the airfields as long as possible. This total of 27,000 troops included about 6,000 Naval personnel under the command of Vice Admiral Kondo.

9 JANUARY - 7 FEBRUARY:

On 6 January, the first day of our preliminary naval bombardment, the enemy began to evacuate the lightly held beachhead area, blowing bridges, defensive installations, and supply dumps enroute. This evacuation extended south of the Agno River and west to Dasol Bay. As a result, on 9 January, Sixth Army, with two corps abreast, landed virtually unopposed on the beaches in the center of Lingayen Gulf.

On the Army right flank, in the XIV Corps zone, negligible opposition was encountered along Highways #3 and #13, and by 16 January our forces moving south had taken Camiling (approximately 80 airline miles northwest of Manila) against slight, scattered enemy resistance. In most instances the enemy evacuated the towns along our route of advance as our troops approached. The following week the enemy interposed little opposition to the Corps advance to the line Bamban--Concepcion--La Paz (approximately 55 airline miles northwest of Manila). The only large engagement was an attack by 200 enemy at Moncada during the night of 16-17 January; 61 Japanese were killed as the attack was repulsed. While enroute the Corps sent patrols as far east as Cabanatuan, south to Angeles, and west to O'Donnell; these patrols met scattered resistance only. During the week ending 31 January our forces continued their rapid movement to the south against very light opposition, occupying Angeles, Magalang, the Clark Fields, and San Fernando (Pampanga). Patrols, probing south in advance of the main body, reached almost to

Calumpit without opposition.

On the Corps right flank, however, the Tsukada Detachment offered stiff resistance in the hills west and southwest of Bamban and in the Ft Stotsenburg area. This force, employing artillery fire and infiltration attacks, was determined to prevent our utilization of the airfields as long as possible. In accordance with the general plan for the defense of Luzon, Lt Gen Tsukada, CG of the 1st Raiding Group, had issued orders weeks, possibly months, before our landing, for the construction of "protective installations" in the Bamban hills. These installations consisting of an elaborate tunnel and cave system extended over a front of 12,000 yards and to a depth of 20,000 yards. Orders stated that full advantage was to be taken of the difficult terrain, and that each position was to be defended until it became untenable at which time troops were to retire to other prepared positions in the rear. In the Stotsenburg area the enemy fought a light delaying action westward across Clark Field and then stubbornly defended from well-emplaced pillboxes in the western outskirts of Ft Stotsenburg. On 29 January, under cover of a counterattack supported by 9 tanks, the Japanese withdrew from this area to their prepared positions in the Bamban Hills. By 7 February the enemy had been pushed back about 5,000 yards into the hills by the U.S. 40th Division.

While the 40th Division was fighting in these hills, the U.S. 37th Division continued its advance south on Highway #3 and the 1st Cavalry Division began to concentrate on Cabanatuan by infiltration preparatory to a push on Manila along Highway #5. One brigade of the 1st Cavalry Division was motorized and on 1 February began to push south toward Manila. The concealed movement into Cabanatuan (approximately 60 airline miles north of Manila) and the speed of the advance gained tactical surprise. On 3 February, 66 hours after the time of departure, leading elements of the brigade entered the northern outskirts of Manila via Novaliches and Grace Park. There were from 1,500 to 2,000 Japanese along the route of advance but the speed and violence of the advance caught the enemy unprepared. During the advance the Novaliches Dam and the Balara Filters were taken intact. A Japanese battalion, located in the north cemetery area of Manila, failed to man the bulk of their defenses and two 120-mm guns sited to cover the highway east of the airstrip were never fired. The 37th Division, meanwhile, continued its rapid advance down Highway #3 toward Manila, and entered the city simultaneously with the 1st Cavalry Division. During this stage of its advance the 37th Division encountered strong opposition from stubborn enemy groups defending successive delaying positions south of Plaridel (approximately 18 airline miles northwest of Manila).

Within Manila, north of the Pasig River, the enemy fought a stubborn delaying action for several days. All approaches to the bridges over the Pasig were defended from well-constructed pillboxes, from buildings, and from other emplacements. Sniper and artillery fire harassed our troops while the enemy was destroying all buildings and installations that could be used by our troops for military purposes. By 7 February the majority of the Japanese north of the Pasig had withdrawn across the river blowing the bridges behind them.

Concurrently with the movement south on Manila, the 11th Airborne Division pushed north from Batangas Province and Tagaytay Ridge. On 31 January elements of the Division (under Eighth Army control) made an amphibious landing at Nasugbu on the west coast of Batangas Province. On 1 February leading elements contacted an estimated enemy battalion on Highway #17 approximately 5 miles west of Tagaytay City. On 3 February one regiment of the Division jumped near Tagaytay Ridge, encountered little opposition and joined troops moving north from Nasugbu. The next day, leading elements reached Paranaque (approximately 10 miles south of Manila) where they encountered strong enemy positions covering the bridge in the town. This opposition was quickly overcome and the troops moved north to Nichols Field where they were held up by heavily-defended caves and pillbox positions. On 7 February the Division was engaged in the slow and difficult task of reducing these positions.

The situation on Sixth Army's left flank, in the I Corps zone, presented a different picture from that on the right flank. Although here too our troops landed virtually unopposed, they immediately encountered strong enemy defenses in the hills to the east and northeast. These defenses, manned by the 23rd Division with the 58th IMB attached, extended along the line Pozorrubio—Rosario—Aringay. For two weeks stubborn and skillful enemy resistance along the Damortis—Rosario road held up our advance. Although by 24 January the main Japanese defenses along the road in the vicinity of Amlang had been overcome, the enemy still controlled the Rosario corridor. Defenses consisted of bunkers supported by fire pits, trenches, and numerous tunnels.

The pocket of Japanese in elaborate defenses in the Cabaruan Hills was eliminated by elements of the 6th Division. Several days of heavy ground fighting and artillery and air bombardment were necessary to dislodge them; a total of 1,232 enemy troops being killed during the two weeks of fighting in this area.

During the next week enemy infantry, supported by artillery and mortars, bitterly contested our advance east along the road, but by 31 January Rosario was taken and the entire road secured. Other elements of the reinforced 23rd Division strongly resisted our advance in the Pozorrubio and Mt Alava areas; however, by 31 January enemy opposition had been overcome. By 7 February our troops were mopping up enemy stragglers and repulsing numerous minor infiltration raids.

During the week ending 17 January other elements of I Corps attacked east towards Binalonan and San Manuel just south of the foothills. This area was defended by the 2nd Armored Division plus two attached battalions of miscellaneous infantry troops. Our advance to the general line San Manuel—Asingan—San Leon was impeded by strong delaying positions at the main road junctions, and by 24 January our troops were meeting heavy resistance on the outskirts of San Manuel from infantry troops supported by tanks and artillery. South of San Manuel, our troops overcame a tank-supported defense at Urdaneta and continued eastwards. From 24 to 28 January a bitter fight for San Manuel took place. Enemy tanks, infantry, and artillery defended each intersection and house; during the five-day engagement 755

Japanese were killed and 45 enemy tanks were destroyed. Simultaneously, other troops moving east from San Leon toward Umingan encountered heavy opposition from elements of the 2nd Armored Division at Pemienta (just west of Umingan). In the town of Umingan the enemy stubbornly clung to his defenses and resisted all our attacks for two days; meanwhile, other troops outflanked the town and moved southeast toward San Jose. These troops met and bypassed strong resistance at Lupao. By 7 February our troops had occupied San Jose against light opposition. Southwest of San Jose, the enemy held the town of Munoz against our attacking troops from 1 to 7 February. During the night of 6-7 February the enemy mounted a tank-infantry counterattack to cover a withdrawal east from the town. The withdrawing troops were annihilated by our forces who, though the enemy was unaware of it, had meanwhile occupied San Jose. In the battle for Munoz 1,242 Japanese were killed and 48 medium tanks, 4 light tanks, numerous trucks and artillery pieces were destroyed. East of San Manuel the enemy withdrew to the mountains and our troops occupied Tayug, San Nicolas, and Natividad.

Thus, by 7 February I Corps troops controlled the north end of the Central Plain except for a few isolated strongpoints which were being cleaned out. During the period between 9 January and 7 February the bulk of the 2nd Armored Division was destroyed. The piecemeal enemy commitment of tanks in repeated counterattacks, while admittedly delaying our advance, cost the enemy heavily; a total of 192 tanks were destroyed in the period.

8 FEBRUARY - 10 MARCH:

Throughout this entire period the 40th Division engaged the "RAN" Group under Lt Gen Tsukada in the Bamban Hills. In these hills the enemy had numerous AA guns ranging from 20-mm to 120-mm taken from Clark Field and hundreds of airplane machine guns removed from the wrecked planes. The guns, emplaced so as to be mutually supporting, were sited to cover the barren approaches. A majority of the positions were so well concealed that they were disclosed only when the guns opened fire. The many tunnels and caves were well stocked with supplies, each position being self sufficient in this respect. These cave positions had to be eliminated one at a time; foot troops had to cross barren ridges in the face of murderous crossfire from all types of automatic weapons and machine guns. Consequently, the reduction of these defenses was a slow, difficult, and costly job. By 10 March, however, the main defenses had been overcome. Isolated strongpoints only remained, and mopping up extended into mid-April. In this action, 22,336 of an estimated 27,000 enemy troops were killed by our forces, approximately 4,000-5,000 of these being killed after 10 March during mopping-up operations.

As for Manila, it soon became clear that such enemy forces, as were still there, were committed to a suicidal defense of the city, by way of denying our use of it as a base as long as possible. The city was divided into two defensive areas; the area north of the Pasig was the responsibility of the Army and the area south of the Pasig was the responsibility of the Navy. The main stand was planned by the Navy south of the river; in the north part of the city the Army was to delay, destroying all buildings and important installations before retiring across the river. In their withdrawal across the Pasig, they were to blow all bridges behind them. The Japanese force south of the Pasig, called the Manila Naval Defense Force, was commanded by Admiral Iwobuchi and was composed of 13,000 Naval personnel. There were approximately 5,000 Army troops in the Manila area, some of whom retired across the river and joined the Naval Defense Force. The troops were a heterogeneous group and were short of weapons. South of the river, Admiral Iwobuchi chose the Intramuros and Ermita Districts as the core of his defense. Though the enemy's plan worked according to schedule, he was able to hold out only for about one month.

Our forces attacked Manila from three directions: the 37th Division attacked south across the Pasig; the 1st Cavalry Division moved southeast through Quezon City and then west to Manila Bay, thus, isolating the Japanese in the Intramuros and Ermita sections; and the 11th Airborne Division attacked north across Nichols Field. Although during the week ending 14 February the Japanese offered heavy resistance to the 37th Division, the 1st Cavalry Division met little opposition in its enveloping movement southeast and then west to Manila Bay. Farther to the south our troops overcame stiff resistance on Nichols Field and on 13 February occupied Cavite without much opposition. During this week the stiff enemy resistance in the Polo--Obando area just north of Manila was also overcome. In the next 7 days organized enemy resistance was broken except in the Intramuros and Ermita areas. Throughout the week small groups of Japanese, unable to reach the main enemy defenses in the city, were contacted while attempting to evacuate to the hills east of Manila.

Inside their main defenses in the Intramuros and Ermita area, the Japanese defended from street-to-street, house-to-house, and room-to-room. By 25 February, however, the entire city had been cleared except for three buildings just outside of Intramuros. The last enemy stand in the fanatical defense of the city took place inside these three buildings. Early in the first week of March, however, these were taken and the siege of Manila was ended. During the violent action in the city 17,342 out of approximately 18,000 Japanese defenders were killed.

While the XIV Corps was sweeping down the Central Plain toward Manila, the 38th Division, reinforced, under command of XI Corps landed at La Paz (west coast, northwest of Subic Bay) on 29 January. No opposition was offered by the enemy to our landing and our troops pushed inland to Olongapo where they made first contact. The enemy withdrew and our forces continued their advance. The enemy was first engaged in strength in the Zigzag Pass. In the Bataan area enemy troops numbered approximately 5,000, the main unit being the 39th Infantry Regiment, 10th Division.

The terrain in the Pass was well suited to defense and, as usual, the enemy took full advantage of it. Caves and pillboxes overlooking the Pass had been constructed and the Japanese offered fanatical defense; however, by 14 February this opposition was overcome and our forces pushed through the Pass and south into Bataan without much opposition. During the action in the Pass and during the subsequent mopping up in Bataan, which continued into

April, 4,412 out of the estimated 5,000 Japanese were counted dead.

Figure 1 - ZIGZAG PASS

On 15 February, in a move designed to open Manila Bay to our shipping, elements of the XI Corps landed unopposed at Mariveles (south tip of Bataan Peninsula) and moved rapidly inland to join troops moving south along the east coast of the Peninsula. The next day, 16 February, elements of the 34th Infantry Regiment attached to the 38th Division made a shore-to-shore landing on Corregidor, and simultaneously the 503rd Parachute Regiment dropped on the Island. The Corregidor Defense Force with a strength of 6,700 men was charged with the defense of Manila Bay. About 5,000 were on Corregidor itself and the remainder on the other islands. Although the enemy outnumbered our troops, the surprise of the parachute landing and the speed of our subsequent attack prevented them from organizing effective opposition.

Fighting on Corregidor was unusual in that there was

no "front". Taking advantage of the extensive tunnel system, the enemy was constantly bobbing up in the middle and rear of our troops. When on about 21 February the Japanese recognized that the end was near, they set off large explosions in the numerous ammunition-filled caves in attempts to kill our troops while they themselves were supposedly committing suicide. Prisoners of war later stated that most of the tunnels were compartmentalized, and, although many Japanese lost their lives in the explsions, not every blast constituted an act of mass suicide. Ten days after the initial landing, 26 February, the island was secured and about 4,800 out of the 5,000 original defenders had been killed. The other small islands in Manila Bay were quickly captured against light opposition and the Bay opened to our shipping.

    The mountains east and northeast of Manila, fortified in the same manner as the Bamban Hills and for the same purpose, namely to delay, were occupied by 30,000 troops under the Shimbu Shudan, later 41st Army Corps, commanded by Lt Gen Yokoyama, CG of the 8th Division. The Corps was divided into three sectors—1) the Noguchi Heidan located around Antipolo, 2) the Kobayashi Heidan around Montalban, and 3) the Kawashima Heidan in the vicinity of Ipo. The Noguchi Heidan was composed mainly of 3 battalions of the 105th Division, one battalion from the 17th Infantry Regiment, 8th Division, and some provisional battalions plus miscellaneous Gyoro (suicide boat) troops. Several provisional infantry battalions, the 31st Infantry Regiment (minus 1 battalion) of the 8th Division, and one battalion of the 105th Division comprised the main force of the Kobayashi Heidan. The main part of the Kawashima Heidan consisted of one battalion from the 105th Division, one Gyoro battalion, and two regiments formed from miscellaneous signal troops.

    About the middle of February elements of the U.S. 1st Cavalry Division and the 6th Division moved into the hills east of Manila to secure the city from artillery fire and harassing attacks. Initially, little opposition was encountered and our troops occupied Marikina. During the week ending 21 February, however, our forces received numerous small attacks at widely separated points. These attacks, according to captured documents, were intended as part of a large scale counterattack by the Shimbu Shudan to retake Manila. Failure to stage the large scale attack as ordered was probably due to lack of communications and to failure of the command structure in this polyglot formation.

During the last week in February our troops continued their eastward advance against light opposition and took Montalban. By 28 February, however, heavy resistance developed as our forces reached the main enemy positions northwest and southwest of Antipolo and east of Montalban. During the first ten days of March strong resistance was encountered in the center and south end of the Shimbu Line, but by 10 March our troops had occupied Antipolo, thus securing Manila from artillery bombardment from the east. At the north end of the line, patrol clashes characterized the activity throughout February and early March.

Figure 2 - WAWA--MONTALBAN AREA

The area south of Manila and Laguna de Bay was defended mainly by Gyoro (suicide boat) battalions, 2 battalions of the 17th Infantry Regiment and a battalion of the 31st Infantry Regiment, both of the 8th Division; the colonel of the 17th Infantry being in command. Starting about mid-February the 11th Airborne Division later joined by the 158th Regimental Combat Team moved south from the Manila area into Laguna and Cavite Provinces. By 10 March they had cleared these two provinces and most of Batangas Province except for small groups of stragglers attempting to evacuate to the east.

By mid-February our forces completely cleared the east portion of the north end of the Central Plain with the capture of Rizal and Bongabon. Thus, I Corps was in position to push north along Highway #5 toward Balete Pass, along the Villa Verde Trail toward Santa Fe, and along the Kennon Road toward Baguio. The Japanese initially defended these areas with combat troops disposed as follows: the 11th Independent Infantry Regiment, less one battalion, on the Old Spanish Trail (east of Highway #5), the equivalent of two regiments of the 10th Division along Highway #5, approximately 1,500 2nd Armored Division remnants along the Villa Verde Trail, and remnants of the 23rd Division and of the 58th IMB on the approaches to Baguio. The 19th Division, then in the Baguio area, never took part in the fighting and about 10 March moved north to Bontoc---Cervantes.

Throughout the last three weeks in February and during the first ten days of March our forces met heavy resistance in all three areas. Probably the greatest difficulty to be overcome was the terrain which afforded the enemy his most favorable opportunity on Luzon to emplace his weapons. With excellent artillery and air support our troops made some progress but the final job was one for the infantry. By 10 March the 25th Division moved north along Highway #5 to just south of Kapintalan, the 32nd Division moved up the Villa Verde Trail toward Imugan, and the 33rd Division advanced in the Sapit---Lawican area and along Highway #11 up to the vicinity of Camp 3.

Farther north, U.S. Army Forces in the Philippines, a guerrilla unit under Sixth Army direction, was encountering heavy resistance as it attacked San Fernando, La Union, and Vigan.

11 MARCH - 31 MAY:

During this period east of Manila, in the enemy 41st Army Corps area, our troops slowly and painstakingly eliminated the elaborate cave and tunnel defenses. It took approximately three months to overcome all organized resistance along the whole Shimbu Line.

During the last two weeks in March and throughout April heavy fighting took place in the center and south end of the line. By 21 March the enemy had been cleared from the Antipolo—Teresa—Morong areas; in the next seven days our troops continued to advance east against moderate to heavy resistance; and by 28 March New Bosoboso, a former enemy base, was occupied. Troops, attempting to advance northeast from New Bosoboso met heavy opposition from enemy forces protecting the escape route to the northeast.

During April and May the backbone of the Shimbu Line was broken, and the disorganized withdrawal of the remaining forces in this area started.

Attacking behind devastating napalm air strikes and intense artillery barrages, the 43rd Division, advancing from the south and southwest over the Metropolitan Road, and guerrilla forces closing in from the north, captured Ipo Dam and its installations intact on 17 May. From this date to the latter part of June small groups of Japanese were contacted attempting to evacuate to the east coast via the Umiray River; however, due to the rugged terrain and the lack of supplies this evacuation only postponed the inevitable death of the remaining stragglers from the northern portion of the Shimbu Line.

In the center and southern portions of the defense line occupied by the enemy 41st Corps, stubborn resistance including intense mortar and artillery fire was encountered in the first days of May in the Wawa Dam—Montalban area; however, during the latter half of May the mountainous area extending from Mt Oro southeast to Sampoloc was taken. Wawa Dam was secured intact and the escape route through San Andres was compromised.

Of the estimated 30,000 troops in the 41st Army Corps, our forces killed approximately 25,000. The remaining 5,000 evacuated into the mountains where many no doubt died from sickness or starvation. The total of 25,000 includes those killed in mopping-up activities during June.

During this period the 43rd Division and the 1st Cavalry Division effected a junction at Santa Cruz, thus, cutting off the withdrawal route of the enemy forces south of Laguna de Bay and forcing them to use cross-country routes to reach the east coast.

During the latter part of April and throughout May a hodge-podge enemy force was assembling at Infanta. These troops consisted of Naval forces and stragglers from the area east of Manila. An air strike on Infanta destroyed all available shipping and prevented the planned evacuation of these forces into northern Luzon via water. Meantime, the 1st Cavalry Division advanced up the Infanta road to the east coast against only small delaying detachments. By the latter part of May all organized resistance was broken and the remaining enemy troops withdrew into the hinterland northwest of the Agnos River; some attempted to reach northern Luzon via the east coast but were thwarted by guerrilla forces operating in the Dingalan Bay area.

South of Laguna de Bay composite Gyoro and infantry forces offered stiff resistance in the Lipa--Santo Tomas area for about four weeks. During the second week in April, however, enemy resistance weakened and a withdrawal, screened by stiff opposition in the Alaminos--San Pablo area, was made towards Mt Malepunyo. Although the terrain on Mt Malepunyo favored defense, the enemy's defense was not coordinated and the Sixth Army action consisted of numerous contacts with isolated strongpoints. Eenemy opposition collapsed early in May and the remaining Japanese withdrew in small groups eastward toward Mt Banahao. During the rest of May our forces mopped up enemy straggler groups moving in that direction.

On 1 April the 158th RCT made an unopposed landing at Legaspi in the Bicol. After two weeks of hard fighting in the Camilig area, enemy resistance collapsed and elements of the 158th RCT moved north to make contact with 1st Cavalry Division elements sweeping south through the northern Bicol provinces. During May mopping-up operations were in progress. By 30 June, 3,450 Japanese had been killed of the 4,000 enemy troops estimated to have been in the Bicol on 1 April.

From 11 March to 31 May, I Corps continued its attack to the north along Highway #5, the Villa Verde Trail and on the approaches to Baguio. Heavy opposition from enemy troops entrenched in caves and pillboxes and supported by considerable artillery made progress slow. By 1 June, however, Highway #5, as far north as Santa Fe, and the Villa Verde Trail to Imugan, were cleared and Baguio had been liberated.

Figure 3 - VICINITY OF BAGUIO

In the Baguio area stiff opposition was encountered by the 33rd Division on the Kennon Road from remnants of the 23rd Division and two provisional infantry battalions formed from service units. Our forces made slow but steady progress toward Baguio against tenacious opposition. Early in April the 37th Division elements moved to the San Fernando area, which area had been recaptured by USAFIP, Northern Luzon, on 14 March after heavy fighting. The division then launched an attack over Highway #9 to capture Baguio from the west. Heavy delaying action by the remaining elements of the 58th IMB and provisional infantry units impeded our rate of advance. By the middle of April advance elements of the 37th Division had taken the town of Philippine and the high ground adjacent to Baguio on the west and southwest.

During the advances of the 37th Division from the west

and the 33rd Division from the south a large-scale enemy evacuation of the major combat units in Baguio was started. The heavy movement of vehicles and troops along the Mountain Trail toward Bontoc, observed during the first part of April, represented the withdrawal of the 19th Division, last remaining enemy reserve on Luzon. The heterogeneous Baguio Defense Force, elements of the 58th IMB and the 23rd Division constituted the strong delaying force on the approaches to the mountain "stronghold".

By the latter part of April advance elements of the 37th and 33rd Divisions entered Baguio and found it almost completely evacuated. The capture of the town cut off the escape route of the enemy forces along the Kennon Road and in the mountainous area west of the road, and mopping-up of these enemy forces continued throughout May and June. Our forces continued their advances to the north securing Trinidad and Acop's Place along the Mountain Trail against only slight opposition from enemy strongpoints.

Farther to the east during this period our forces closed the vise on the bitterly-contested Balete Pass. By the last of May the 32nd Division advancing over the Villa Verde Trail joined forces with the 25th Division moving over Highway #5. In this action, one of the toughest of the Pacific War, the enemy defended from organized defensive installations in jungle-covered mountains over 5,000 feet in altitude.

Figure 4 - CAGAYAN VALLEY, VICINITY ECHAGUE

In attempting to prevent our entry into the Cagayan Valley, via Highway #5, Lt Gen Okamoto, Yasuji, commander of the enemy forces defending this route, committed the last remaining reserve from this sector. The remaining elements of the 10th Division, raiding units, Air Force units, service and shipping troops were pulled out of the Bagabag and Bayombong areas in a futile effort to stem our advances. This commitment militated against any future enemy capability in defending against our subsequent advances northward during June.

During this period Filipino guerrilla forces operating in Northern Luzon secured the entire coastal area from San Fernando to the west bank of the Cagayan River at Aparri. During May, guerrilla forces and composite American task forces secured the west bank of the Cagayan River from Ilagan to Aparri, thereby denying the enemy use of the river for transport of troops and supplies.

During the latter part of April and throughout May the Japanese 79th Brigade was practically wiped out while attempting to defend the Cervantes area. The Japanese 19th Division which had withdrawn from the Baguio area was continually harrassed by the guerrilla bands along the mountain trail in the vicinity of Bontoc. By the end of May combat patrols entered Cervantes; a southward trek by the enemy forces in the northern extremes of Luzon had begun and the remnants of the Japanese 19th Division and the 79th Brigade, depleted and starving, began heading for the Central Cagayan Valley. Nowhere in Luzon were there any Japanese troops not committed to the fight; even the so-called reserves constituting the 103rd Division and the 80th Brigade in the north Cagayan Valley were being contained by guerrilla forces. General Yamashita had withdrawn with his staff into the mountain fastness near Kiangan. The disintegration and destruction of the remainder of the enemy forces was only a matter of time.

1 JUNE - 30 JUNE:

In the southern area during the month of June our forces continued to meet slight resistance from isolated enemy groups in the Mt Purro and Santa Ines area. By the end of

June Santa Ines and the Lenatin River valley had been occupied by our forces and small groups of enemy attempting to reach the coast had been eliminated.

In the Infanta area 1st Cavalry troops and guerrilla forces compressed the remaining enemy into the upper reaches of the Agnos River where mopping-up activities were carreid out during the month of June. Elsewhere in the south, isolated enemy groups continued to be encountered throughout the month.

The month of June in the I Corps zone was marked by the utter destruction of all organized resistance in Northern Luzon. During the first 6 days of June, the partially motorized 37th Division jumped off from the recently-won Balete Pass area north on Highway #5 and advanced swiftly for a total of 17 miles. In the advance, 11 enemy medium tanks and approximately 500 Japanese troops were killed. The swiftness of the advance and the disorganization of the remaining enemy forces did not permit any substantial resistance to this advance; much enemy equipment and supplies were captured.

The 25th Division, during this same period, while conducting wide-spread, mopping-up operations in the Villa Verde Trail area, killed approximately 1,000 Japanese. The 6th Division, following the advance of the 37th Division up Highway #5, met considerable opposition from enemy strongpoints and defensive positions on either side of the highway. Numerous groups of enemy were engaged attempting to escape from the encirclement made by our forces along the Villa Verde Trail--Highway #5 trap.

Between the 6th and 20th of June the momentum of the drive by the 37th Division carried them through Cordon, Santiago, Echague, Cauayan, Nagulian and Ilagan. This drive was high-lighted by the relatively light resistance offered by the enemy to our flying column. However, to the rear of the column, bypassed enemy groups offered considerable resistance to elements of the 25th and 6th Divisions.

The last ten days of June were high-lighted by the

junction of our northern and southern forces and the complete domination of Highway #5 from Aparri south. On 21 June, the Connolly Force consisting of U.S. and guerrilla forces crossed the Cagayan River and occupied the town without opposition; the enemy having withdrawn to the south. Other elements of the Philippine forces crossed the river farther south and occupied Tuguegarao. A subsequent enemy attack against the town forced the guerrilla units to withdraw to more tenable positions west of the Cagayan River. On 23 June, paratroopers of the 11th Airborne Division dropped just south of Aparri without enemy interference, and on 24 June occupied Gattaran, 30 miles north of Tuguegarao. By 25 June, the paratroopers had reached the Dummun River Bridge. The next day, they made contact with the 37th Division, 3,000 yards east of Alcala. During this advance, from Balete Pass to the junction, 5,328 enemy were killed, and 421 Japanese and 911 Formosans were taken prisoner.

After the fall of Bagabag elements of the 6th Division moved northwest along Highway #4 toward Kiangan against light to moderate resistance to a point up to 1,800 yards southeast of Bolog. Here, approximately three enemy battalions manned strong defensive positions, which on 30 June our forces were still attacking.

During this period Philippine Army units continued their attack along Highway #4 on the Cervantes--Bessang area against units of the 19th Division. On 12 June Bessang was taken and shortly thereafter enemy resistance in the Cervantes area collapsed. The 19th Division, depleted by battle casualties, sickness and starvation, retreated east. For the rest of the month Philippine Army units mopped up the Cervantes area and patrolled to the east. On 22 June, patrols located well-prepared and well-organized defenses in the Tadian--Kayan area and spent the last week of June probing these positions.

During the Luzon campaign a total of 257,890 Japanese was identified on Luzon. This figure does not include 13,000 Formosan labor troops. Of this total, 173,563 were counted dead; an additional 57,605 were estimated to have been killed by artillery fire and aerial bombardments, sealed in caves, or to have died from sickness or starvation; 4,072 Japanese, 3,112 Formosans, and 113 Koreans were taken prisoner.

CHAPTER II

ENEMY TACTICS EMPLOYED

JAPANESE DEFENSE DOCTRINE - THE THEORY:

In October 1944 the Japanese General Staff Headquarters and Inspectorate General of Military Training published a "Manual for Defenses Against Landings (Provisional)"--translated by ATIS as Enemy Publication No. 384, 2 June 1945. The preface to the captured copy of the manual stated that it "contains important matters relative to the direct defense of vital coastal areas of Japan proper." Although published in October 1944 and thus predating the Philippine campaign as well as the battles for Iwo Jima and Okinawa, this document was the most important single expression made of the enemy's defense doctrine. First, since it was published by the Japanese General Staff Headquarters and Inspectorate General of Military Training, it had the stamp of approval of the highest military headquarters. Second, the treatise was one of the most complete and detailed tactical manuals published by the Japanese to come into our hands.

The main principles promulgated in this manual were as follows:

First and foremost, the doctrine of "annihilating the enemy at the water's edge" was formally abandoned. In fact, one would search in vain even to find this ancient and well-worn phrase in the treatise. Instead, the manual frankly conceded that "annihilation at the beach frequently fails; for example, in a situation where the enemy has air-superiority and command of the sea, and attacks with a vastly superior force." Thus, at this late date, Japanese commanders finally acknowledged that Allied forces would not attack with less than a "vastly superior force" or without air-superiority and command of the sea. "Annihilation at the water's edge" was therefore, with Oriental obliqueness, thrown out the window.

Beach positions were to be very lightly defended; the prescribed frontage for a company in defensive position along the coastline was 1,500-2,000 meters, and for a platoon 300 meters, figure which can be compared with the U.S. prescription of 500-800 yards maximum frontage for a company on the defense. The Japanese manual went on to state that in order to create a false illusion of strength, "it is especially advantageous to deceive the enemy into believing that dispositions are directly on the beach". This stratagem of employing dummy positions was successfully employed at Iwo Jima.

Secondly, heavy emphasis was placed upon the importance of developing an inland defense in depth (i.e., in the hills) with only rear guard and covering detachments on the beaches themselves. "Positions of the main line of resistance constitute the nuclei of the defense systems. They are usually key positions disposed on important ground favorable to withdrawal from the coast." Centers of resistance for units of battalion size were to be constructed in underground positions on high ground. They were to be self-sustaining, and organized not only for all-around defense but even for internal defense against the possibility of an Allied breakthrough and penetration of the position. Some artillery was to be assigned to battalions and companies and placed within the positions, so that in effect the garrison occupying a center of resistance was to be a self-contained task force.

Level terrain where our tanks and other mechanized equipment could be employed was verboten to the Japanese: "It is important to avoid being forced into open warfare with the enemy". Banzai charges were also frowned upon: "Whether performed during the day or night, major hasty and unorganized counterattacks often incur tremendous losses".

Thirdly, the role of artillery was clearly defined to be primarily for support in defense at the MLR (i.e. in the hills inland from the beach), and with the secondary mission of firing at landing craft and beachhead positions, in an effort to break up Allied landing attempts. Most of the artillery was to be emplaced behind the MLR; only limited quantities to be deployed at beach positions. "The opening fire of concealed guns should be withheld, and surprise weapons like the rocket gun must be kept under strict supervision", presumably to avoid the effect of our naval gunfire and counterbattery fire.

Fourthly, the manual stressed the importance of "Yugeki" (mobile attack) tactics—the suicide penetration squads, the individual soldiers with demolition kits and lunge or shoulder pack mines who dart out of foxholes into the paths of M-4s or swim out to LSTs, or who contrive in other ways to commit suicide in melodramatic style. Their behavior, familiar to every Pacific doughboy, was a nuisance threat deserving of respect and vigilant countermeasures. The manual advocated that specially picked and trained men should be used for these tactics and that they be trained as a separate arm, raised to status almost equivalent to the infantry and artillery branches. Plans for their use were to be well integrated with the general defense plan.

Enemy activity in the Philippines and, as far as could be gathered from reports, in the Bonins and in the Ryukus, amply bore out the conclusion that the tactical principles enunciated in this manual were carried out.

The manual itself, however, recognized some basic defects in cave defense, notably the problem of maintaining morale. It stated that "...personnel may become unexpectedly dispirited and their fighting spirit greatly sapped when forced to remain underground for days and months at a time..."

The effect of our psychological warfare was accorded a healthy respect: "When fighting is prolonged, enemy ideological tactics become increasingly skillful and telling. Officers and men must be on guard against this and intensify their fighting spirit so that they will not be taken in by the enemy. This is especially true of those surrounded by the enemy and cut off."

Finally, there was a broad, basic criticism. The Japanese were offering a solution to a dilemma which they admitted was inherently insoluble. On the one hand, the manual was written to devise a method of defeating an Allied invasion; on the other hand, the enemy was compelled to direct that the beaches be practically undefended and to place the main reliance upon delaying actions conducted from the mountains. This "solution" would certainly prove embarrassing if important objectives were located near the coastline.

JAPANESE DEFENSE DOCTRINE--THE DEVELOPMENT AND PRACTICE:

Enemy tactics on Luzon served to illustrate the enemy's defense doctrine as outlined above. Furthermore, because of the recent evolution of these defense tactics, it is possible to trace their development, in part at least. In this connection it is interesting to note that while Imperial Headquarters was compiling its "Manual for Defense Against Landings (Provisional)", and after this treatise had been published but before dissemination could have been accomplished, field units were feeling their way towards a like doctrine.

During the early years of the war "attack" and "surprise" were the twin slogans of the Japanese Army and the word "defense" an anathema. Commanders neither studied the technique of defense nor trained their soldiers in the art of defense. As events then suggested, such study and training would have been superfluous. Japanese armies swept through the Malayan States, the Dutch East Indies, the Philippine Archipelago and the Central Pacific islands; "attack" and "surprise" were gaining the day; the "banzai" charge seemed irresistable.

When the tide of war changed and the exigencies of the situation demanded knowledge of defensive tactics, the enemy was unprepared. From this unpreparedness, the Allied soldier profited; for the Jap, forced on the defensive, did the only thing he knew -- he attacked. Abandoning defensive positions and rushing headlong into interlocking bands of machine-gun fire, his sole accomplishment was that he "embraced honorable death."

The waste and futility of the "banzai" attack was strikingly exhibited in the Admiralties campaign. During the first few nights of this campaign the enemy abandoned well-emplaced, coconut-log pillboxes and charged screaming across the Momote strip. Each morning hundreds of enemy bodies covered the airfield.

Though slow to recognize fact and accept defense as normal tactics and strategy, once the enemy began to think and act in terms of defense rather than attack, his conversion program proceeded with remarkable swiftness. His speed in converting was particularly remarkable since he not only had to develop a physical technique of defense, but his troops had to be prepared psychologically for this about-face.

The following instructions, captured on Leyte and issued by a battalion of the 26th Division, clearly represented the beginnings of the mental reconditioning of the enemy's program.

"Instructions by the Unit CO:

"a. Japan is a divine land! We will surely win the final victory.
"b. Live to the last and win through.
"Our philosophy of life is not solved by death, but rather by the degree of success in accomplishing a mission."

(Translation by Sixth Army Language Detachment)

In a publication dated 15 October 1944, entitled "Combat Regulations of the 14th Area Army", the prodigality of the "banzai" attack was clearly deprecated.

"Defense combat must be active and offensive in nature. However, because such actions as massed counterattacks, unprepared and hasty, are apt to end in sudden defeat and so hinder the execution of subsequent combat, they must be avoided."

(Translation by Sixth Army Language Detachment)

Thus the checkrein was tightened on the "banzai" spirit; its wastefulness was pointed out; and the enemy

- 25 -

soldier was told that to seek death in such a manner was "too easy." The Japanese soldier was instructed that when he died he must take ten Americans with him.

When our troops landed in Lingayen Gulf on 9 January 1945, they found that the enemy soldier had been well schooled in defensive tactics, that the enemy commander had adopted an overall strategy of defense. During the first week of the Luzon campaign an estimate of the situation, published by the Japanese 26th Division in September 1944 when it was garrisoning Lingayen Gulf, was captured. In this document, which obviously reflected the contemporary thought of higher headquarters, the enemy realistically conceded his inability to stop an advance through the Central Plain "by the overwhelmingly superior power, in particular (the) armored forces" of the Americans, admitted that the Japanese would have difficulty in "checking them in an all-out engagement," and therefore implied that a decision had been made that "if the battle situation developed unfavorably, the Japanese must be able to hold a route of withdrawal to the mountainous terrain around Baguio...in order to hang on doggedly and await the plans of later years." In broad strokes this accurately foreshadowed General Yamashita's strategy.

Pursuant to General Yamashita's overall plan, major enemy forces withdrew to the mountains west of Stotsenburg, east of Manila and northeast of the Central Plain. In these areas the enemy conducted a fanatical defense from cave and tunnel positions. Enemy commanders evoked the doctrine of "10 to 1." Time and time again troops were instructed to remain within their positions so as to avoid needless casualties; it was emphasized that this "is definitely not a cowardly action." In countless orders of both major and minor units, the enemy recognized that delay and attrition of our forces were his mission. With these two objectives firmly in mind, and taking full advantage of terrain eminently suited for defense, cave and tunnel positions were constructed.

The physical aspect of these cave and tunnel positions is covered in another article; here it is sufficient to mention that the Japanese in their extensive use of caves and other subterranean positions devised an essentially novel technique of defense. Not only were these defenses used as firing points, but living and working quarters were built underground and in many instances the positions were interconnected, enabling the enemy to go from one to another without appearing above ground. Supplies were stored in the caves, and blast walls were constructed to protect the interior from bomb and artillery hits. The enemy even sited artillery pieces within the caves, rolling them to the cave mouth to fire and then withdrawing them into the interior. These practices reduced the effectiveness of our artillery fire. In most cases a direct hit was needed to inflict material damage.

Wherever possible the enemy prepared these defenses in belts. When one position became untenable, he retired to prepared defenses in the rear, and the battle began anew. The enemy followed this practice in the hills east of Manila, northeast of the Central Plain, and west of Stotsenburg. The Bamban hill area, west of Stotsenburg, was the best example of this defense from successive, prepared cave positions; for here the enemy defended on a 12,000 yard front to a depth of 20,000 yards.

Recognizing that our control of the air and our artillery observation technique rendered maintenance of supply lines to front line troops a virtual impossibility, the enemy, particularly in the area west of Stotsenburg and east of Manila, developed a logistical technique which partially compensated for this deficiency and which accorded with his defense tactics.

In the hills west of Stotsenburg the enemy established supply dumps echeloned in depth upon which contiguous units could draw. Furthermore, in addition to establishing these decentralized dumps, the enemy amply provisioned each cave and tunnel position. In almost every position overrun in the hills west of Stotsenburg, a residue of supplies and ammunition was found.

Similarly, in the hills east of Manila, the enemy applied this technique. On 5 February, as our troops were penetrating the outskirts of Manila, the Shimbu Shudan, controlling headquarters of the polyglot units in the hills east of the city, ordered that the two main ration and supply dumps within its area be cleared and that the supplies be "dispersed within the positions." Relevant portions of this order follow:

"Shimbu Gp Opn Order D-73, 5 Feb, Wawa.

"1. The Gp will immediately disperse its military stores now in the vicinity of the Montalban and Antipolo Ration and Supply Depots.

"2. Supply depots and Branch Depots will temporarily suspend their duties and by requisitioning men from their own unit, attached units and local people, will transport the military stores by man-power when necessary. The Montalban Supply Depot must be cleared by 8 Feb, the Antipolo Supply Depot by 10 Feb, and the entire war supplies must be dispersed within the positions."

(Translation by Sixth Army Language Detachment)

Although the enemy made maximum use of favorable terrain and of cave and tunnel positions to minimize casualties, his tactics of defense were by no means passive. Rather, as was expressed by 14th Area Army, they were "active and offensive in nature." Experience on Luzon demonstrated that he punctuated his defense of subterranean positions with well co-ordinated counterattacks and numerous suicide penetration attacks.

Although possibly overemphasizing the offensive nature of this combat, instructions published under the heading "Combat Methods" by the 137th Airfield Battalion for the purpose of preparing the men of this service unit for combat in the hills west of Stotsenburg, sum up the enemy's doctrine.

"II. Counter-measures:

"1. In the first phase of (the American) attack, utilize caves advantageously so as not to lose our men...

not even one. If the enemy enters our effective zone of fire or assault distance, annihilate him by severe firing and daring assault. At night annihilate the enemy by penetration units.

"2. Detailed explanations on above methods are as follows:

"a. During bombardment, all men will take shelter in caves. However, look-out posts will guard against the advance of enemy ground forces by taking advantage of lulls in enemy bombardment.

"b. After bombardment, if coordinated attack of enemy infantry, tank, artillery, and air commences, artillery and combat personnel will take up positions immediately and if the enemy enters our effective zone of fire, commence attack immediately. For this purpose each position will provide one guard who will observe enemy ground forces. Place various weapons in trenches so as to avoid damage by enemy bombardment.

"3. Firing Methods:

"a. Sniping is the main objective for rifles and heavy infantry weapons. For this purpose, place markings from your position to the front edge of the firing limit; when the enemy approaches the markings, open fire. Reckless firing is prohibited. Each unit CO must instruct his men so that ammunition on hand will last in combat for more than a year.

"b. Remember the enemy's halting positions in daytime and reconnoiter again at night. Then, send penetration units to annihilate him. Objectives for penetration units will be enemy heavy weapons, tanks, CPs, and dumps."

(Translation by Sixth Army Language Detachment)

Having wholeheartedly adopted cave warfare as his defense tactics, the enemy constantly attempted to improve the technique. Documents describing the most effective methods of protecting the occupants of caves against our flamethrowers and instructions on how to construct positions proof against artillery and aerial bombardment were captured in quantity. The following document captured on Kerama Island, Ryuku Group, and constituting a critique of defenses on Iwo Jima is of interest because of its comprehensiveness.

"Observations Based Upon Inspection of Positions of Various Units.

"1. Organization of Positions:

In organized positions, some small arm ports and gun embrasures are conspicuously exposed to naval gunfire. Others have been constructed in high positions where they can be easily discovered by the enemy. Furthermore, others have a maximum of dead space and a minimum of shelter. In view of combat experiences on Iwo Jima (in the three day period prior to landings, six out of eleven casemates were destroyed), it becomes obvious that under such conditions casualties will increase. It is therefore necessary to improve and organize positions, so that cover will be provided by natural terrain features and so that flanking and reverse fire can be delivered.

"2. Weak Points of Underground Positions Will be Strengthened:

    a. By eliminating dead spaces and by constructing connected, mutually supporting and self-guarding positions.

    b. By establishing anti-flame, anti-gas defense installations.

    c. By effecting measures to protect gun ports and embrasures against tank fire (75-mm) and shells.

"3. Construction of Dummy Positions:

The construction of a great number of dummy positions will not only force the enemy to disperse and waste his abundant resources over a wide area, but will also decrease damage to our positions. This will increase our power of resistance.

"4. In Attacking Tanks, Firepower and Suicide Attacks Must be Closely Co-ordinated:

Because firepower assists suicide attacks, full use will be made of automatic weapons to annihilate infantry troops riding or accompanying enemy tanks. Suicide attacks will be co-ordinated with fifteen seconds of surprise fire; active mine attacks will be carried out. Suicide attackers and automatic weapons men will operate as one unit to effect destruction of enemy tanks. Reorganization is therefore extremely important in order to coordinate firing and suicide attack teams.

"5. Construct Surprise 'Jack-in-the-Box' Type Positions (Key Attack Points) Within Anticipated Bridgehead Areas:

Because of the difficulty of infiltrating into enemy bridgehead areas which are covered by intensive nets of fire and obstructed by obstacles, establish surprise 'Jack-in-the-Box' positions (caves as attack key points) in advance. In coordination with attacks from our positions, our men will appear unexpectedly among the enemy, create confusion and annihilate them. Theirs will be the extremely important mission of confusing and annihilating the enemy from within. When these surprise 'Jack-in-the-Box' type positions are numerous and superior, they are of extreme value in affecting the outcome of battle.

In view of the present situation in which the Army is increasing its personnel by defense mobilization and the existence of favorable terrain in coastal areas of anticipated attack, double consideration should be given to the practical application of these surprise 'Jack-in-the-Box' positions. Thus to establish a road to victory by tactics peculiar to the Army is of vital importance. Therefore, troops should endeavor to camouflage fully entrances to hidden caves. It is believed that one good plan is to deceive U.S. troops by constructing naturally sited outhouses, which U.S. troops thoroughly dislike, near the entrances to the caves, thereby causing them to avoid these areas.

Because of modifications in the construction of M-4 tanks (louvers protecting air intake and exhaust tubes have been moved from the front to the rear), flame attacks should be made from the rear of enemy tanks."

(Translation by XXIV Corps Language Detachment)

Two suggestions, to construct dummy and "Jack-in-the-Box" positions, are of particular interest since neither was encountered on Luzon. It should be noted that the "Jack-in-the-Box" position is merely another manifestation of the enemy's penchant for suicide penetration attacks.

In conclusion it is well to note that the enemy gave the widest possible dissemination to these "lessons learned". A case in point is the above mentioned document captured in the Ryukyus commenting on the defense of Iwo Jima. Critiques of the Saipan operation were captured in the Philippines. All evidence indicates that the enemy was making the greatest possible effort to circulate throughout the entire Imperial Army these battle lessons, so that his troops could benefit from the mistakes of the past.

TYPICAL JAPANESE CAVE AND TUNNEL DEFENSES ON LUZON:

It is clear that the Japanese perfected his subterranean refuge by taking advantage of the natural defenses afforded by the mountainous terrain, and by his untiring efforts to construct elaborate artificial fortifications for the protection of personnel, equipment and supplies, and for the emplacement of his weapons.

The underground positions encountered during the Luzon operation revealed many new types varying in size, construction and general elaborateness. Defenses were found to range from the individual protective position to the elaborate bombproof cave and tunnel systems which in many cases housed large forces and contained huge stores of supplies.

It is believed that the following illustrations of

typical defenses, in the form of photographs, sketches and diagrams, will serve to indicate the thoroughness demonstrated by the enemy in his attempt to resist the acknowledged superior might of our forces through the chosen medium of cave warfare. Although the particular fortifications described in this section are limited to specified areas, they are typical of those encountered in other mountainous areas suited for defense.

Figure 5 - "chose to defend from these ridges"

After overrunning the town of Bamban, our troops were confronted with the task of cleaning out strong Japanese forces from their dug-in positions in the hill mass just west of the town.

During the conduct of his defense, the enemy fought tenaciously from cave positions such as those portrayed in the sketch on the following page. Many of the entrances housed automatic weapons which were mutually supporting, and which in some cases served as emplacements for heavy field pieces. Huge stores of supplies were contained in underground dumps which were connected by intricate tunnel systems.

The larger tunnels measured 100 feet in length and 10 to 15 feet in diameter. Since the inward path of each tunnel was constructed so as to curve away from the entrance face, protection against direct fire was good. Further protection was afforded by blast walls.

Figure 6

Northwest of Ft Stotsenburg, and particularly in the Snake Hill West—Storm King Mt area, our forces encountered cleverly concealed individual emplacements. Common among these was the protected rifle position dug-in under the heavy growth of cane break and timber. Because of the almost perfect concealment afforded by the terrain as well as the particular construction of the defense, the enemy was often detected only after he had commenced firing his weapons.

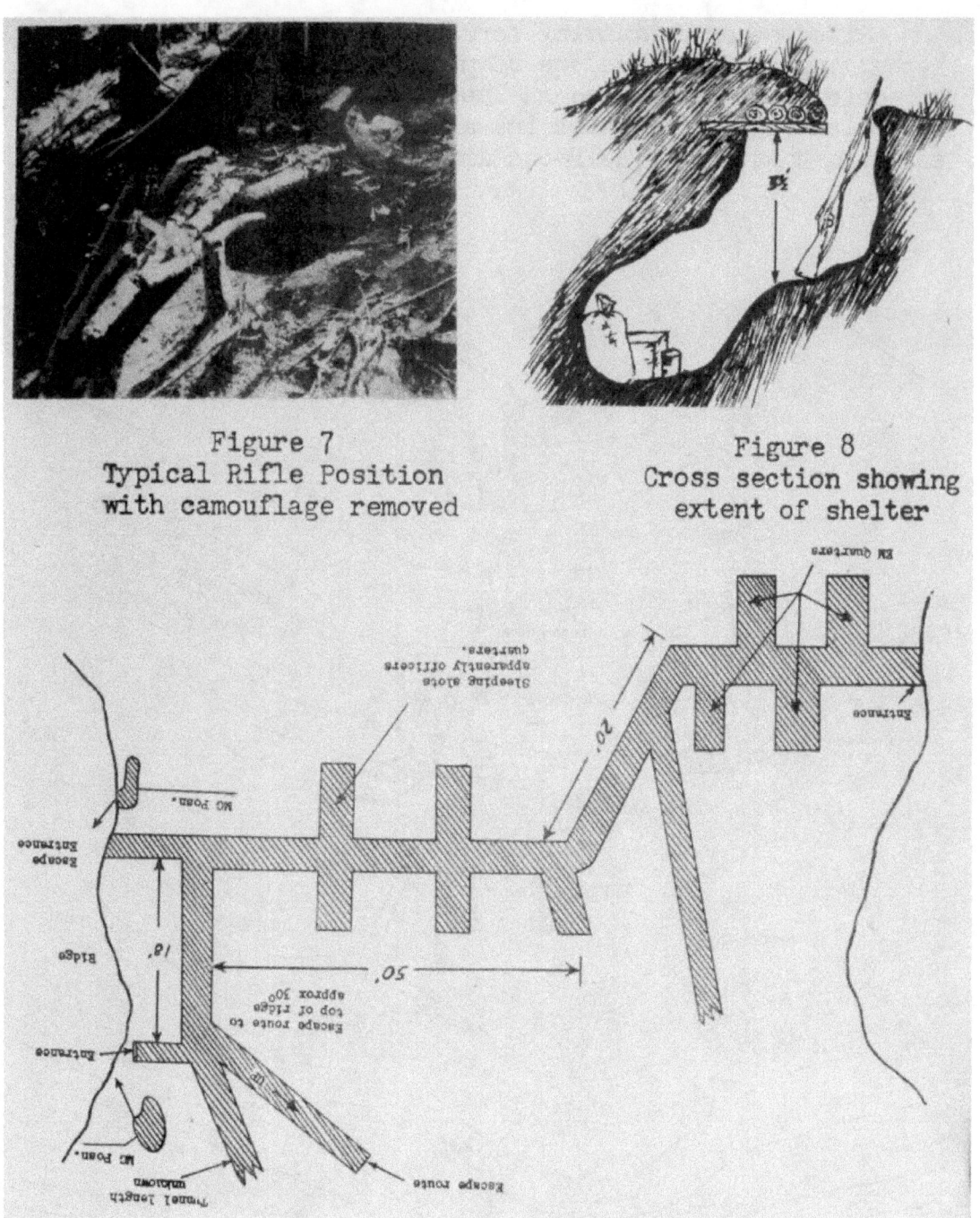

Figure 7
Typical Rifle Position
with camouflage removed

Figure 8
Cross section showing
extent of shelter

Figure 9 - UNDERGROUND COMMAND POST

The diagramatic sketch shown above represents a battalion command post which was encountered on Hill 508, flanking the Villa Verde Trail.

Situated on commanding terrain, west of Highway #5, the Kenbu Ridge defense was one of many points of resistance encountered by our forces in their advance on Balete Pass. The illustration indicates the attempt on the part of the enemy to construct a self-contained installation below ground.

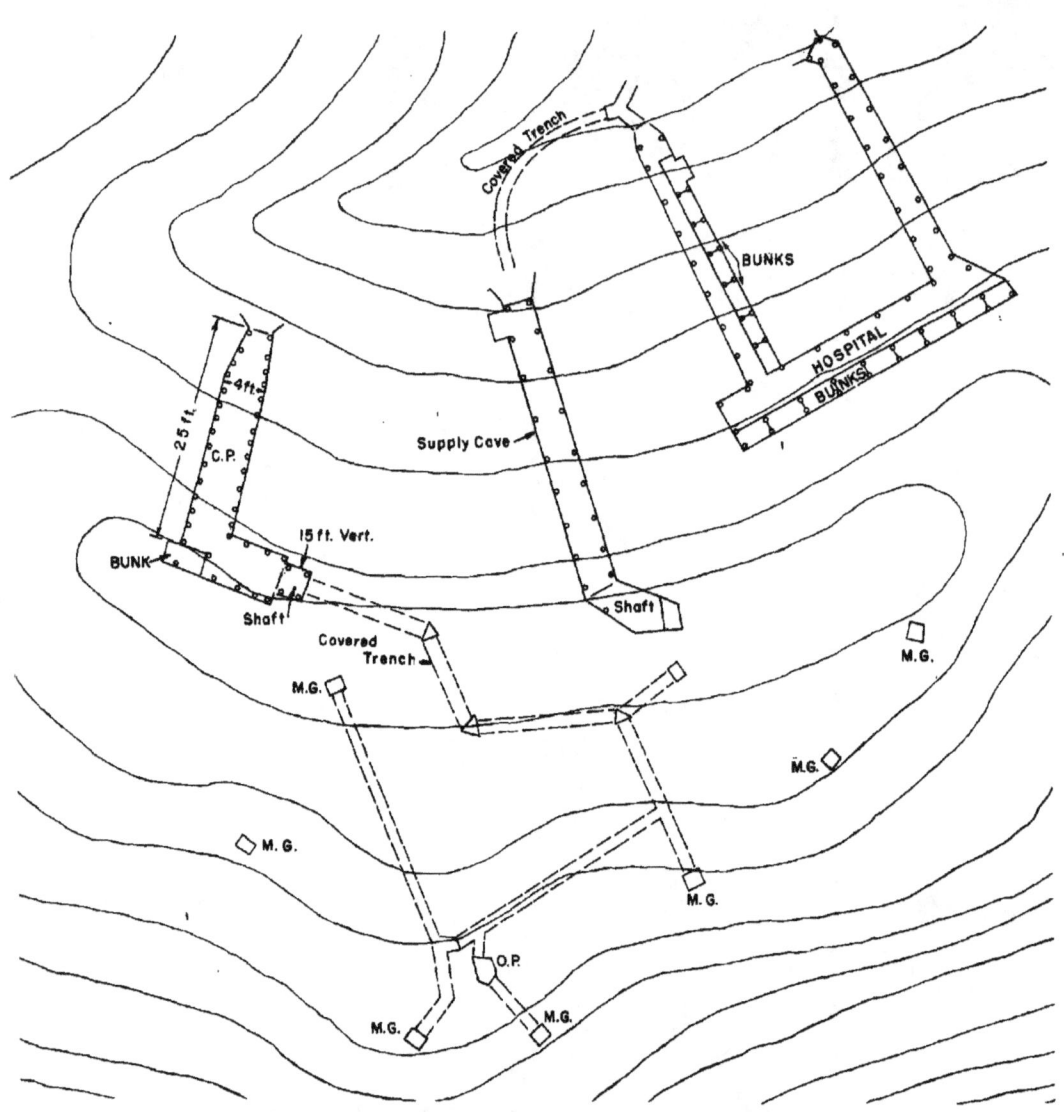

Figure 10 - KENBU RIDGE INSTALLATION

Figure 11   TYPICAL JAP STRONGHOLD   Figure 12

    The sketches shown here illustrate typical cave positions encountered in the hills northeast of Taytay. These caves generally had their portals located in small ravines in the hillside. Good fields of fire and excellent concealment were afforded by the terrain features. In some instances, tunnel positions extended from one side of a hill to the other.

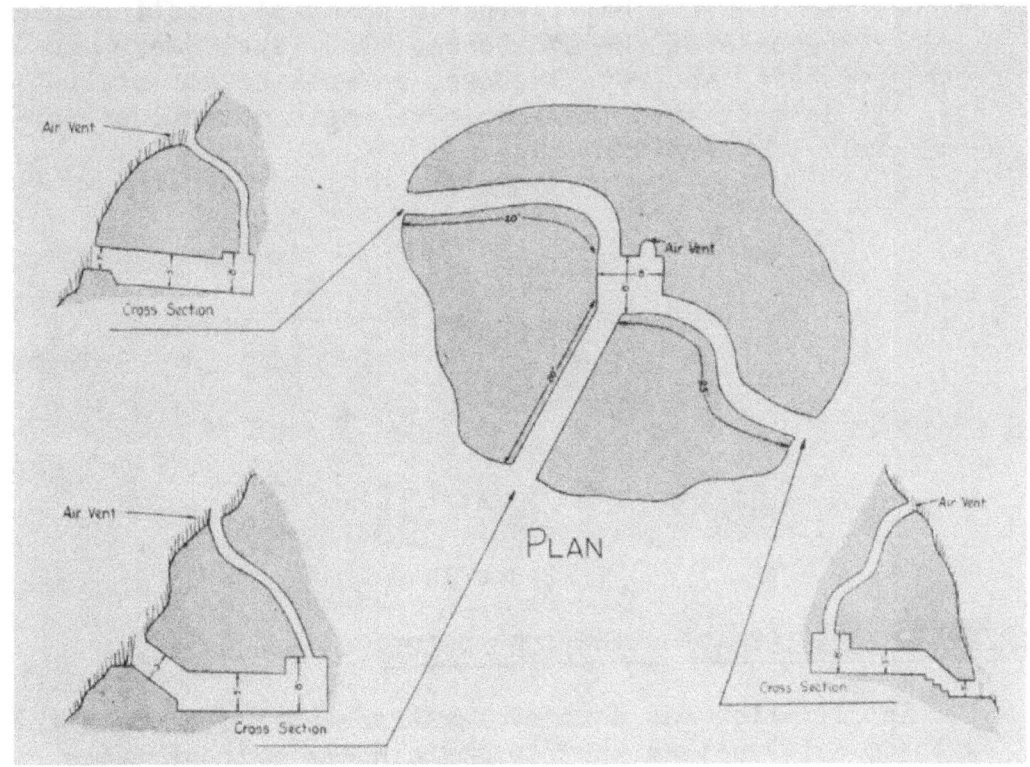

Figure 13

The mountain bastion prepared by the enemy in the foothills extending from Ipo Dam south through Wawa to Antipolo provided one of the most formidable strongholds encountered on Luzon. That the enemy was able to effect a delay in our advances is attributable to the thoroughness of his prepared cave and tunnel positions.

In most cases the ground into which the caves and tunnels were fashioned was a hard brittle shale and did not require much timber support. Normally, 10 to 15 feet of shoring was found at the entrances, thereby offering protection against the possible caving in of loosened surface rock. A common feature of the construction of the tunnels was the protection against direct fire afforded by curving the tunnels away from the entrance.

A mammoth cave was used as a headquarters by the Japanese forces defending Ipo Dam. This cave was of natural formation and was unique in that it consisted of four levels. It is believed that the main level was used by the Japanese as a lecture hall, since a speaker's platform was found at the base of the staircase. The levels were connected by shafts and rope ladders, as well as the staircase. It is estimated that the cave could accommodate approximately 1,500 men.

Figure 14.

JAPANESE INFILTRATION TACTICS ON LUZON:

Infiltration was a mode of warfare well-suited to the Japanese. It enabled them to sustain the myth that the Japanese soldier is always on the offensive, even though committed to the defense. It offered him the opportunity of testing his powers as an individual fighter--and he was trained to believe that he excelled as such. It gave him the chance to engage in hand-to-hand combat, his favorite method of fighting.

It is not surprising, then, that the only planned offensive action by the Japanese on Luzon, was a series of infiltration raids, launched from strongly-held defensive positions.

Infiltration groups were given a variety of names, such as: "Raiding Units", "Suicide Penetration (Kirikomi) Units", "Harassing Units", and "Special Attack Forces". These groups operated mostly at night, with varied objectives, in an effort to destroy our fighting strength.

The objectives of these penetration raids were many and varied. Obviously "annihilation of U.S. fighting strength" was the ultimate desideratum and many operations orders illustrate the high hopes held for these raids and the grandiose results they were expected to attain. A headquarters northeast of Manila issued the following order:

"The 3rd 'Iron Heart' Infiltration Unit with a mission to endeavor to diminish the enemy's fighting strength by raiding in the vicinity of Novaliches at 1900 on X-day is preparing for infiltration."

A 2nd Armored Division Staff Telegram, 31 January 1945, reads in part as follows:

"1. The army is expecting this group to reduce the enemy combat strength and positively harass them.

"2. The group will...accomplish its mission by relying on active raiding operations."

A 10th Division Operations Order, 19 February 1945, follows:

"The duty of the Puncan Guard Unit is to destroy the enemy in the present position (hills southwest of Puncan).

In order to do this, numerous suicide penetration attacks must be carried out."

Instructions from a high headquarters indicated the motivation which prompted such infiltration missions.

"It is most useless to become cannon fodder for enemy artillery. It is better to----crush him by penetration. Convey the above point to every soldier."

Infiltrating units were sometimes given no more specific mission then that of proceeding to a given area where they were to "destroy U.S. fighting strength." The majority, however, were assigned specific missions such as the destruction of artillery, mortars, tanks, airplanes, and bridges in specific locations.

The enemy, having learned to respect the quality, quantity, and accuracy of our artillery fire, realized they could not hope to combat it with the limited amount of artillery in their possession. Consequently, they took great pains to guard against our artillery fire by making their tunnels and caves as shell-proof as possible. Infiltration raids apparently were decided on as the best method of reducing our overwhelmingly superior artillery. The following extracts from captured documents and reports denoted the scope and persistence of Japanese infiltration attacks against our artillery:

OKA Operation Order, 24 January 1945:

"2nd Lt Kagayama will organize four groups of a suicide unit and attack enemy artillery positions in the vicinity of Mabalacat airfield."

Operation Order (unit unknown), February 1945:

"The CO's of Maintenance Company and 4th Company will penetrate into the enemy's artillery positions at Pococ."

Daily Report XIV Corps, 13-14 March 1945:

"In the Ternate area 8 enemy attempted to infiltrate an artillery position...."

Since the enemy relied heavily on mortars to repulse our attacks on their pockets of resistance, they appreciated the effectiveness of this weapon. As a result our mortar positions ranked high as an objective of infiltration units.

The enemy, recognizing the quantitative and qualitative superiority of American armor, had to devise some method of reducing this superiority. The "daring suicidal penetration unit," whose members were armed with Molotov cocktails and the suicidal "lunge" mine, was one answer. The following are typical operation orders:

Maeda Force Order, 25 January 1945:

"At dawn tomorrow, the 26th, 1st Lt Tsugita will lead 8 men and make a suicidal penetration attack upon the enemy tanks in the vicinity of the grade school house (San Manuel)."

Figure 15

2nd Armored Division Operation Order, 8 February 1945:

"A penetration raiding unit composed of a leader and 14 men will be dispatched toward Santa Maria to reconnoiter the enemy situation and attack enemy artillery and tanks."

Since the Japanese had no planes to counter U.S. aircraft, our planes and airfield installations were a lucrative and tempting target. Unfortunately for the enemy, our principal airfields were generally out of reach of his raiding parties; however, during the night of 10-11 March one party did destroy the tail assemblies of five C-47s on Clark Field. Artillery liaison planes based near the front lines were more accessible targets. Since these planes were primarily responsible for the accuracy of our artillery fire, their destruction was of great importance. For instance, it was the overwhelming weight of XIV Corps artillery fire that evoked the following operation order from the Fukumi Force on 19 February 1945:

"Our positions on the high ground east of Marikina have been subjected to an intense artillery barrage for the past several days.

"1. Some of the enemy (observer) planes are using the Caloocan airstrip and the Wackwack Golf Course.

"2. The force will select a small number of men to infiltrate into the above mentioned airstrips and destroy the enemy planes."

Since the enemy lacked air power with which to interdict road and trail approaches to his pockets of resistance, this responsibility fell upon infiltration units. Thus, bridges, bridge-construction equipment and road-making equipment were among the objectives assigned penetration units. The following extracts from operations orders illustrated this:

Omuro Operation Order, 7 February 1945:

"On the night of the 7th, the Detachment will send a raiding unit and will disrupt the enemy's bridge-construction work south of Kitakita.

"WO Hiruda of Yoshida unit will organize a raiding unit of 15 EM, depart by midnight tonight, and demolish Maniyushi Bridge by 0300 hours."

Yoshi Operation Order, Left Sector Unit, 25 March 1945:

"The main strength of the Mori platoon will carry out suicide penetration attacks to destroy the enemy road construction equipment northwest of Hill 300."

"By striking at enemy rear areas, bivouac areas, and supply lines, it will naturally be easier to bring about weakness in front line strength."

The idea contained in the above order was the motivating force behind the many Japanese efforts to penetrate our flank and rear positions during the campaign. Small enemy groups were constantly attacking our dumps and supply lines, and during the night of 19-20 January made one large raid on one of our principal beachheads.

There was no uniformity in the strength or organization of the enemy infiltration groups. They ranged in size from the major portion of a regiment down to lone infiltrators. The enemy as a rule favored the three-man groups. Orders of the 14th Area Army illustrated this:

"Frequent employment of infiltration units is encouraged. The ideal strength of each unit will be 2-3 men."

"All ranks must carry out suicide penetration raids. Therefore, all forces will immediately organize suicide penetration units. These will be formed of squads consisting of approximately 3-5 men to a group and three groups to a squad."

On Luzon the enemy relied heavily on the raiding tactics of these small groups.

The quality of the personnel and the degree of specialized training of these infiltration groups varied considerably and were usually proportionate to the extent to which the supervising unit was approaching disintegration. Whenever circumstances and time permitted, personnel for these units were specially picked men and were given specialized training in assault tactics, terrain appreciation, use of demolitions, and the like. In the Caraballo mountains an enemy paratroop unit was used on these ground missions to disrupt our supply lines and rear areas; the high state of training of these troops made them ideal for the task. On the other hand, as units approached disintegration, the sick, the lame, and the lazy were used on these infiltration attacks. The theory behind this, as expressed in operations orders, was that these men were of no use and that, since rations were getting short, they should get rid of men whose usefulness had passed.

Thorough and detailed planning characterized the organization of large infiltration groups. An example of this is the organization of the infiltration attack launched against our positions in the Rosario--San Fabian area in mid-January. According to a captured 23rd Division operation order this attack was to involve elements of several infantry battalions with engineer personnel attached. Routes of approach and assembly areas were reconnoitered ahead of time by officer patrols.

The equipment of this infiltration unit was additional evidence of the care and study with which the attack was planned. Five days of rations were found on all enemy dead. Demolition kits, magnetic mines, flame throwers, grenades, mortars, rifles, and automatic weapons were carried. The group was prepared to operate behind our lines as a self-contained unit for an extended period of time.

The raiding party which attacked the Binday area consisted of four platoons from the 3rd Battalion, 71st Infantry Regiment, with an attached engineer demolition platoon. It was one of three parties organized by the 23rd Division operation order. This raiding party moved from the hills east of Sison to a point west of Pozorrubio, and thence west towards San Fabian. Although the raid proved abortive, it was significant for its size and careful planning.

For the organization of small infiltration units, planning consisted of little more than picking a leader and his men. Units of 12 or more were commanded by a lieutenant or a warrant officer; the number of officers killed during these raids was extremely large. Indeed the 14th Area Army deprecated the high casualty rate amongst officers and suggested, "It is not necessary to include an officer in a penetration raid. It is advantageous to organize several small penetration parties of which each part consists of three men with a suitable NCO or EM in charge."

The following I Corps report on the operational methods of the larger infiltration units illustrated the tactics of such groups.

"The method of operation is very simple. Patrols locate and reconnoiter lucrative objectives in rear areas, and then report to unit headquarters. A platoon, organized into five groups, infiltrates to the objective; three groups advance on the front of the objective, the other two encircling the flanks. The assault groups, operating against the front, infiltrate into the heart of the position or until they are discovered, then attack with bayonets, grenades, and demolitions. The flanking groups launch a similar attack against the rear simultaneously. When the mission is accomplished, the groups disperse to reorganize at a predesignated assembly area for return to the unit bivouac."

Operational methods for the favored three man group are outlined by "Battle Instructions" issued by the Kobayashi Heidan on 14 March 1945:

"An example of a method of suicide penetration attack, with 'A', 'B', and 'C' operating as a team. 'A' will be armed with hand grenades and smoke candles in a frontal attack. 'B' will be provided with improvised or mattress mines. He will await in readiness on the opposite side from 'A' and attack, taking advantage of the enemy's unguarded moments. 'C' with explosives will await in readiness on the same side as 'B'. If the 'B' attack is a failure, 'C' must carry out the decisive attack. However, if 'B' succeeds, it is necessary to annihilate the withdrawing enemy troops."

Enemy infiltration units usually operated from heavily fortified areas and the employment of infiltration units was an integral part of the enemy's defense tactics.

Obviously, Japanese infiltration attempts did not accomplish their mission of the "destruction of enemy fighting strength." Only in a few instances, and then when minor objectives, such as small bridges, isolated gun positions and the like, were assigned, did they achieve anything like total success. Some damage to our "fighting strength" was caused and some casualties inflicted, but, considering the large part infiltration was to play in "annihilating the enemy," these tactics failed. Early in the Luzon campaign the Japanese themselves realized that their infiltration tactics were unsuccessful. Captured diaries and PW interrogations reflect the extent of the failure.

Captured diary, 24 January 1945:

"Again it is said that we are to go on a raid tonight, but I wonder how effective it is to make infiltration attacks against enemy artillery. What success did they have last night? They have not come back as yet, and we have no news of them."

A Japanese soldier made the following entry in his diary on 18 January 1945: "It is regrettable that our suicide penetration mission resulted in failure---the main strength of the 2nd Company was annihilated."

The most virulent criticism of infiltration tactics reported was by a Japanese soldier to Major General Fujishige. Extracts from the interrogation report follows:

"A prisoner of war, as leader of an unsuccessful penetration mission, came back to make his report to the Group (FUJI) Hq. Gen Fujishige appeared at this point and upon hearing of the failure of the mission, reprimanded the PW in the harshest terms, accusing him of being cowardly, incompetent, and unworthy of his NCO rating. 'It's because we have to rely on NCOs like you that we are now in the circumstances we find ourselves,' said the General.

"At this point the PW replied, 'Why you blundering brass hat, it's very easy for you to sit all day in your especially built foxhole, while you order us out on impossible missions. If you'd get out there where the bullets are flying, you'd find out how futile your so-called penetration missions are.'"

The prisoner of war stated the Chief of Staff of the group wished to behead him on the spot, but was prevented by Major General Fujishige who wanted time to think up a more fitting punishment. In the meantime the prisoner of war escaped and surrendered to our troops.

Throughout the Luzon campaign infiltration raids persisted in every area where fighting was taking place and even though they failed they had a large nuisance value. Only by being constantly on the alert did our forces prevent a much larger success. The slightest relaxation on our part would have immeasurably increased the enemy's chances of "destroying U.S. fighting strength."

Figure 16 - Results of Banzai Attack.

JAPANESE ANTI-TANK TACTICS:

When our troops landed on Luzon, sufficient time for the enemy to devise and develop countermeasures had elapsed since he first encountered our M-4 and M-5 tanks. Furthermore, the nature of the terrain—the broad, open Central Plain of Luzon—necessitated local study by the enemy of anti-tank measures. In view of these two factors it was not surprising to find that the majority of the enemy's anti-tank weapons and tactics were new.

The problem of how best to stem the advance of our superior armored might was studied by the enemy's Luzon tank division, the 2nd Armored, and on 15 November 1944 the division headquarters published a combat manual which outlined both an offensive and defensive doctrine. Pertinent extracts from this document follow:

"I. Overall Principles.

"These instructions outline the basic principles for wiping out the American devils; and are to be followed by subordinate units to make their orders as concise as possible.

"The Philippines battle has but two alternatives: for the Americans to be annihilated, or for the whole Japanese forces, officers and men alike, to die in the attempt. Such an honorable death may be the ultimate goal; but no man should sacrifice himself unless he destroys ten of the enemy.

"II. General Rules.

"This is an anti-tank war, especially a battle against heavy tanks. Any lack of equipment must be made up by the skill derived from long training and by our superiority in diversionary surprise plans.

"The main point in anti-tank combat is to know the weak points of enemy tanks, and by surprise plans to magnify these weaknesses and then to attack suddenly.

"Skillful planning can put enemy tanks at a disadvantage and present a good opportunity for a sudden surprise attack through use of trenches and camouflaged positions to prevent detection, and by distracting enemy attention to objects, movements, smoke, or explosions in other sectors. Officers and men must at all times be proficient in the use of such surprise tactics.

"Our tank-destroying weapons are the Type 90 Field Gun and the hollow-charge shaped explosive with attached handle (known as 'hollow-charge explosive') which have their maximum destructive effect within 500 meters and within 2 meters respectively.

"In contrast to the above, the weapons listed below are known as 'surprise tactics weapons' (KISAKUKAKI). Because these weapons are highly mobile, can use terrain features readily, and can inflict some damage upon the enemy tanks' mobility and fire power through sudden attacks, they can thus facilitate the attacks by the tank-destroying weapons. They are effective within the following approximate ranges:

      47-mm gun - 1,500 meters
      37-mm gun - 1,000 meters
      Machine guns - 300 meters.

"It takes exceptionally good skill for the gunners to be able to destroy enemy tanks completely. Officers and men alike, without exception, must become proficient in handling explosives, especially hollow-charge explosives.

"To bring the tank-destroying weapons into range before the enemy can damage them is the prime consideration. This can be done by ambush, by seizing the right moment to attack during tank advance, or by diverting the enemy through use of a plan of surprise. In such a plan of surprise, smoke, faked explosions, dummy men and the like can be used on one side to distract the enemy's attention so that a close approach from other quarters may be rapidly made. Both the diversionary attack and the main assault should be very closely keyed together and greatest precautions taken to maintain communication and liaison between them.

"In attacking with the tank-destroying weapons, the first attempt must produce direct hits. Wait fearlessly and patiently for the range to close. Keep under cover, expose positions only long enough to fire carefully, and then disappear before the enemy can take aim."

(Translation by I Corps Language Detachment)

The principal anti-tank artillery used by the enemy in the Luzon campaign were the 47-mm Anti-Tank Gun, Type 1, and the 75-mm Type 90 Field Gun with armor-piercing ammunition. These were augmented by the 70-mm Battalion Howitzer with hollow charge ammunition. Both combat reports and field tests made by technical intelligence personnel proclaimed the effectiveness of the first two weapons. No combat reports were available on the third; however, preliminary field tests indicated that this ammunition will penetrate at least 3 inches of armor. Since hollow charge ammunition does not depend on velocity for penetration, effective anti-tank range equals the range of the howitzer. In addition to these artillery weapons the enemy employed the Hollow Charge Rifle Grenade, 30-mm, Type 1; however, because of faulty design, a high percentage of these grenades failed to detonate.

Little that is unique was observed in the enemy's employment of this anti-tank guns. In general, when employing them in "tank" terrain, he chose positions affording excellent fields of fire, dug in the individual gun and provided the individual piece adequate small-arms protection. He did not, however, provide alternate positions for the guns. The medium tank with the 47-mm gun was frequently employed as an anti-tank gun, dug-in and sited as described above.

Enemy doctrine in the employment of anti-tank guns emphasized the "ambush." The Japanese gunner was directed to "lure" the unwary American tanker close to his position, then "to annihilate him with one shot." This cunning often took the form of allowing our tanks to advance beyond the well-camouflaged gun positions and then firing upon our tanks from the rear.

Figure 17 - "firing upon our tanks from the rear..."

During the Luzon campaign the enemy employed such well-known mines as the Type 93 Tape-measure mine, the Type 99 Magnetic Mine and the Yardstick Mine. Hitherto unknown mines, such as the Type 3 Pottery Mine, were used. In addition to these he employed many improvised mines and continued the practice of using bombs as mines. In one instance, the enemy employed naval depth-charges as land mines.

The official Japanese doctrine on the tactical use of anti-tank mines was generally the same as ours, according to captured documents on the subject. By the employment of minefields, the Japanese commander was expected to canalize our tank attack onto terrain dominated by anti-tank guns. This doctrine apparently was ignored, however, and little training appears to have been given along those lines.

Minefields, though more numerous than in previous campaigns, were relatively few and were ineffectively employed. Poor camouflage enabled our troops to locate and remove the mines with ease. Several instances were noted where small unit commanders deprecated this serious deficiency and attempted corrective action. The following extract is from instructions of a battalion CO to his troops issued 1 June 1945:

"The camouflage of buried mines on the road by all units is not thorough. They must be buried and thoroughly camouflaged so that anyone passing will not be suspicious."

(Translation by I Corps Language Detachment)

It will be noted that this admonition was by a battalion CO; no instance appeared of a major command noting the deficiency. Officially, the enemy apparently did not appreciate the tactical importance of minefields--at least he did not consider them sufficiently important to give adequate training to his troops.

Though inept in laying minefields, the enemy exhibited considerable skill in his use of the individual mine. During the Philippine campaign, he employed electrically-controlled mines buried in the shoulders of a road. Concealing himself in a nearby foxhole, the individual Japanese soldier awaited the approach of our tanks and, at a critical moment, detonated the charge. As an individual weapon the anti-tank mine was principally used in night infiltration attacks. Carrying mines or other explosives on these night raids, the enemy placed the mine on or within the tank, detonated the charge and attempted a getaway. Often no attempt was made to detonate the charge. It was placed under a tank track or along a much-used road, and on the following morning the movement of the unsuspecting tank or of vehicles along the road set off the mine.

Figure 18
"...at a critical moment, detonated the charge..."

The "suicide" or "penetration" attack was the most distinctively Japanese of the enemy's variegated anti-tank measures.

There follows an enemy account of a large infiltration attack executed by the 58th IMB in the Rosario area, Luzon, on 16 January 1945.

"SHOBU (14th Area Army) Battle Lesson No. 33, SHOBU GP Hq, 18 January 45:

"Investigation of the effect of the 'Blanket' (Shoulder Pack) mine. According to the result of MEI (58th IMB) Gp Suicide Penetration Unit attack at Arakan (Phonetic) on the 16th (presumably January) it is effective against M-4 tanks.

"The results are as follows:

1. Completely destroyed eight M-4 tanks with 'Blanket mines.
2. Completely destroyed 46 mobile guns.
3. Eight vehicles completely burned."

The 14th Area Army's account of this raid was distributed to all major units under its command and no doubt the recipients of the report were duly impressed. However, investigation failed to disclose any tanks or artillery pieces even damaged by members of the 58th IMB in infiltration attacks on the date in question.

It is not intended to leave an impression that these suicide penetration units were always unsuccessful. Such is not the case. American tanks and artillery pieces, in small quantities, were destroyed in this manner. Experience proved, however, that once the enemy entered our perimeter he usually either lost his nerve or got so excited that he threw his explosives wildly at the first object which caught his eye. As a result little damage was sustained.

A more out-and-out suicide method of destroying tanks involved the use of the "lunge" mine and the "shoulder pack" mine. Soldiers employing these weapons were taught to wait in ambush and "destroy the oncoming tank with one stroke." Sometimes lone soldiers attacked. At other times the user of the explosive was covered by a small group of riflemen. Such attacks were but loosely coordinated, and in general, it may be said that the enemy developed no "tank-hunting" teams as such.

In one instance, however, the enemy employed a "tank-hunting" team in conjunction with the 47-mm anti-tank gun. During the morning of 4 March 1945, as three of our tanks were rounding a hairpin turn 2,500 yards west of Antipolo, a well-camouflaged anti-tank gun scored a direct hit on our lead tank. Immediately, from 15 to 20 Japanese, armed with satchel charges and incendiary grenades, swarmed around the tanks. One of the satchel charges blew a track off the second tank and incendiary grenades set fire to both leading tanks. The two squads of supporting infantry were pinned down by fire from an enemy machine gun during this attack.

JAPANESE ARMORED TACTICS:

During the planning phase of the campaign the Japanese 2nd Armored Division was identified in the Central Plain of Luzon. Since no sizeable armored forces had been encountered in the Pacific war, the presence of this division caused some concern. Would the enemy mass his armor for one sledgehammer blow or would he fritter it away in minor counterattacks? Although precedents were lacking, captured Manchurian maneuver problems indicated that the enemy contemplated using armored task forces smaller than ours, most frequently centering around a tank company.

On 6 January 1945 our preliminary bombardment of the Lingayen Gulf beaches commenced. On 7 January the CG, 2nd Armored Division, mobilized his command into three task forces and prepared to meet an invasion at widely separated points. These task forces were composed as follows:

Shigemi Force	Harada Force
3rd Tank Brigade Hq	10th Tank Regt (bulk)
7th Tank Regt	1st Co, 2nd Mobile Arty Regt

Shigemi Force (Cont.)	Harada Force (Cont.)
1st Bn, 2nd Mobile Inf Regt (bulk)	One Platoon of Infantry
3rd Bn, 2nd Mobile Arty Regt (bulk)	One Platoon of Engrs
3rd Co, Div Engr Regt	
2nd Co, Div Tank Maint Unit	

Ida Force

6th Tank Regt	3rd Co, 25th AT Bn
8th Ind Tank Co	3rd Co, Div Transport Regt
3rd Bn, 2nd Mobile Inf Regt (bulk)	1st Co, Div Engr Regt
2nd Bn, 2nd Mobile Arty Regt (bulk)	1st Co, Div Tank Maint Unit

The Shigemi Force was ordered to assemble in the vicinity of San Manuel (Lingayen Gulf area) and to be prepared to annihilate an invasion force. The Ida Force was ordered to Bataan on a similar mission. The Harada Force was to remain under Division control and, with the units of the Division not assigned to one of these three task forces, apparently constituted the reserve.

When it became clear that our main effort was the Lingayen landing, enemy plans were altered and the entire division was used to screen Highway #5, along which enemy units were withdrawing from south and central Luzon through San Jose into the Caraballo Mountains. The Shigemi Force proceeded per schedule to the San Manuel area where it engaged our troops. The Ida Force, instead of going to Bataan, joined the remainder of the Division and was committed piecemeal west and northwest of San Jose. Apparently, the 8th Tank Company and the 3rd Battalion, 2nd MLR, both originally assigned to the Ida Force, were already enroute to Bataan, could not be recalled, and so were committed west of Stotsenburg.

First contact with the 2nd Armored Division occurred during the night of 14-15 January when three tanks of the 7th Tank Regiment attacked our positions at Malasin, a barrio 2,000 yards southwest of Pozorrubio. On 16 January 6 tanks supported by infantry attacked Potpot (west of

Binalonan); four of these were destroyed; and documents taken from dead crew members identified the 4th Company, 7th Tank Regiment. During the night of 16-17 January tank battles developed at Binalonan and Urdaneta. Both attacks were repulsed with a loss to the enemy of 19 medium and 3 light tanks.

Apparently these contacts were with advance elements of the Shigemi Force, the main body of which dug-in for defense of San Manuel. An order to defend San Manuel to the death had been issued by Major General Shigemi.

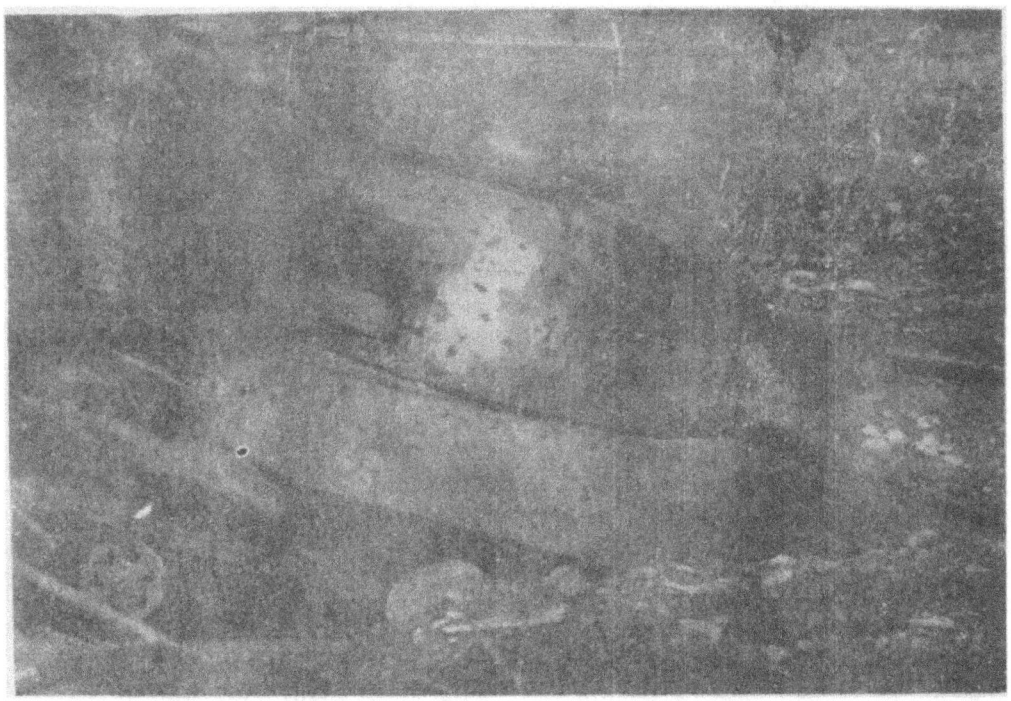

Figure 19 - "dug-in for defense of San Manuel..."

"Force will defend present positions to the death, the enemy must be annihilated, we must hold San Manuel at all costs. We are only prepared for a frontal assault. If the enemy should encircle us or threaten our line of communication, we shall lose. The reason the enemy will not take this course is that he is too timid."

The battle for San Manuel which raged from 24 through 27 January ended in a last desperate spasm on 27 January, when the enemy launched a counterattack with 13 tanks and supporting infantry at dusk. This thrust was defeated; that night beaten remnants of the Shigemi Force evacuated the town. During the battle the enemy lost 41 medium tanks, 4 light tanks, six 105-mm guns, seven 75-mm guns, two 47-mm anti-tank guns, three 37-mm anti-tank guns and two 75-mm field pieces.

Figure 20 - "the enemy lost 41 medium tanks..."

The bulk of the remainder of the 2nd Armored Division was committed piecemeal in the area southeast of San Manuel. Although the enemy launched several minor counterattacks, his greatest effort was expended in the defense of towns--notably Lupao, San Isidro, and Munoz. The enemy's efforts in this area were hampered by the unexpectedly swift advance of our troops. Captured orders and diaries indicated that enemy units spent considerable time in marching and countermarching throughout this area, that in the general confusion of the situation units became disorganized, and that men became separated from their officers and officers from their units.

By 7 February, three weeks after first contact, the

2nd Armored Division had lost 192 of its 234 tanks. Not only its tank, but its infantry and artillery elements had been reduced to remnant status. The entire division had been employed defensively; the largest counterattack had been with 13 tanks.

In surveying the enemy's armored tactics two facts are clear: he recognized the importance of the tank-infantry-artillery team; and he did not appreciate the importance of the principle of "mass."

When our invasion convoys were sighted off the coast of Luzon and the enemy prepared to meet threats at widely separated points, he broke up his Division into three task forces. As was shown, the Shigemi and Ida Forces were equally balanced tank-infantry-artillery teams with necessary engineer and maintenance units attached. The third, the Harada Detachment, deficient in infantry and artillery, significantly was retained under Division control. If its employment at some distant point had been necessitated it would have been possible to attach the necessary infantry and artillery.

Further appreciation of the importance of the tank-infantry-artillery team was exemplified by the Manchurian maneuver problems mentioned in the first paragraph of this section. Each maneuver problem was designed for a task force composed equally of the three arms.

The size of these task forces, as has been mentioned before, was small---the nucleus usually was a tank company. The conclusion drawn from an examination of the Manchurian problems prior to the Luzon campaign, i.e., that the enemy did not appreciate the principle of "mass" in the use of armor, was confirmed on Luzon not only by actual combat experience---no more than 13 tanks were ever used in an attack---but also by a Combat Manual issued by the 2nd Armored Division, dated 15 November 1944, published in obvious preparation for the coming Luzon campaign. Pertinent extracts follow:

"Raiding combat will take place at night. Attacks by tanks (including infantry riding on tanks) will be against airfields, warehouses and tents, etc. Attacks by infantry and engineer troops will be against headquarters, artillery, tanks and other mobile targets....

"After the infantry groups have broken through the enemy front lines our concentrated power will smash through to enemy interior positions and destroy enemy CP and main fire power systems. This will be termed 'main strength combat.' A tank platoon as nucleus, with various branches of service in cooperation with infantry groups in raiding attacks, is termed a 'tank combat group'."

(Translation by ADVATIS)

An interrogation of a Japanese 2nd Lieutenant, 2nd Mobile Artillery Regiment, reveals the theory held by 14th Area Army on armored warfare. Pertinent extracts from this interrogation follow:

"General Yamashita, being an old time infantry soldier, did not believe in mechanized warfare. When the 2nd Armored Division landed in Manila, General Yamashita expressed great displeasure and was immediately prejudiced against the unit. There were no tank tacticians attached to General Yamashita's headquarters. Therefore, when the Division landed, it was split up and the pleas of the CG of the Division to keep it as a unit were not backed by anybody in the headquarters. Yamashita thought that if the Division was split up it could attack U.S. troops wherever they landed on Luzon. One unit would engage them and would later be reinforced by other units of the Division. If it were assembled in force Yamashita feared that air attacks would annihilate them. He also wanted them dispersed as protection against possible U.S. airborne landings. Constant movement of the unit and consequent use of gas and rations and wear on equipment and personnel convinced the General that they were more trouble than they were worth."

(Interrogation by I Corps Language Detachment)

In conclusion, it would appear that combat instructions, the comments of a Japanese armored officer, and combat experience all agree that the Japanese did not appreciate the principle of "mass" in the employment of armor. It would further appear that a tank platoon or company was considered the largest unit that would enter combat at any one time. On the other hand, the enemy did appreciate the importance of the tank-infantry-artillery team and recognized that tanks were most effectively employed after a breakthrough, i.e.: "...will smash through to enemy interior positions and destroy enemy CP and main power systems."

In the Luzon campaign, by reason of our complete air supremacy and numerically superior ground strength, the enemy was forced to use his armor in a defensive role. An examination of his combat instructions, however, indicates that his tactical doctrine is that armor should be employed offensively.

Figure 21 - "forced to use his armor in a defensive role..."

GROWING JAPANESE SECURITY CONSCIOUSNESS:

As the Luzon campaign progressed, it became apparent that the enemy had at last realized the need for security of military information, and had embarked on a counterintelligence program to eliminate the laxity and total disregard for security which had so long been characteristic. The lush days of easy conquest, when a hasty retreat from a CP and sudden abandonment of a headquarters in the face of superior opposing forces were unknown, had become relics of a distant past. The Japanese found it necessary to recognize the "facts of life", and to admit finally the possibility of retreat and even capture. In any event, it became clear that the enemy, towards the end of the Pacific war, was well aware of the valuable information we obtained from captured documents and prisoners of war and that he made a sustained effort to close these sources of information.

Figure 22 - "destruction of documents..."

On Luzon the enemy issued many directives dealing with the destruction of documents and limiting the issuance of written orders. It also appeared that commanding officers' names, instead of the compromised code name and number system, were most frequently used in orders to designate units. Furthermore, improvised code names were used for geographical locations and it was not uncommon to find the enemy giving admonitions such as the following one issued by the 8th Division:

"It is desired that the following instruction be carried out if a soldier becomes a prisoner of war. If a soldier unluckily falls into enemy hands, he must not give out any military information.

"Furthermore, he must use every means to seek out enemy military information, and endeavor to escape and return to his unit. If the above mentioned instructions cannot be carried out, the prisoner will commit suicide."

Another typical enemy directive is one issued by the 8th Division on 28 November 1944 as follows:

"According to special intelligence, the enemy has obtained extremely accurate and detailed information on movements, armament, organization, and strength dispositions of our land and air forces within and without Japan. It is concluded that most of this information has been obtained from our captured 'Top Secret' documents. There is also some evidence that a part of the intelligence is from notebooks, etc, of an officer belonging to a high headquarters. A considerable amount of information is noted as obtained from prisoner of war sources.

From the above, the need for adequate counterintelligence measures in the handling of 'Top Secret' documents can be readily realized. Hereafter, the strictest care will be taken in counterintelligence measures for the restriction of copy numbers and distribution of printed documents, immediate decrease in number of documents carried, and careful burning of documents after use. Strict enforcement of these measures will be required so that there will be no mishap in disposing of 'Top Secret' documents under any circumstances. Thorough spiritual training will be given for those unfortunate enough to be taken prisoner."

A memorandum issued by the 54th Independent Mixed Brigade 10 December 1944 reads:

"Recently the Allies have had information on the strength, disposition, and movement of our forces on the mainland as well as in conquered countries. The reason the enemy has this knowledge is that they have captured large quantities of our secret documents. Prisoners of war may have contributed much information.

"Now that the war is reaching its climax, it is necessary to bear in mind the idea of security. The number of printed documents and their distribution must be limited. Only limited numbers of documents should be kept on hand, others must be burned.

"All soldiers must receive thorough spiritual training with regards to their conduct if captured. In the China Expeditionary Army, the opinion has prevailed that, if a soldier is captured due to conditions beyond his control (for example, when he falls from a cliff and is rendered unconscious), in the case of noncommissioned officers, he must exert every effort to inflict as much damage as possible upon the Allies and escape. If he returns he will not be stigmatized as a prisoner of war. If escape is not possible, he should commit suicide. Officers in every case must commit suicide if captured.

"Thus, those who penetrate into enemy territory should carry very few if any documents.

"The group (SHUDAN) concurs in this opinion."

Another memorandum illustrating this trend was issued by Shimbu Staff, 22 January 1945, as follows:

"Memorandum concerning thorough counterintelligence measures:

"1. Recently, upon withdrawal of troops, secret documents have been left behind in houses.

"2. Each unit must take thorough counterintelligence measures to safeguard secret documents. It is desired that neighboring houses used for military purposes be thoroughly examined to prevent the leaving behind of secret documents."

The following detailed instructions appeared in orders issued by intelligence organizations of the Okuyama Force and the Kawashima Heidan (both near Manila) from 20 January to 13 February 1945:

"In keeping with the spirit of counterintelligence, each officer must be sure to prevent the leakage of matters concerning the essence and operational plans of the organizations. It is expected that conflicts will arise in military discipline and officers are responsible for keeping this matter secret.

"Items which must be heeded in counterintelligence activities:

"a. It will be a general rule that no one except persons concerned will know the composition of the organizations. The residence of the commanding officer and names of the officers will not be disclosed. Assumed names will be given. Officers will have secret names.

"b. Vehicles will not be marked with the insignia of the special organization. Plate numbers will be changed once a week beginning the 10th.

"c. Matters of secrecy will not be disclosed over the telephone.

"d. The knowledge of the whereabouts of special organizations will never be disclosed, and telephone calls concerning this will not be made.

"e. Concerning the custody and burning of secret documents: A responsible man will be selected and he will be charged with managing these matters. Methods will be quickly devised for the burning and disposition of worthless documents.

"f. Telephone numbers will only be given to persons concerned.

"g. Important printed papers will be kept by responsible persons. In case important papers are lost, that fact will be reported to the responsible higher officer.

"h. Projected moves and the names of places will not be disclosed. If it is necessary to disclose such matters, secret language - mountain (yama), valley (tani), river (kawa) will be used.

"i. Each organization will carry out an investigation of counterintelligence matters within its own unit and will issue a counterintelligence report once a week."

The existence of an extensive security program of enemy units on Luzon, by order of 14th Area Army, was also confirmed by prisoner of war interrogations as shown in the following excerpt:

"The 14th Area Army issued an order to all units on Luzon in regard to security measures. Commanding officers of all units were responsible for seeing that operational orders and all official documents were either burned or buried in order that such documents would not get into the enemy's hands. Prisoner of war stated that if any of these documents did get into U.S. hands it was because of the carelessness of the officer concerned. Stated that most Japanese officers are easy to excite; therefore, many times they will leave documents half-burned or buried. However, security measures were closely followed in Manila. A business receipt or even the slightest thing that would give their units away were burned before troops fled from their defensive positions."

In some instances, the enemy has resorted to concealment and deceptive measures in order to attain security, as is shown in the following orders of the 58th IMB. One dated 23 March 1945 follows:

"1. In order to conceal our plans the following is to be noted hereafter:

"a. Place names will not be used for CPs; instead, numbers will be used. Present CP will be called No. 1 CP hereafter.

"b. All units must be careful not to pinpoint locations of commanders, CP locations and other important data on maps."

Another, dated 3 March 1945, reads:

"1. Intensification of enemy reconnaissance plane and artillery activities is an indication of enemy's intention to carry out an all-out attack.

"2. The Salacsac Sector Unit will endeavor to mislead the enemy by carrying out feint movements in other sectors, thus giving the enemy the impression that a strong force is opposing him.

"3. The Okuda Unit CO will establish a diversionary base (one platoon) in the jungle 3 km northwest of Geri. He will construct dummy positions to attract the enemy in the Mt Ruzu area. Simultaneously, he will destroy all enemy guerrillas in the vicinity of Mt Geri. Also, he will investigate the road leading to Natividad.

"4. The Inui Force will establish a position in the vicinity of Mt Matsu to distract the enemy.

"5. Following precautions must be taken in construction of dummy positions:

"a. They should be constructed at least 500 meters from real positions.

"b. Use dummy troops."

It must be conceded that these instructions were to some extent at least, effective. With surprising regularity enemy troops in the Philippines entered combat without paybooks, identification discs and other documents. Many abandoned command posts and headquarters did not yield the usual rich assortment of documents. Fortunately, however, the enemy's security program was a complete failure in respect to prisoners of war. Japanese prisoners of war continued to speak volubly and to furnish valuable information, and in some cases even volunteered to participate in missions against their former comrades in arms, and to endeavor to induce their surrender.

Evidence accumulated from other sectors indicated that the trend toward security consciousness was widespread, and was undoubtedly the result of a general policy announced by Imperial Headquarters. Documents captured on Okinawa and Iwo Jima contained detailed directions for destruction of documents and records likely to fall into our hands and also instructions to follow in the event of capture. A typical document found at Okinawa dated 30 December 1944 is of particular interest. After listing excerpts from Allied intelligence reports which disclosed considerable information concerning Japanese units and installations, it states that the enemy could only have obtained this information from prisoners of war interrogation or captured documents. After pointing out the necessity for greater attention to the care of secret and top secret documents, the following countermeasures were suggested: (1) limitation of the number of departments preparing the documents and limitation in distribution, (2) greatest possible decrease of documents on hand or carried along, (3) burning of documents after using, and (4) preparations to cover unforseen circumstances. The report further advised indoctrination in the idea of "shrewd and exhaustive counterintelligence as well as nurturing the capacity for carrying out counterintelligence serously," and urged thoroughness in instruction to promote security consciousness. Specific recognition was taken of the fact that in a "great number of instances" important information was revealed by Japanese prisoners of war and that since it was likely that more would be captured as the conflict progressed to its "violent extreme" troops should be fully indoctrinated as to their conduct in the event of capture. The carrying of notebooks and diaries was commented on adversely and it was also suggested that individuals should only be given the minimum information necessary for proper performance of their duties.

The effectiveness of such a security program was confirmed by a report received from XXIV Corps on the Okinawa campaign stating:

"One of the outstanding features of the Okinawa campaign is the dearth of enemy documents and identifications. Captured orders now make clear the strenuous security effort which has been carried out by the CG 32nd Army. Diaries were ordered burned and identification discs turned in. In addition, all unit records were ordered deposited with the 32nd Army."

Figure 23

Documents found in the Southeast Asia Command indicated the same trend in that area. A communication addressed to a lower echelon by the Mori 18700 Butai Staff gives detailed precautions to be taken to prevent documents from falling into Allied hands:

"Only when absolutely necessary will information be

committed to writing. Burning of secret papers must be planned when a withdrawal is ordered; diaries and notebooks will not be used to record secret data; code books and tables of organization will be kept tied by cord to the persons of responsible officers. Troops must be impressed with the importance of committing suicide before being captured to avoid being interrogated for information."

It is obvious that this pronounced tendency of the enemy toward security consciousness posed a serious problem for all Allied intelligence officers. At least insofar as documents were concerned, the enemy was able to make considerable progress in closing these fertile sources of intelligence. Fortunately, his efforts were not successful with respect to prisoners of war.

The fact that the enemy had indisputable knowledge in many instances of the extent of our information concerning him, and did as a result seek to plug the leaks, suggested strongly a laxity and need for security in our own forces. The full significance of this development was shown vividly in the enemy treatment of identification discs, which, in addition to identifying the individual soldier, also identified his unit in the form of its code name and number. Presumably the enemy had always considered this code name and number system secure, but the directives and action in having these discs turned in, and the increased use of officers' names in field orders for unit identification, clearly indicated an awareness by the enemy of our knowledge of his former system.

The possible outcome of the loss of this important source of information should have been obvious to all of our intelligence officers. The value of such items and other documents certainly proved important in every campaign and engagement. The detailed records which the Japanese kept gave the most accurate possible information of the enemy's strength, dispositions, status of equipment, status of supply, and tactics; they pinpointed important camouflaged installations and often outlined future enemy intentions, all of which contributed to easier, more economical victories.

Figure 24
" have not yielded the usual rich assortment of documents..."

CHAPTER III

COUNTERINTELLIGENCE PROCEDURES

CIC OPERATION IN A FAST-MOVING SITUATION:

The speedy advance of XIV Corps in the drive from Lingayen to Manila affords an excellent opportunity to study the effectiveness of CIC in a fast-moving situation. CIC detachments with XIV Corps and its two divisions, the 37th and 40th, included 30 agents and six officers. In addition, each of the three detachments had six Filipinos from the 2nd Filipino Battalion (U.S. Army) attached as interpreters, and the 214th Detachment (Corps) had an officer from the 2nd Filipino Battalion attached as an assistant. Additional personnel, in the form of an area team were expected to join the initial force, but were assigned by higher headquarters too late to be included in the operation.

The original plan contemplated that the three combat detachments would be sufficient to handle the counterintelligence situation for the first two to four weeks. However, the rapid advance of the 37th Division down the Central Plain was not anticipated. Early calculations were considerably upset and a serious strain was placed on CIC facilities.

In the initial landing operation, it was anticipated that the division teams would effectively cover all towns within the immediate area of the beachhead, with their strength augmented by personnel from the 214th Detachment. In the second phase, that of expanding the beachhead, it was planned that the Corps detachment would assume control in the coastal towns, while the division detachments followed closely behind the front line troops. Lastly, when sufficient ground had been recovered, area detachments were to take over from Corps, permitting the 214th Detachment to move forward with the Corps CP. As the operation developed, however, this plan could not be followed. What actually took place is set forth below.

The 40th Division CIC Detachment established an office in the town of Lingayen on S-Day. Since the 40th Division advanced slowly, the demands on CIC personnel were not excessive and they were able to operate in an orderly manner. When the detachment reached Bamban, Tarlac Province, it remained stationary and was later able to lend the 214th four of its investigators to cope with CIC problems in Manila.

The operation of the 37th Division Detachment, however, was a different story. Within a period of 28 days the detachment was forced to cover the entire distance from Lingayen to Manila, establishing sub-offices as closely behind the various combat elements as possible in the wake of the advance. It called constantly on the 214th Detachment for the loan of personnel. As they followed the 37th Division in its headlong plunge down the Central Plain, CIC agents concentrated on establishing order from the chaos in each newly liberated town, apprehending the most serious collaborators and dangerous subversive elements, and giving as close support as possible to each regiment of the 37th Division. In rapid succession, Dagupan, Calasiao, Malasiqui, San Carlos, and Urbiztondo, Pangasinan Province, were occupied and vacated by the 37th far ahead of schedule.

By this time it was obvious that the existing SOP was inadequate. The 214th found it necessary to skip towns completely that the 37th Division Detachment had rapidly passed through. In order to provide for continuity of action between the outgoing detachment and the relieving detachment, an effort was made to assign a liaison agent from the 214th to each sub-office of the 37th Detachment. His duties were to acquaint himself with the CIC situation in the town so that the division team would not have to leave detailed records behind, but the plan did not work. Liaison agents had to leave the town before the next detachment arrived in order to keep up with the rampaging 37th Division. Because a multitude of other tasks fell to CIC in each occupied town, very little actual CIC work was done and, since scant records were kept for the information of relieving detachments, what little had been accomplished was often lost and had to be done over by the next team.

One of CIC's biggest jobs on entering a new town was to establish a provisional government. Puppet officials were panelled by a board of reliable citizens. If they were found to be loyal, they were permitted to retain office. If not, CIC agents reinstated pre-war officials in their former positions. CIC then helped the officials draft a proclamation to calm the populace and set forth regulations concerning military restrictions, black-outs, curfews, turning in weapons, and the like.

Other duties included, if time permitted, processing alleged collaborators held by guerrillas, interrogating guerrillas and informants for tactical information, using every means available to get this information into intelligence channels, and making physical surveys of the town, when possible. CIC teams found it necessary to perform other missions not properly within the scope of CIC. These included the procurement of civilian labor for U.S. Army engineers, arranging for the hospitalization or medical care of Filipinos wounded by shellfire or aerial bombardment, the establishment of guerrialla guards to prevent looting, and cooperation with civil authorities in setting up a program for refugee control.

Conducting real investigations, however, was out of the question. There was simply not enough time, and the situation became progressively worse as the combat detachments continued their advance. It became increasingly difficult for agents of relieving detachments to reach a new town before the CIC combat personnel had departed. However, the 37th Detachment itself followed the practice of calling in its agents from the sub-offices every few days to make written reports of their town surveys and other action taken. While this provided the detachment with a fairly complete record, it rarely reached the following detachment in time to be of immediate use. Often, both the 37th and 214th were cut off from all communication with their sub-offices for long periods. Liaison between the 214th and the 37th was also difficult and succeeded only because of the decision of the 214th Commanding Officer to give close support to the 37th Division and to worry about the rear areas later.

The detachments were also hampered by inadequate provisions for rationing. A food shortage developed, due principally to the fact that numerous informants and guerrillas had to be fed by CIC--an unforeseen circumstance.

At the end of two weeks it was found that the attached Filipino personnel were not suited to the job for which they were intended, mainly because they spoke dialects foreign to the area in which they were operating. They were therefore assigned administrative jobs in which they proved helpful.

Lastly, it became obvious that a lack of sufficient clerks hampered the operation of the 214th Detachment. Two civilian clerks were hired, as well as civilian interpreters better qualified for the work than the 2nd Filipino Battalion personnel. Two additional Army clerks were also added.

CIC OPERATIONS IN THE BATTLE FOR MANILA:

The battle for Manila presented a new set of problems for the CIC detachments which took part. The wartime population of the city had reached approximately 1,400,000, many of these persons being without permanent homes. Included in this figure were some 3,000 enemy nationals representing five major European powers. There were also 18,000 Chinese and many persons from India, Korea, Formosa, the Netherlands East Indies, and the U.S.S.R.. The problem of security was further complicated by the presence of active German, Italian and Spanish agents.

Confusion among the civilain populace, encountered by CIC in every newly occupied town, reached chaotic proportions in the teeming city of Manila. The guerrilla problem was particularly vexing. Nowhere in the Philippines did CIC encounter so numerous and so diverse a collection of guerrilla groups as it did in Manila. They ranged from well-trained military units to little groups of hoodlums on a looting spree. CIC agents wasted valuable time in establishing the authenticity of guerrillas and in evaluating the information they volunteered to detect claims and charges that were groundless. These are but a few of the headaches that awaited CIC in Manila.

Responsibility for the Manila operation rested with XIV Corps. CIC detachments under Corps jurisdiction included the 214th, 37th, 11th (11th Airborne Division), and 801st (1st Cavalry Division). These units were assisted by a special metropolitan force composed of agents from the 306th, 450th, 457th, and 493rd CIC Detachments. Approximately 50 agents were committed to the initial invasion of the city. During the first two weeks, nearly 100 agents were on duty.

By agreement of all detachments, the 214th and the three division teams under it undertook searches and seizures in the city, the screening of refugees coming from enemy territory, and the investigation of alleged collabortors in the hands of guerrillas at the time of the entry of American troops.

Figure 25 - "Investigation of alleged collaborators..."

The 214th directed the work of search squads whose duty it was to comb Japanese-occupied buildings for documents. Several thousand pounds of documentary material were seized by CIC agents in the city, and a wealth of information concerning the Japanese and the activities of pro-Japanese agencies and other national groups was obtained. Three Nisei from the Army Language Detachment were attached to CIC to assist in scanning these documents for immediate tactical and counterintelligence information.

Hundreds of civilians who were displaced from their homes or freed from Japanese internment streamed through the lines to seek the protection of American forces. The 37th CIC Detachment was assigned the task of interrogating these civilians for tactical information. During the height of the battle, between 2,000 and 3,000 persons a day passed through its screening point. The 214th was responsible to the Corps G-2 for getting tactical information.

The 214th Detachment, with the help of four agents borrowed from the 40th Detachment and excess personnel from the 37th, undertook the more difficult task of processing approximately 150 alleged collaborators held by guerrillas and initiating investigations when charges appeared to be substantiated.

The remaining personnel from the other CIC detachments which took part in the operation were pooled in a central location from which their work throughout the city was directed. These men concentrated, for the most part, on the investigation of collaborators. Scores of persons were brought to CIC headquarters by guerrillas and other well-intentioned Filipinos with vague charges of collaboration. Many of these persons were temporarily cleared and released when insufficient evidence could be found. But many others were interned, and one of the later jobs of the 493rd (regional) CIC Detachment was to re-process and classify the large number of prisoners sent by CIC to Bilibid Prison. They included Japanese espionage agents who had been left behind to gather information, Filipino collaborators who had actively aided the Japanese, enemy nationals (German and Japanese), Indians and Chinese sympathetic to Japan and its puppet governments, and Kempei Tai agents.

Still another problem was posed by the approximately 8,500 civilian internees who had been left by the Japanese in Santo Tomas University and the Muntinglupa internment camp on the outskirts of the city. It was necessary to screen these persons for tactical information and to issue clearances before they could be evacuated for repatriation. CIC agents performed these duties.

All of this work was accomplished under conditions that were adverse, to say the least. The job of locating food, shelter, and sanitary facilities taxed the ingenuity of CIC personnel to the utmost. Detachments were woefully ill-prepared in this respect and were obliged to use all sorts of makeshift arrangements to prepare food and establish decent quarters. Another distracting factor was the fact that a fierce battle for control of the city was raging not many yards from where the first CIC detachments set up their headquarters. Snipers, artillery and mortar fire, land mines, Japanese demolition charges, and fierce fires curtailed many CIC activities.

COUNTERINTELLIGENCE SCREENING:

An important function of CIC throughout the Luzon campaign was the screening of the vast number of civilians who came from Japanese territory into American zones as the operation progressed. Two things were accomplished by this screening: valuable tactical information on enemy strength, disposition, and installations was obtained and forwarded to appropriate G-2 sections; and many collaborators, enemy agents, spies and Japanese sympathizers were apprehended.

CIC screening activities did not follow a universal pattern. Combat detachments with a division committed to front line action employed certain methods, while detachments in a static situation in rear areas used others. Both will be discussed below.

The 43rd Division CIC Detachment probably handled more civilian evacuees than any other detachment in Luzon; thus its experience in the field is a good example of forward area screening.

Not many civilians were encountered by the 43rd Division in the first few days after its landing at Lingayen Gulf. Although some suspicious persons were brought to

CIC headquarters, most were cleared locally after reference to a few informants hastily contacted. Records of these persons were kept and white (cleared civilian) passes issued to those investigated, but no reports were sent to higher headquarters. The detachment at the same time contacted or recruited guerrilla guides and auxiliaries; these, upon clearance, were issued blue (guerrilla) passes. Later, when the division had worked out a definite procedure for recruiting, supplying and paying guerrillas, this practice was discontinued.

Within two weeks after the landing, however, civilian evacuees began crossing the division lines by the thousands. Some were driven by curiosity or the desire to contact Americans, but the majority came in because of the increased brutality of the enemy toward non-combatants. These people were not laborers or auxiliary soldiers, but families, bringing with them livestock and household possessions. They were screened by CIC agents placed at strategic road blocks along the main highways leading from Japanese territory. These travelers were interrogated for tactical information only, with relatively poor results. Very few pro-Japanese were apprehended at this stage, as they were not disposed to leave the Japanese and surrender so early in the invasion.

When the 43rd Division moved into the area east of Manila, a new factor began to assert itself. Large numbers of Makapili and Pampars, auxiliary Filipino soldiers recruited from local Ganap organizations, Butais and the Yoin (United Nippons) taken by the Japanese in their retreat from Rizal and Laguna Provinces were encountered. Most of them were armed, uniformed and trained to assist the enemy. Many of these persons had incurred the wrath of local guerrillas by their past pro-Japanese activities and could not afford to remain behind once the Japanese garrisons had withdrawn. Consequently, taking their families with them, they evacuated with the enemy to the Sierra Madre range via Antipolo, Tanay, and Santa Maria, Laguna Province. Although they had systematically looted all lakeside villages of food before retreating, their supplies soon dwindled, and it was not long before hunger drove hundreds of these people to surrender to our troops. Others were captured while accompanying Japanese patrols.

The following procedure was used in screening these persons: line companies passed civilians back to their regimental headquarters where they were questioned by a CIC agent, assisted by an interpreter. If at all suspicious, the agent filled out an interrogation sheet listing name, address, personal description, education, and circumstances of capture. With reference to the latter, the following information was obtained: time, date, place of capture (with map coordinates, if possible), name of captor, documents and other materiel possessed by prisoner at time of capture, exact details of apprehension (whether with an enemy patrol, for instance). clothing worn, and any other pertinent details. Sometimes the agent obtained a longhand affidavit from the captor describing the capture. The interrogation often elicited tactical information of value to the regimental S-2. Maps and aerial photographs were used to pinpoint Japanese installations.

Next, the suspect was forwarded to the detachment or division headquarters, where CIC agents conducted a more thorough interrogation. The suspect was questioned concerning his activities before and during the war, and encouraged to talk about himself. His story was taken down, and if sufficiently incriminating, reduced to a written confession and duly executed in the presence of witnesses. If the suspect came from a locality within the division zone, or had been active there, his story was checked with local informants known to be loyal. Witnesses to incriminating acts by the suspects signed affidavits describing the incident. These affidavits were attached to the confession or used to induce a more complete confession. A memorandum was then prepared summarizing the evidence and listing undeveloped leads. In the event the suspect came from another section of the country. a copy of the report and confession was forwarded to the CIC detachment operating in that area. If a large number of suspects from another detachment's area came in, arrangements were made to ship them to that detachment, together with a roster and a description of the circumstances of capture.

Suspects who confessed, or against whom a complete case had been made, were interned at Bilibid Prison or the Muntinglupa detention camp. Those against whom cases were unfinished were detained at a local jail pending completion. When the division moved, all such persons were interned with interim case reports. If subsequent investigation failed to substantiate charges, these prisoners were released.

The most damaging evidence that fell into the hands of CIC agents screening evacuees were the papers and documents possessed by the suspect at the time of capture. The Filipino had a tendency to retain personal papers long after it was safe to do so. Typical documents found included Ganap party membership cards, Makapili membership certificates, Matsuyama Butai passes, Yoin membership cards, Kempei Tai passes, Kalibapi cards, clippings containing pro-Japanese propaganda, and damaging personal correspondence.

In the final phase of the Luzon campaign, the 43rd CIC Detachment tried some novel stunts. One was to set up a public address system and broadcast invitations to surrender. Makapili were addressed in their native tongue by a loyal Filipino. When the detachment learned that Pio Duran, guiding spirit of the Makapili organization, was in its sector, it prepared leaflets inviting him to surrender, and dropped them from a Cub plane in the area where he was reported to be hiding. Duran eventually gave himself up to 38th Division troops, but he carried with him one of the 43rd's leaflets.

CIC detachments in static areas behind the fighting fronts were faced with acute screening problems in large centers of population. Refugees and persons displaced from their homes by the exigencies of war invariably congregated in the nearest city in the hopes of finding food and shelter. Residents of a city who evacuated their homes when it became a battleground, streamed back into town at the first opportunity. CIC agents were obliged to screen these people to obtain tactical information and to detect enemy agents or collaborators attempting to get through American lines. In the Luzon campaign, the city of Baguio was an outstanding example.

Baguio operations were conducted by a special CIC detachment composed of three officers and 24 agents from the 478th, 33rd, 37th, and 201st CIC detachments. Tactical screening points through which thousands of evacuees had passed as they fled the city prior to American re-entry had been operated at Naguilian, La Union, by the 37th CIC Detachment, and at a point near Baguio on Route 9 by the 478th. Consequently, CIC had on hand a large file of suspects and persons wanted in Baguio. These names were augmented by a blacklist compiled during the Japanese occupation by Volckmann's guerrillas (USAFIP, Northern Luzon).

The situation in the city immediately after its occupation by American troops was complicated by these factors: a substantial percentage of the population had previously evacuated, thousands of non-residents from mountain communities were seeking refuge in the city, practically all public records had been destroyed, civilian government was non-existent, and few of the people had any permanent address, since a majority of the dwellings had been demolished. In addition, the populace was starving, confused, and suffering from battle shock. There was this advantage for the CIC, however: the people naturally turned to and cooperated with a visible authority, and CIC quickly established itself as that authority.

Figure 26 - "Refugees...congregated in the nearest city..."

Because Baguio had been the Japanese military headquarters and the seat of the puppet Philippine government after the evacuation of Manila, search parties were given top counterintelligence priority. Consequently only three agents and three enlisted men from the 2nd Filipino Battalion were available for screening duty. The agents were carefully selected and had devoted intensive study to the blacklist.

The American forces entered Baguio on 28 April 1945 and by noon of that day a CIC screening point was established in the Baguio Cathedral. The location was suitable as it was the nerve center of the city, the Cathedral being the one building in the business district which had not been a target for bombing and was, therefore, a place of refuge. When our forces entered, it was also used as a hospital, a civilian aid station, and a food distribution center.

The screening team set up two offices, one, manned by one agent and two Filipinos, as a registration desk at the entrance of the Cathedral, the other, in the interior, for more detailed interrogations of suspects and informants. Initially, all persons in the city were required to register. As each person appeared he was given a hasty interrogation. If a suspect was spotted, or if the individual possessed tactical or counter-intelligence information, he was routed to the interrogation desk. All persons were told when they registered to turn in all weapons and to report the location of arms or ammunition.

It soon became obvious that it was impossible to register every civilian in the city; therefore, the people were told that one member of a non-resident family could report for the whole group. It was also found that checking each name against the blacklist required too much time. Accordingly, four informants were stationed behind the desk or among the crowd as "spotters" to point out collaborators. This proved to be a very efficient method of apprehending suspects.

Members of the Military Police detachment and various guerrilla groups cooperated by rounding up known suspects and bringing them to the Cathedral. Four Filipinos were given arms and employed as guards to control the crowd milling about the church. As movement out of Baguio was rigidly controlled and also because guerrillas were shooting prominent collaborators on sight, many persons on the wanted list remained in the vicinity of the Cathedral. Most suspects were restricted by parole only, being required to report daily to the registration desk. Many civilian informants reported on their own volition and were given brief loyalty checks by the interrogation team.

By 5 May the search targets had been covered and the CIC detachment was well established in a permanent headquarters. The screening point in the Cathedral was closed. In conjunction with the Military Police a pass system was established to control movement of civilians out of Baguio. Passes were issued by the Military Police (later by the Mayor) but were checked and stamped at the CIC office before they were valid. Thus all persons seeking exit from the city could be checked against CIC wanted lists before they departed.

In the first ten days of operation nearly 1,200 individuals were screened, 33 of them being detained. In addition, approximately 100 names were added to the suspect and "wanted" files, and a large informant net was created. One of the outstanding accomplishments of the Baguio detachment was the apprehension of Kisaburo Nisikawa, a Japanese spy, who was attempting to slip through American lines on an espionage mission.

Figure 27 - Apprehension of Kisaburo Nisikawa

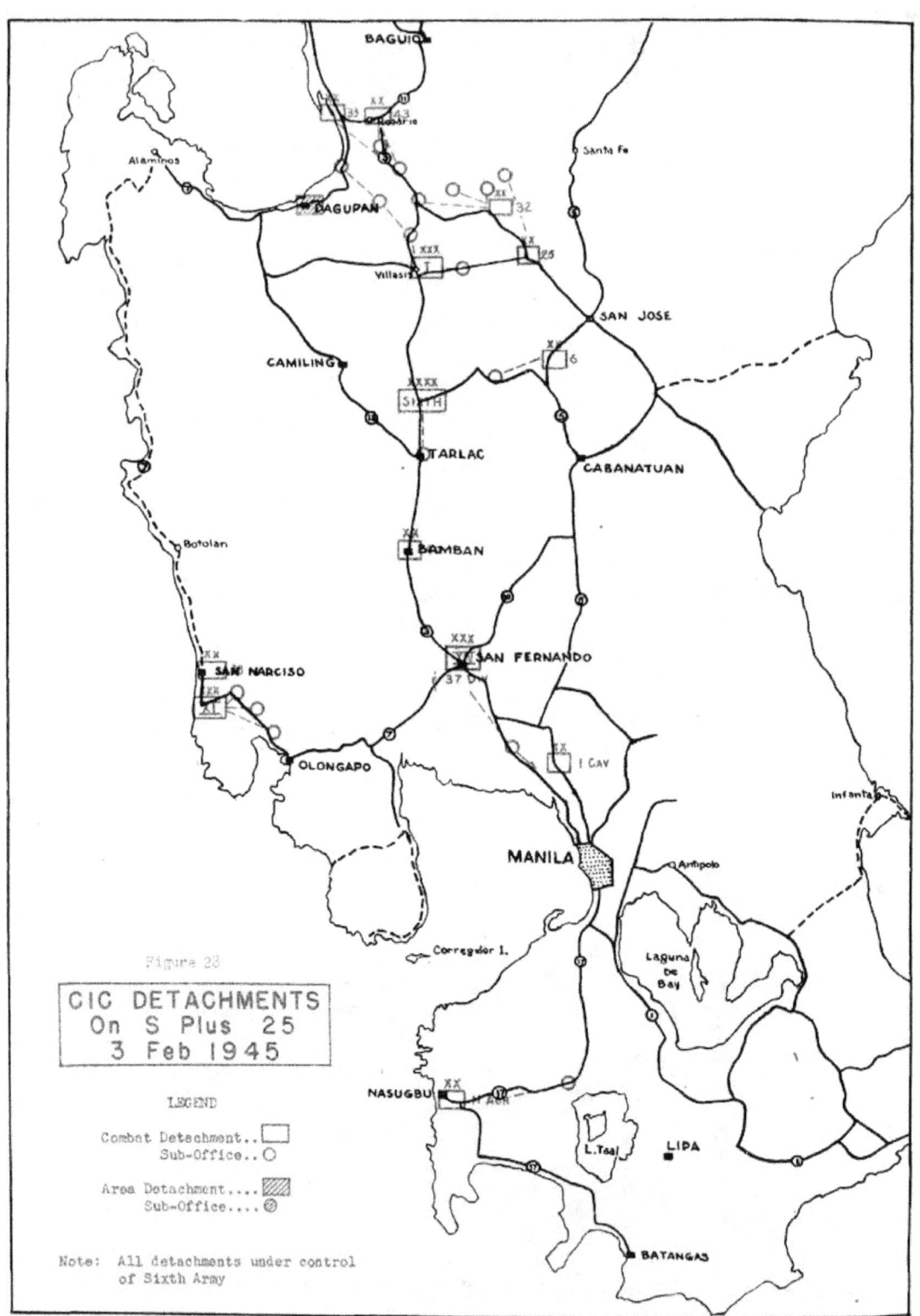

Figure 23

CIC DETACHMENTS
On S Plus 25
3 Feb 1945

LEGEND

Combat Detachment.. ☐
  Sub-Office.. ○
Area Detachment.... ▨
  Sub-Office.... ⊘

Note: All detachments under control of Sixth Army

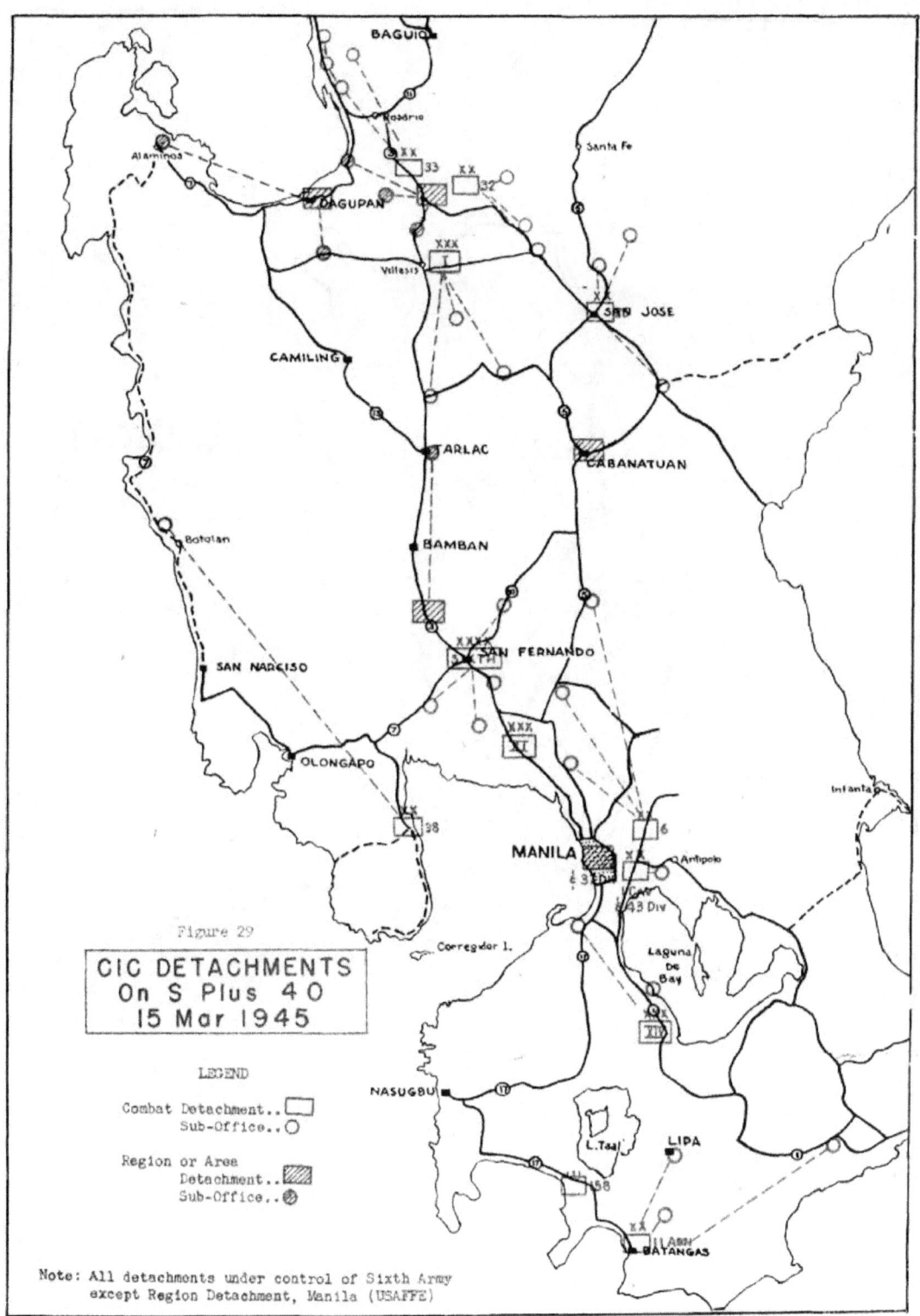

Figure 29

CIC DETACHMENTS
On S Plus 40
15 Mar 1945

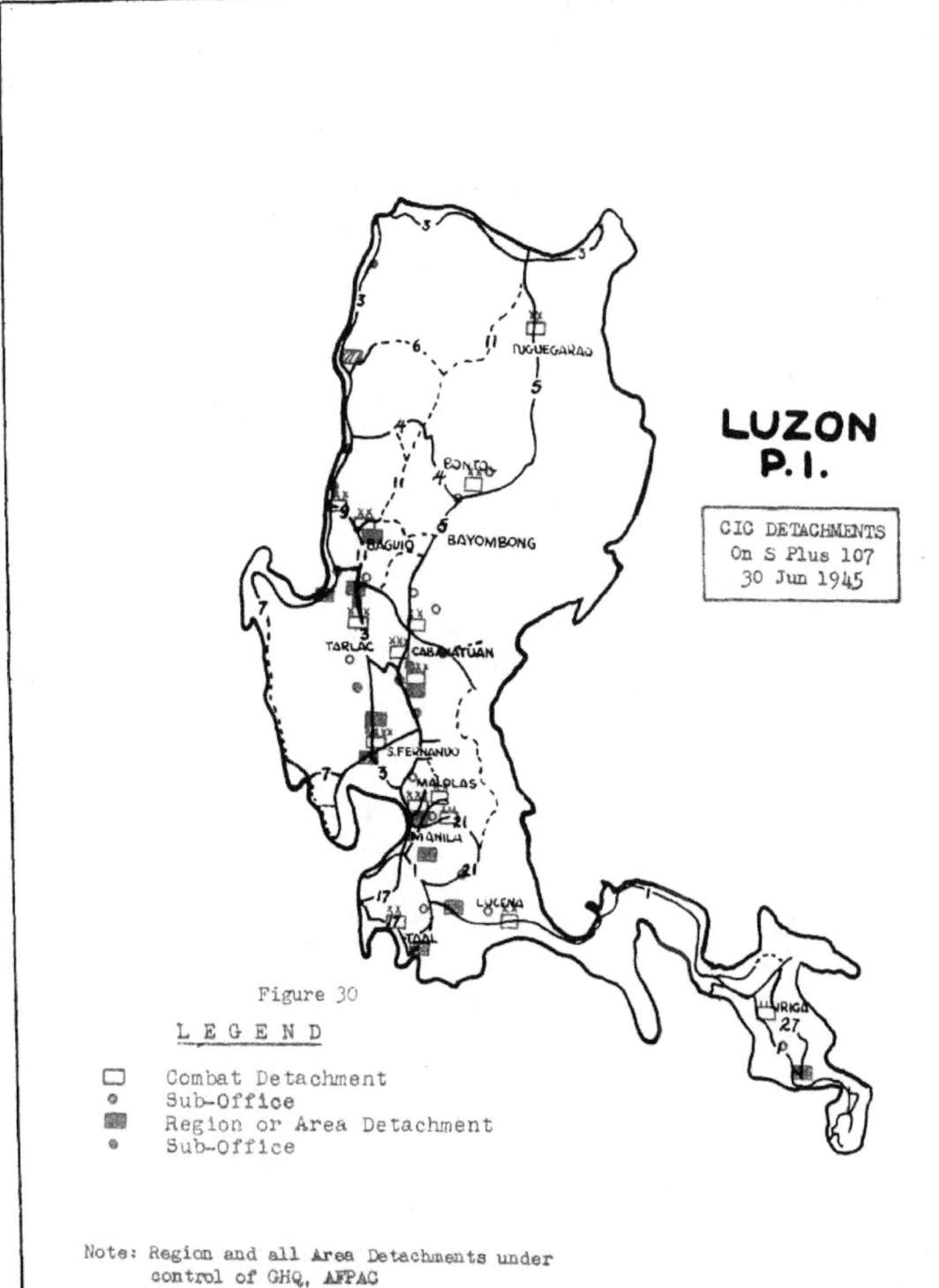

Figure 30

CHAPTER IV

SPECIAL RECONNAISSANCE OPERATIONS

GUERRILLA SUPPLY ADMINISTRATION AND COMMUNICATIONS ON LUZON:

Prominent in the history of the campaigns which removed the Japanese from the Philippine Islands will be the role taken by native guerrillas. Handicapped through the years of occupation for want of food and clothing and even the arms and ammunition with which to fight, they came into their own when American troops swept into the islands.

Effective employment of these scattered guerrilla bands, however, involved major problems in logistics and administration. While many units were well organized, others were loosely knit. Although units were officially recognized, others were of indeterminate status. Common to all was the pressing need for arms and supplies, and for an efficient and adequate system of communication.

With the landing of Army troops in Luzon, the Special Intelligence sub-section of G-2 arranged for delivery to organized units of arms, ammunition, clothing and field equipment as well as an extensive assortment of signal equipment. Requests for supplies came in by radio. Air drops or delivery by C-47 to strips constructed by the guerrillas were then arranged.

Requisitions were submitted first to G-3 to establish priority status, to G-4 for approval, and finally to the appropriate staff sections. Arrangements for delivery were made through the Transportation Section.

An uninterrupted flow of supplies was thus potentially assured, but difficulties arose in connection with delivery. At first air-drops were frequently lost or not delivered, either because the recipient unit moved into a new area after making its request without informing G-2 or because the unit failed to display proper recognition signals. Through patient and repeated instruction by radio, guerrilla units learned the necessity of keeping headquarters constantly informed of their movements and to show recognition signals when drops were scheduled.

Figure 31 - "air drops ... were then arranged..."

Radio communication with guerrilla units on Luzon was established from Leyte and continued while our forces steamed north toward Lingayen Gulf. The communications enroute were accomplished through a monitoring circuit set up aboard the Command ship.

Three of these stations were in the area taken over by Sixth Army on S-Day. Through them flowed information from Northern Luzon and the Central Plain. Within two weeks, three more stations were added and by March all guerrilla radios on Luzon were operating in Special Intelligence nets. Through the channels of this network came intelligence reports from 70 widely scattered stations.

Here again there were difficulties. Guerrilla operators were accustomed to a procedure of their own, partly military, partly civilian. Handling of such traffic in the Sixth Army Message Center would have involved serious delays in the transmission of intelligence. Therefore, a Filipino Message Center with operators experienced in guerrilla procedure was established and proved to be the effective solution.

There were other communication "bugs", chief of which was the problem of providing repair parts for the off-standard radio sets being used by the guerrillas. Experience on Leyte taught that standard signal equipment would be inadequate; therefore, stocks of spare parts for all the various types of radios used in the nets were shipped with the first echelon of G-2 equipment. If these stocks had not been brought in, no immediate solution of the guerrilla radio supply problem would have been possible, since no dumps of signal supply were available early in the campaign. Supplies taken from Army stocks were later replaced when the guerrilla shipment arrived.

From the outset, a troublesome obstacle to the efficient operation of guerrilla units was the nebulous status of many organizations. Since little was known concerning many of these organizations, there being no overall command as in Mindanao and the Visayas, several months passed during which scores of Filipino fighting men were neither "fish nor fowl". Considerable dissatisfaction was the inevitable result, but the situation cleared when it was determined to recognize bona fide units as components of the Philippine Army. Officers and men then received formal status and proper pay.

No sooner had the "recognition policy" been announced than a flood of claims threatened to inundate the Special Intelligence section. Since many were known to be spurious, it was necessary to determine the legitimacy of every claim.

American units employing guerrillas submitted rosters

to the Sixth Army G-1 and these in turn were passed to the Special Intelligence section for verification. Approved rosters went forward to USAFFE with a request for formal recognition of the units involved. Lists of recognized units were then published.

Not the least serious of guerrilla operational problems were the inability of many units to coordinate their efforts, the various political frictions, and, in some cases, the lack of recognized leadership. These problems were solved through the employment of Alamo Scout teams as coordinating agencies. Where guerrilla leadership was absent or disputed, Scout officers assumed command. Where political frictions existed, diplomatic appeals for unity of effort and expulsion of chronic agitators were effective.

Concern of the Special Intelligence section over all these problems ended as American troops contacted and assumed control of guerrilla units. The contacting American unit, along with the assumption of command, also assumed logistical and administrative responsibility.

COORDINATION OF GUERRILLA ACTIVITIES:

During the Luzon campaign, Alamo Scout missions were generally of two types: 1) collection of information from guerrilla and civilian sources and by personal reconnaissance and 2) organization of guerrilla activities. The following account, written by an Alamo Scout team leader assigned the mission of coordinating guerrilla activities in the southern Bicol, is included in this publication as an example of the second type of mission:

"When we landed at Magallanes, Sorsogon Province, (12 miles north of Bulan) by seaplane on 8 February 1945, our mission was to develop intelligence in Albay and Sorsogon Provinces, to requisition necessary supplies for guerrilla units, and to advise the Escudero and Lapus units to become active in the Bulan---San Francisco area. My team consisted of three American soldiers, two Filipino soldiers educated in the United States and a Filipino radio operator from the Philippine Message Center at Sixth Army headquarters.

"During the occupation considerable friction had existed between Escudero and Lapus, guerrilla leaders in Sorsogon Province. Escudero, Lapus, and Zabat (a guerrilla leader from Albay Province) had all aspired to be commander of the Fifth Military District (the Bicol provinces, Tayabas Province and part of Batangas). Several conferences on this subject had accomplished nothing since none of the three would subordinate himself to any other. As a result of this rivalry, bad blood existed between Escudero and Lapus, causing firefights in several instances.

"Escudero, the former governor of Sorsogon Province, had refused to surrender to the Japanese in 1942, had gathered available Philippine Army officers and enlisted men, and, supplementing these with civilians, had formed a regiment. Prior to the Lingayen Gulf landing he had accumulated 350 small arms, four 81-mm mortars, 4 light machine guns and 16 bazookas, the bulk of these being U.S. arms sent in by PT boat during the Leyte campaign.

"When Escudero first organized his unit he established a training center in the hills where classes in military courtesy and discipline, tactics, weapons, and marksmanship were run by experienced Philippine Army officers. At the completion of the training program the armed men were retained and employed actively in harassing the enemy; some of the unarmed men were retained as service troops to secure rations; the others were sent home and called in as additional arms became available. The method of organization and training of this unit was typical of all guerrilla units in the area, and efficiency varied greatly.

"Lapus was the former inspector of Sorsogon Province. He also had organized a regiment, two battalions of which were in Camarines Sur and the third in Sorsogon. His Sorsogon unit possessed 60 arms. Lapus had some able Philippine Army officers, his training program had been good, and he was on good terms with the civilian population.

"Immediately upon the landing of my unit, the Escudero unit was contacted and an arms and ammunition drop arranged. Escudero was instructed to proceed with 200 armed men to the Bulan area; the remainder of the arms were to be employed in northern Sorsogon Province to prevent enemy stragglers from moving north into Albay.

"After these arrangements I dispatched three of my team to Jovellar (15 miles southwest of Legaspi), Albay Province, where they were to collect information and maintain daily radio contact with Sixth Army. They travelled that night by banca across Sorsogon Bay and up the Jovellar River to Jovellar. The remainder of the team and I walked to the Bulan area which we found occupied by approximately 200 Japanese and 160 Formosans.

"Prior to leaving for Bulan, Major Sabarre, Philippine Army, was contacted. He had been sent in prior to the Lingayen landing by GHQ. He had several radios and his mission was to coordinate the collection of intelligence in the Bicol.

"When I arrived in the Bulan area I contacted Lapus and, upon the arrival on 28 February of Escudero with his 200 men, a meeting was held. Due to the rivalry between the two, neither Lapus nor Escudero would operate in the Bulan area with the other; however, they agreed to cooperate under my command. I established the Irosin--Bulan road as the boundary between the two units; Escudero was to be on the north and Lapus on the south. By 3 March four enemy garrisons in the barrios of Bulan had been driven into Bulan town and on 4 March the town was taken. The remaining Japanese went to San Francisco, the last remaining permanent enemy garrison in Sorsogon.

"In order to avoid friction, I had to divide Bulan town into two districts and each unit was ordered to police one half. Escudero was to operate north of Bulan and to contain the enemy garrison at San Francisco; Lapus was made responsible for the coast south of Bulan to Monito, as stragglers were still coming from Capul and Samar Islands (south of the Bicol).

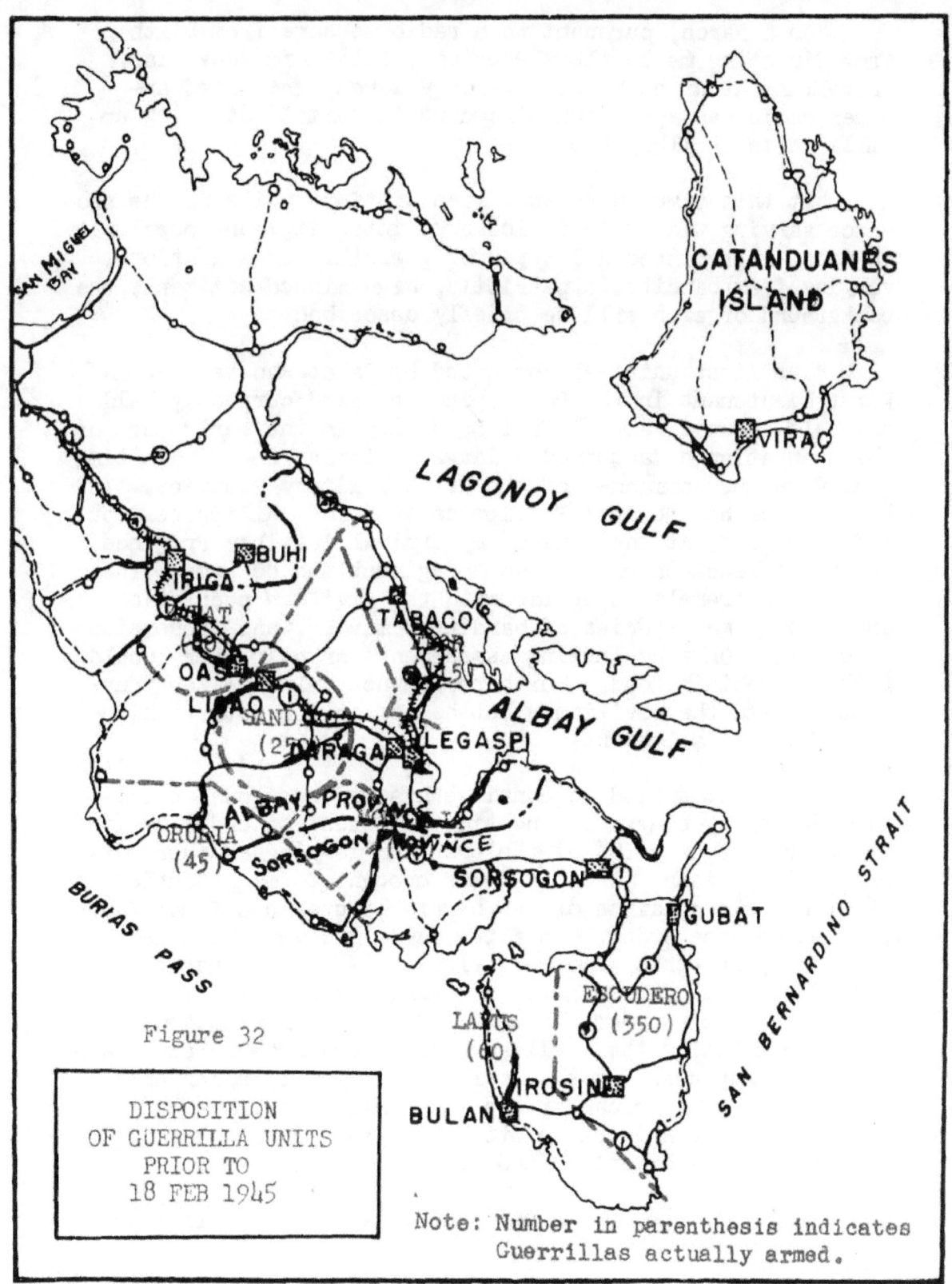

Figure 32

DISPOSITION OF GUERRILLA UNITS PRIOR TO 18 FEB 1945

Note: Number in parenthesis indicates Guerrillas actually armed.

"On 4 March, pursuant to a radio message from Sixth Army directing me to Albay Province, I left for Jovellar, travelling at night by banca. On 9 March I received another radio message which placed me in command of all guerrilla units in Albay Province.

"At this time there were five distinct units in the province varying widely in efficiency, integrity, and popularity. As these represented all types of guerrilla organizations, varying from bandits to patriotic, high-minded citizens, the background of each will be briefly described.

"The first unit was commanded by Zabat who had been a First Lieutenant in the Philippine Army and currently held the self-assumed rank of full Colonel. In the early part of the occupation he acquired a large following and at one time nearly became commander of the Fifth Military District. In his unit he had several Philippine Army and Philippine Scout officers, and, at the time of my arrival in Albay Province, Zabat, at least on paper, had a regiment and 80 arms. The unit was extremely unpopular with the civilian population and unconfirmed stories of banditry, murder, and oppression were rife. Only by levying assessments or by robbery could this unit obtain food. Furthermore, not only was Zabat unpopular with the civilians, but he was on the outs with the other guerrilla leaders.

"Zabat attempted to continue his unscrupulous activities during my stay. At one time he issued an order taxing the share croppers 20% of the crop and levying another 20% on the land owner. When this was brought to my attention through the complaints of the barrio lieutenants I had Zabat retract the order. In a few days, however, he tried the same game--this time he levied a 20% tax on the gross of all cabarets, cockfights, and gambling houses. I made him retract this order. A week later, in a last attempt to continue mulcting the civilians, Zabat ordered all civilians to accept Japanese invasion currency as legal tender until the arrival of American troops. In this manner he thought to unload his considerable stock of this paper. This order soon came to my attention and was retracted.

"Next was the Orubia unit. Orubia had the self-assumed

rank of Brigadier General, no military background and few Philippine Army officers in his organization. His strength was one regiment on paper and 45 arms. The unit was loosely knit, poorly trained, and completely undisciplined. Relations with civilians and other guerrilla units were bad. The area occupied by this unit was hardly ever entered by the Japanese; the men of this organization apparently had made no attempt to harass the Japanese, but contented themselves with pillaging the civilians.

"The third unit, the Monillia unit, was commanded by the mayor of Jovellar. Monillia was largely of Spanish blood, spoke no English and held the self-appointed rank of Lieutenant General while two of his staff members were self-appointed Brigadier Generals. The roster of this unit showed six regiments and 45 arms. Few regular Philippine Army officers were in the unit, and discipline was very lax. Monillia, however, was a clever politician. The civilians in the area were behind him and voluntarily donated food. He was on good terms with all other guerrilla units except the Zabat and Orubia units. Generally speaking the Monillia organization caused little harm, but was incapable of doing much good.

"The fourth unit was headed by Sandico, formerly the provincial inspector of Albay Province, who held the Philippine Army rank of Major and had the assumed rank of full Colonel. The unit had a large number of Philippine Army officers and enlisted men, consisted of two regiments and had 250 small arms, two 81-mm mortars, and 3 bazookas. The training of this unit had been exceptional. Relations with the civilians were excellent and Sandico was on good terms with all other guerrilla leaders except Orubia and Zabat.

"The fifth unit was commanded by Flor who had been a non-commissioned officer in the Philippine Army and who currently held the assumed rank of Lieutenant Colonel. His force consisted of two regiments and possessed 115 small arms, 4 light machine guns and two 50 caliber machine guns. The unit was on excellent terms with the civilians who looked on it as their protector and as civil police. When I arrived in Albay this unit had secured the entire coast north from Libog (10 miles north of Legaspi) to the

Camarines Sur border and had cleared the bulk of the Japanese from nearby islands.

"As can readily be supposed, many factors militated against the voluntary combination of these units under one leader. Two of the most potent factors were the desires for self-aggrandizement politically and militarily. Obviously anyone who had been an important guerrilla leader during the occupation would have a good start in politics after the war. Furthermore, a commission in the Philippine Army was most desirable. Guerrilla leaders in the Bicol had heard that several guerrilla leaders elsewhere in the Philippines had already been recognized and given commissions in the Philippine Army. As leaders of their own unit they expected to attain a higher rank in the Philippine Army than they would otherwise. By submitting to another leader they felt that they would lose stature.

"These factors which kept the guerrilla units from combining worked in my favor; for, since I was the Sixth Army representative in the southern Bicol, all realized that recognition would come either by my direct recommendation or through mention in my reports. Furthermore, their only means of getting arms and ammunition, which they were all clamoring for, was through me. Undoubtedly these factors are responsible for the complete cooperation that I received from all units. No sooner had I arrived in Albay than I was flooded with intelligence reports, reports of action against the enemy, requests for arms (including equipment for six full regiments of the Monillia unit) and petitions seeking redress against other units for past wrongs.

"When I entered Albay there were approximately 2,200 Japanese in the Camalig—Legaspi—Gapo—Mt Bariwy area (generally 10 miles west and southwest of Legaspi), referred to by the Japanese as little Bataan. Though the Japanese were actively patrolling the surrounding country and taking large quantities of foodstuffs from the civilians, we were still able to send agents into the little Bataan area. These agents would talk with the enemy officers while selling chickens and the like. Quantities of intelligence information were obtained in this manner until the heavy bombings commenced which preceded the 1 April landing at Legaspi.

"Upon arriving in Albay, I established a CP near Guinobatan (15 miles northwest of Legaspi) and immediately called a conference of all guerrilla leaders. At this conference I made it clear that units causing trouble with other units or pillaging the civilians would receive no further supplies from me and would not be mentioned in intelligence reports to higher headquarters. On the other hand, units supplying reliable intelligence reports and taking part in actions against the Japanese would be mentioned favorably and would receive supplies. I further emphasized that all charges and accusations among themselves for past conduct did not concern me, but that CIC would take these matters up when they arrived with our troops.

"At this same meeting I assigned each unit, except the Zabat unit, a sector around the little Bataan area so that the enemy could be harassed if they attempted to withdraw. The Zabat unit was placed to the north to prevent the enemy forces in the north from filtering south and joining the little Bataan troops. In assigning sectors to units I attempted to place each as near as possible to their old sectors. In all cases, except that of the Orubia unit which had to move a considerable distance, I was able to do this. The reason for effecting such an arrangement is a practical one. Guerrilla units of necessity depend on the civilian population for food. When assigned a mission in another unit's area, not only does serious friction over this matter develop between the civilians and the new unit, but incidents between the new and old units are bound to arise.

"When these guerrilla organizations were redisposed Major Sabarre was called in and arrangements were made whereby his net control station moved to my CP and one of his radios was placed with each guerrilla unit.

"A permanent drop area was established at Jovellar and a supply dump was maintained in the hills. Two of my team members were placed in charge, and on 13 March we began to receive supply drops of arms, ammunition, and medical supplies. It was essential to check very carefully on all requests for supplies. Furthermore, it was found to be poor policy to issue much ammunition at one time; as a rule, guerrilla troops are prone to fire large amounts for morale effect.

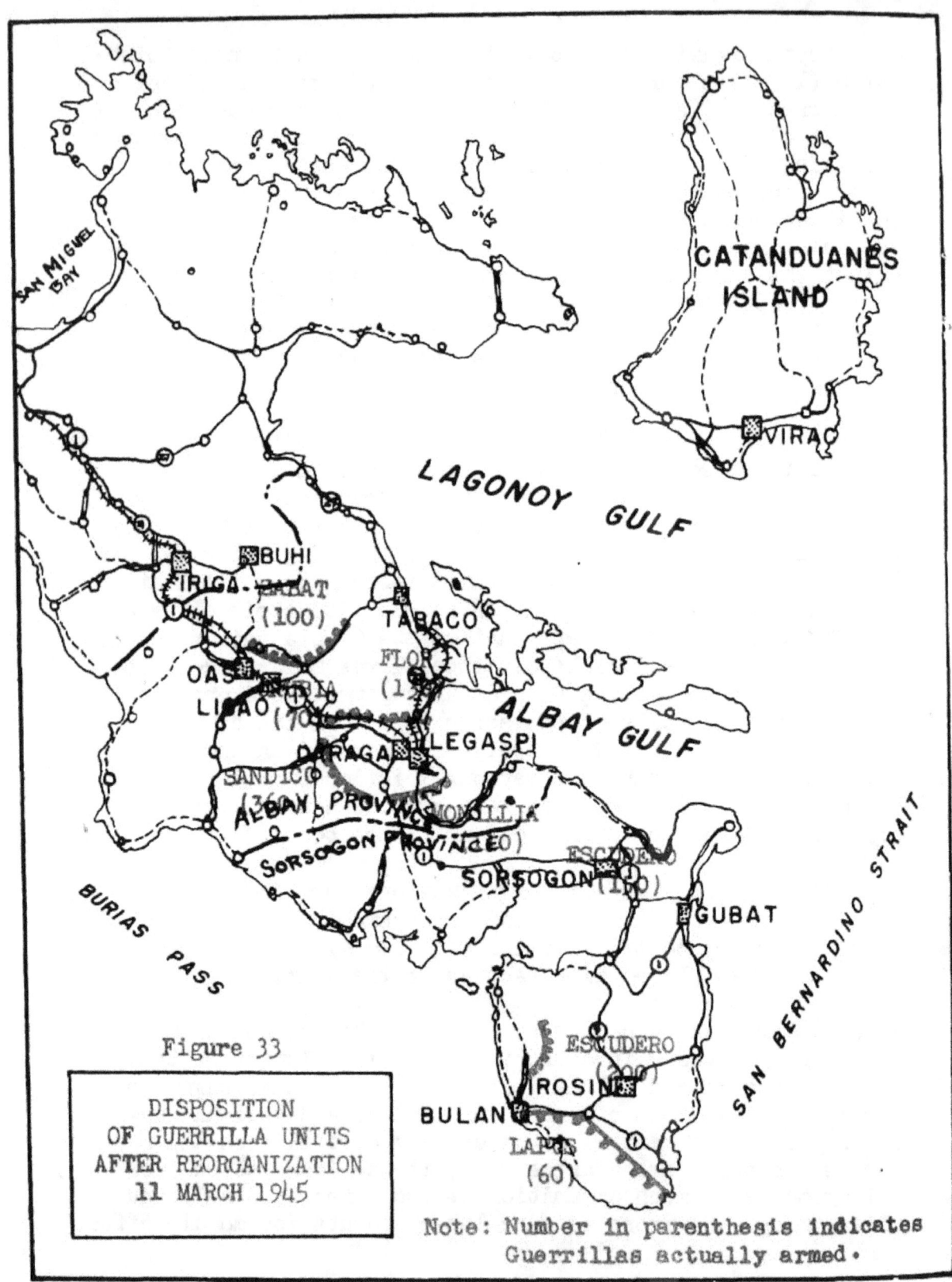

Figure 33

DISPOSITION OF GUERRILLA UNITS AFTER REORGANIZATION 11 MARCH 1945

Note: Number in parenthesis indicates Guerrillas actually armed.

After I determined what was needed, the commander making the request was given a chit authorizing him to draw the determined amount.

"In spite of my having assigned definite sectors to each unit, some friction persisted. I received many complaints from guerrilla leaders regarding maltreatment by other units, and about the disarming and arrest of their men by other units. The bulk of incidents of this nature was caused by the Zabat and Orubia units. A typical example occurred on 17 March near Malacbalac (southwest Albay Province). I had proceeded there on a civilian motorcycle to meet another Alamo Scout officer coming in by seaplane and to send out sketches, captured documents, and intelligence reports to Sixth Army. Zabat had sent a lieutenant and 5 armed men to contact me at Malacbalac about supplies. Orubia disarmed and held prisoner Zabat's men so that they couldn't speak to me about supplies. Fortunately I found this out. Orubia's story was that the arms that Zabat's men had were his. Having no time to investigate the matter thoroughly, I took the arms to guard my own supply dump.

"By 13 March all units, except the Orubia unit, were in position and had commenced ambushing enemy patrols and attacking outposts. Due to the excellent intelligence obtained from civilians and by reason of their thorough knowledge of the terrain, the guerrillas had all the advantage in this type of action. This fact was thoroughly appreciated by the Japanese and enemy outposts were driven in with surprising ease. On numerous occasions guerrillas raided the enemy's prepared positions, usually at night. Occupied huts were machine-gunned and 81-mm mortars were used for harassing fire. The enemy's return fire was heavy on these occasions, and it was not unusual for the Japanese to continue their fire 20 to 40 minutes after the guerrillas had left the area.

"On 23 March I discovered that the Orubia unit had held a parade with their new arms, four days after they were supposed to be in position, in Dansol, 20 miles from their assigned sector. On 24 March I intercepted half of the Orubia unit. They informed me that they had pulled out of their sector because they could not harass the enemy since he was numerically superior. This part of Orubia's unit was disarmed on the spot; Orubia was relieved of his sector and ordered to disband his unit.

"Since being disarmed and disbanded was a major calamity for Orbuia, I was not at all sure that he would obey my order. Thus to give added weight to the original order, I attached a memorandum stating that, if the order was not complied with immediately, I would send Orubia out by seaplane to Sixth Army where an investigation would be made of his past activities. Since an investigation of his previous activities was something that Orubia was most anxious to avoid, the unit was disbanded and all arms were turned in to me. These arms were then given to the Sandico unit which extended its lines and took over Orubia's area.

"On 1 April, when the 158th RCT landed at Legaspi, I contacted the RCT headquarters. I had been in radio contact with the 158th RCT since 17 March and had been sending them daily intelligence reports as well as beach information and recommendations for air strikes. My instructions from Sixth Army were to be of what use I could in regard to coordination of guerrilla activities. Upon order of the CG, 158th RCT, I moved my net control station to the headquarters of the RCT and handled all guerrilla matters for them.

Figure 34 - "recommendation for air strikes..."

"While the 158th RCT was attacking west from Legaspi, guerrilla units were instructed to remain in their assigned positions to prevent stragglers from escaping the little Bataan area. When needed for guides, patrols or road blocks, guerrilla detachments were assigned directly to 158th RCT elements. About 16 April 100 guerrillas were assigned to each battalion.

"In Sorsogon the Japanese garrison at San Francisco was still holding out against the Escudero unit. Elements of the 158th RCT were sent south to break organized resistance and mopping up was left to the guerrillas.

"On 26 April I was ordered back to Sixth Army headquarters. The guerrilla radio net, however, was left under control of the 158th RCT.

"In conclusion there are several points that should be brought out. First, guerrilla units had neither sufficient training nor equipment to attack prepared defenses; they were best employed in raiding or in harassing patrols and small outposts. Second, it was necessary to have an American officer or non-com constantly checking guerrilla leaders; for these men did not understand that orders should be immediately complied with. Their attitude was that tomorrow or next week is just as good a time to carry out an order as today. Third, guerrillas were best supplied with weapons that could take a great deal of abuse. The Springfield was an ideal guerrilla rifle, for it will take more punishment than the M-1. Moreover, 60-mm mortars would have been better than 81-mm mortars; for carrying 81-mm mortar ammunition by hand presented a difficult problem."

TYPICAL ALAMO SCOUT INTELLIGENCE MISSIONS:

Alamo Scouts on Luzon not only organized guerrilla activities but continued on their previous mission, the collection of information--gathering new and confirming information derived from other sources. The intelligence which was reported by this agency and which could have been obtained in no other way enabled the Army G-2 accurately to follow the movement and activities of the enemy behind his own lines.

During May American forces were assaulting the enemy's

cave defenses astride the Villa Verde Trail and Highway #5 in order to break into the Cagayan Valley. Philippine Army troops were attacking east astride Highway #4 towards Cervantes and U.S. troops were maintaining pressure north of Baguio along Highway #11. At this time the enemy's 19th Division was concentrated in the Bontoc---Loo---Cervantes triangle; remnants of the Japanese 58th IMB guarded Highway #11 north of Baguio; troops of the 23rd Division were deployed east of Baguio and west of Highway #5; the 10th Division, 2nd Armored Division and a polyglot assortment of service troops and air units were defending Highway #5 and the Villa Verde Trail. The bulk of the 103rd Division was immobilized in the Aparri area in anticipation of an amphibious landing.

There were many questions which could be promptly answered only by observers planted behind the enemy lines: Would the 19th Division move from the Bontoc---Loo---Cervantes triangle through Bontoc and down Highway #4 to reinforce the Balete Pass and Villa Verde Trail defenders? Would the 103rd Division elements move from the Aparri area to reinforce Balete Pass? Would the heavy concentrations of service and air corps troops in Cagayan Valley move south for the same purpose? These were among the many pressing questions to which the Army G-2 needed an answer.

In order to obtain answers to these and many other questions five teams were originally dispatched to north Luzon in May. For the purpose of simplifying this discussion, however, only three teams will be mentioned. These were placed in the vicinity of Bontoc, west of Santiago along Highway #5, and in the vicinity of Ilagan along Highway #5.

The question of whether the 19th Division was moving, either east into the Cagayan Valley over Highway #11 or southeast to Highway #5 over Highway #4, was soon answered. Daily negative reports from the Bontoc team assured the Army G-2 that there was no movement towards either of these areas. Other valuable information was gathered by this team. The heavy attrition suffered by the 19th Division was first reported by this Alamo Scout team as a result of an interrogation of a prisoner of war captured by civilians. The movement of General Araki's forces from the Vigan area towards Bontoc, reported by guerrillas, was confirmed by this team, and the arrival of this force on Highway #4 was reported 24 hours after the advance guard emerged from the mountains.

Order of Battle information was supplied in abundance. The following radio message, sent 3 June 1945, is typical of many:

"Information from prisoner of war who surrendered to civilians near Tadian on 1 June: Navy, seaman first class. His ship, Esubete, commanded by Shosa, Satokira, ran aground in Lingayen Gulf 1 November 1944, was bombed soon after. Original strength of crew, 126. Present strength 100, all now at Tadian under Araki's command. Believes his unit under Araki, but knows no other officers of other units. Went from Lingayen to Bobong to Vigan to Tadian. Has been in Tadian since May. Knows nothing of Shun Heidan or Yoroi Heidan. All soldiers in Bontoc are from Tora Heidan. Knows nothing of intentions of his or other units. Tadian has radio contact with Cervantes, acute shortage of food and medicine in Tadian area. Is there any other information you desire? Please answer immediately. (signature)"

This particular message, though principally confirmatory, filled in several gaps in the intelligence picture-- such as the current location of Araki's forces and the supply situation in that area. Furthermore, the prisoner of war's negative reaction to the Shun Heidan (103rd Division) and Yoroi Heidan (61st IMB) was significant. Although the bulk of the former was located in the Aparri area and the latter on the Babuyan Islands, movement of either unit was at any time possible. This negative information together with the informant's mention that the soldiers of the Tora Heidan (19th Division) were the only ones in the Bontoc area negated the possibility that new troops had arrived from any quarter.

Equally valuable information came from the two teams echeloned along Highway #5. The following radio message sent on 9 June by the team located west of Santiago is typical of many messages:

"Road traffic on Highway #5 night 7 June observed from a point 2 kms west of Cordon: going west toward San

Luis were 12 trucks, 9 bullcarts loaded with supplies and 330 Japanese. Going east were 3 empty trucks and 21 empty bullcarts escorted by 41 Japanese. (signature)"

Messages of this type soon made it obvious that the movement of supplies and men was west and that only empty vehicles with an escort returned east. Furthermore, since messages of this type had been received daily since mid-May, it was possible to determine the number of reinforcements that could have reached the Balete Pass and Villa Verde Trail areas.

Farther north along Highway #5, in the Ilagan area, the third Alamo Scout team was sending in similar daily reports. Therefore, to determine whether all the troops that passed the Ilagan team were proceeding to the front line past the Santiago team was simple arithmetic. In this manner it soon became obvious that only a portion of the enemy passing through the Ilagan area were proceeding through the Santiago area.

Figure 35 - "possible...to estimate with greater accuracy..."

As has been stated previously, the potential movement of the 103rd Division from the Aparri area into southern Cagayan Valley was a major question. How many of the troops passing south through Ilagan were from this combat unit? It would, of course, have been conservative to assume that all the troops that passed south were members of the 103rd Division. Furtunately this broad assumption was not necessary; for the Ilagan team sent in sufficient Order of Battle information to enable the Army G-2 to state definitely that a certain number of the troops passing this area were not from the 103rd Division. The following message was one of many sent which was helpful on this point:

"Prisoner of war, Sgt Kataoka, captured 3 June near Cauayan interrogation follows: Came on merchant ship Kazura Maru which was sunk 8 January at San Fernando. Is from 32nd Shipping Engineer Regiment. Regiment reached Baguio in January, proceeded to Aparri in February and now is on its way south, passing through Cauayan 28 May. Commanding officer is Lt. Col. Omura. The 24th Shipping Engineer Regiment made same itinerary and is now in Santiago. The 32nd Shipping Regiment had 400 men, mostly armed when it went to Aparri. Majority now going south. The 24th Shipping Regiment has 200 men in Santiago. Morishita in Cauayan.... (signature)"

As a result of this and other messages a certain number of Japanese which moved south through Ilagan could be definitely identified as other than from the 103rd Division.

These incidents are given as examples of the type and usefulness of intelligence derived from Alamo Scouts. As a result of information from this source it was possible to follow the movement of enemy units in north Luzon, to estimate with greater accuracy the size of the various concentrations, to form an opinion of the status of supply in the various areas, and to identify the troops that were moving.

Figure 36 - "...follow the movement of the enemy..."

Brief mention will be made of methods employed by Alamo Scouts in collecting their information. As a rule their first step was to contact local guerrilla units or pro-American individuals, form them into road-watching parties and station them throughout the area. These persons were provided with a checklist on which they could write the number of vehicles, weapons, and enemy that passed their station. These reports, delivered by runner to the Scout team, were checked against one another to determine accuracy. Thus, after proper evaluation, the intelligence was radioed to Sixth Army. If possible, daily visits were paid to each station to insure that it was operating properly.

Figure 37 - "daily visits...to each station..."

When information was desired concerning a particular area several, sometimes as high as six, guerrilla agents or civilians would be dispatched with instructions to obtain the specific information. Their reports would be compared, evaluated and the distillation radioed to Sixth Army. When the information brought back by these agents was particularly startling, or if the area was of considerable importance in the first instance, an Alamo Scout would make a personal reconnaissance of the area. Physical limitations forbade a personal reconnaissance of all areas by Scout team members.

Figure 38 - "personal reconnaissance of the area..."

In setting up these intelligence nets it was found desirable to enlist a local inhabitant of intelligence and high standing in the community. His knowledge of men and women employed as agents was of great assistance in evaluating agents' reports and in selecting suitable persons to be sent on specific missions.

It was always found desirable to send a local man to gather information as he would be able to question civilians with greater ease and would arouse less suspicion than would an outsider. In some instances such persons knew individual

Japanese within his area and could speak freely to them on a personal basis.

As a rule each team picked an interpreter to interrogate the Japanese prisoners captured. These interpreters were found in every locality and were of every age and sex. One team employed an eleven year old girl who spoke excellent Japanese; another team used a venerable Chinese.

ALAMO SCOUT MISSIONS ON LUZON:

	Dates	Location	Mission
1.	17 Jan to 19 Jan	Santo Tomas-San Jose, La Union	Locate enemy artillery.
2.	17 Jan to 27 Feb	Guimba-Gapan, Rizal	Establish road watcher station and collect information.
3.	22 Jan to 16 Feb	Sibul Springs, Bulacan	Locate and observe escape routes from Manila north, and evaluate guerrilla intelligence.
4.	27 Jan to 31 Jan	Cabanatuan, Nueva Ecija	Make reconnaissance of prisoner of war camp.
5.	28 Jan to 20 Feb	South Bataan	Conduct reconnaissance for XI Corps, supervise guerrilla radio, and serve as guerrilla affairs officer with Corps.
6.	6 Feb to 15 Feb	Palauig-Iba Zambales	Organize guerrilla intelligence, conduct reconnaissance of enemy installations in Subic Bay, and secure information concerning Iba airstrip.
7.	8 Feb to 15 Apr	Malolos-Manila Bulacan and Rizal	Establish road-watcher station, supervise

Dates	Location	Mission

7. (Continued) — guerrilla radios and intelligence nets, and conduct reconnaissance of Highway #5.

8. 10 Feb to 6 Apr — Pila, Laguna — Organize guerrillas, report on escape routes out of Manila, and supervise guerrilla intelligence.

9. 17 Feb to 5 Mar — Baler Bay, Tayabas — Conduct reconnaissance of enemy situation in Baler area, report on guerrilla and civilian situation, and supervise guerrilla supply.

10. 17 Feb to 5 Mar — Casiguran Sound — Conduct reconnaissance of air strips, supervise guerrilla affairs, and reconnoiter mountain trails.

19 Feb to 26 Apr — Sorsogon-Albay (Bulan) (Jovellar) — Organize guerrilla intelligence, conduct reconnaissance of enemy situation, serve as guerrilla affairs officer with 158th RCT.

11. 20 Feb to 11 May — Camarines Norte — Organize guerrilla intelligence, road-watcher stations, coastal lookouts, and conduct reconnaissance of beaches and airstrips.

	Dates	Location	Mission
12.	3 Mar to 28 Apr	Mauban, Tayabas	Establish coast and road-watcher stations.
13.	5 Mar to 29 Apr	Tayabas	Organize guerrilla intelligence, set up road-watcher stations, and conduct reconnaissance of enemy escape routes.
14.	28 Mar to 7 May	Iba-Zambales Range, Zambales	Search for General Kondo and Admiral Tsukada, conduct guerrilla affairs, investigate trails in mountains.
15.	28 Mar to 26 May	Infanta, Tayabas	Conduct reconnaissance of enemy installations and of mountain trails, and set up coast-watcher stations.
16.	8 Apr to 20 Apr	Pasacao, Camarines Sur	Conduct reconnaissance of beach, road and bridge conditions.
17.	13 Apr to 28 Apr	Tuao, Cagayan	Attempt to locate and capture General Yamashita.
18.	25 Apr to 30 Jun	Bontoc-Sadanga, Mountain Province	Establish road-watcher station, and collect information.
19.	28 Apr to 22 Jun	Ilagan, Isabela	Establish road-watcher stations and collect information.
20.	1 May to 25 Jun	Pinayag, Nueva Vizcaya	Collect information in the Aritao-Pingkian area.
21.	2 May to 4 May	Ipo and Wawa, Rizal	Conduct reconnaissance of enemy installations and of routes of approach.

	Dates	Location	Mission
22.	2 May to 14 Jun	Cordon, Isabela	Establish road-watcher stations and continue search for General Yamashita.
23.	10 May to 30 Jun	North Cagayan	Establish road-watcher stations, and collect information.
24.	19 May to 30 Jun	Daklan-Kiangan, Mt Province	Collect information.
25.	24 May to 30 Jun	Kibungan, Mt Province	Establish road-watcher station and report on enemy situation.
26.	8 Jun to 10 Jun	Casiguran Bay	Conduct reconnaissance.
27.	9 Jun to 30 Jun	Atok, Mt Province	Establish road-watcher station, and collect information.
28.	10 Jun to 30 Jun	Tuguegarao, Cagayan	Establish road-watcher station.
29.	11 Jun to 13 Jun	Palanan Bay	Conduct reconnaissance.
30.	12 Jun to 22 Jun	Fuga Island	Conduct reconnaissance.
31.	16 Jun to 30 Jun	Enrile, Cagayan	Collect information.
32.	21 Jun to 30 Jun	Banaue, Mt Province	Report on enemy movements and dispositions.

ALAMO SCOUT TRAINING:

Not long ago, the name, "Alamo Scouts" was unknown.

Today the name is familiar throughout the Army and across the United States. Typical printed overstatement has made the name synonymous with heroism, super-daring and super-skill. Alamo Scouts have been compared with "Heroes of the old west", called "super-sleuths", "teams of heroes", and "the most skilled of all Sixth Army's jungle fighters." These are press terms.

The Alamo Scouts was a valuable military organization, designed to give Army headquarters what every Division and lower command already had—an organic reconnaissance agency. It was formed with a view to obtaining strategic and tactical information, primarily for the Army G-2, but concurrently for units being employed or about to be employed.

That the idea was sound and that its new application of standard principles was practical and successful is attested by the results of more than 60 missions. It has been recognized by commanders who benefited from it that information provided by Alamo Scouts saved lives, changed plans of attack, led to the destruction of enemy positions and enemy shipping. They were successful on two prisoner rescue raids; they brought in 60 Japanese prisoners for questioning. They were commended by a division commander who said, "The work of officers and men of the Alamo Scouts has been largely responsible for the success of this and other divisions in the accomplishment of their assigned missions," and by General Krueger's tribute, "This little outfit has never failed the Sixth Army".

The field tested practicability and value of such an organization bears inspection and the foundation of training on which its success was built is worthy of consideration.

There are no guarded secrets in the process of converting a soldier into a Scout, nor in the forming of an organization comparable to the Alamo Scouts. In the making of a scout, basic qualities are sought and standard lessons taught. In the forming of a scout organization there is groundwork to be laid and a gradual building process to be completed.

Any male who wears the army uniform can be designated a scout, but comparatively few can be capable and dependable in this capacity. Reconnaissance, as carried out by Alamo Scouts, is specialized military service requiring particular temperament and talent. Men possessed of the proper qualities are not so rare, however, as to discourage the project.

Foremost of the requisites of a good scout is that he be intelligent. This does not mean "well educated". He need not hold a degree, he need not even have completed high school, though experience has proved that the better scouts are men who have at least completed high school. He must have "horse sense"—be able to think logically and make sound deductions.

Physically, a scout need not be a big man nor have the frame of an athlete. He must be strong enough to withstand fatigue on arduous marches and he must have no physical defects or debilitating diseases. His vision must be clear without the use of glasses and he must be a capable swimmer. This does not mean that he be merely able to swim. It means that he must be able to swim in rough surf or over distances up to at least a half mile. His physical vigor and resistance must be such that he is able to travel for weeks without the need of medical attention, since normally it will be impossible for him to get such attention.

Hand-in-hand with his intelligence and physical fitness, a scout needs courage and an attribute which may be called daring or a spirit of adventure—and this is to be distinguished from recklessness and lack of reasonable judgment.

Scouts are often called upon to make marches over tortuous terrain, up to 30 or 40 miles with little rest and little food. Trails and easy going are normally forbidden him since he must not be seen. A man without grit can not do it. It takes courage, too, to get into a rubber boat with five or six other men, paddle silently through darkness and land on an enemy shore where there are no friendly troops. Scout teams never know whether they have gone undetected or whether they are paddling into the hands of an alert enemy. They do know that, if they are caught, there is virtually no hope for assistance. They must dare the risk.

Figure 39 - "land on an enemy shore..."

Being naturally observant is part of a scout's equipment, and in this respect, men from small communities and rural areas seem most gifted. City-bred men are not excluded, however. Some of them have made excellent scouts. In basic training, all soldiers get instruction in scouting and patrolling, the use of the compass, and the use of cover and concealment. If they have not shown a natural aptitude for these subjects, it is not likely that they would make good scouts and time does not permit "starting from scratch".

Proper temperament or personality is the last requisite, but certainly not the least important. Teamwork is the key to successful scouting and not every man is willing or temperamentally suited to mold himself into part of a small unit. Certainly initiative and individuality are desirable, since no one wants to work with a "deadhead," but a scout must harmonize his individualism with that of other members of his team. Being bellicose, loud, "mouthy"—being self-centered, contemptuous of others' opinions, unamenable to compromise, he will not succeed in this field.

At the Alamo Scout Training Center six weeks proved to be sufficient time to give a scout the training he needed, since most of the things he was taught were not new to him, although in many cases he actually learned them for the first time. Indeed, if he looked upon scouts as supermen, he might have been keenly disappointed to find himself in a classroom during much of the first three and a half weeks of his training—learning such things as map reading, use of radios, sketching, aerial photography, combat intelligence, and message writing. Neither was he far afield when he was taught scouting and patrolling, including use of the compass, handling of rubber boats, night amphibious landings and pick-ups and beach reconnaissance.

His body was hardened through the only known process—sweat and aching muscles. Late in the afternoon each day, after his mental faculties had their workout, he spent from 30 to 45 minutes at vigorous physical training. This was supplemented by conditioning hikes. Daily, too, he swam, did surface dives and improved his underwater techniques.

His marksmanship was sharpened with the weapons he was to carry—the carbine, the pistol, M-1 rifle and sub-machine gun. Night classes taught him radio code, the operation of portable sets and blinker signals.

Nearly every soldier is instructed in the things that are taught a scout, yet surprisingly few of the men who volunteered for scout training really knew them. Many an eager candidate declared his competence with map and compass, only to be lost on training problems. Scout instructors made it their business to see that their charges did learn, understand, and put into practice what they were taught. If they could not, they did not become scouts.

Through the entire course, the men were imbued with

the spirit of the organization, with its pride in its accomplishments. They were spurred with the desire to make good—to make the team—to be one of the chosen. Their final test consisted of two and a half weeks of training problems—missions worked out to be as nearly like a mission "for record" as possible. There were failures, but that was the crucible of scouting. In these problems, all they learned was put to practical application.

In operations, much was learned from experience, from trail and error. Some of the first scouts to be sent out carried too much food on short missions of 48 to 72 hours. They found their nerves were tense—they neither needed nor wanted much food. It was standard procedure, at first, to deflate and hide the rubber boat. A loud, whistling valve, on one mission made it seem more advisable to have a contact crew return the boat to a waiting PT.

One team thought of leaving a rope attached to their rubber boat as they paddled in, so that if they came under fire they could signal the PT to head out to sea, pulling them behind. The idea was discarded. A strong enough line was too heavy a drag on the paddlers—a lighter line broke. Experience taught the carrying of only bare necessities to keep down weight and careful selection of rations. The same teacher proved that mission planning must be as meticulous as fine needle work.

Preference in officers ran to junior grades, since they were normally younger men and because the command of a six-man team, however specialized, did not seem commensurate with higher rank. In addition to the qualities already enumerated, it was desirable that an officer scout leader be able to win and hold the admiration, respect and confidence of his men yet be not apart from them, but one of them. He was the guide, the steadying hand, the responsible man, but not the final voice of authority. Scouts must plan together and operate together. The officer was one of a family, his role being that of elder brother.

Where were such men to be found? They were line privates, platoon sergeants, drivers, radio operators, even clerks. Alamo Scouts were drawn from units throughout Sixth Army. They were infantrymen, cavalrymen, artillerymen, engineers, parachute troopers. A start was made with a class of five officers and 26 enlisted men and from this group, four teams were retained as scouts. Classes varied in size from 60 to 80 men, with one officer to every six enlisted men. Quotas were assigned to several divisions for each class, men in those units being informed that there was a call for volunteers. Volunteers were then interviewed by officers from the Scout Training Center, with an eye to the qualities desired.

Once selected, candidates were placed on temporary duty and given a six-weeks training course at Alamo Scouts Training Center, which was always located near the sea and away from other units so that suitable training ground would be available. As the course proceeded, officer students were called into consultation each week to rate men assigned to them and give opinions of their work. Students were formed into teams of six and were placed in new teams each week. From time to time, during the course, men who did not measure up were returned to their units.

Upon completion of the course, enlisted men were given ballots upon which they named in order of their preference the three officers they would be most willing to follow on a mission. In turn, the officers named in order of their preference the six men they would choose from the entire class as members of their team. To these votes, instructors and staff officers added their observations. Thus, the top men were selected to remain as scouts, the number depending on current needs for scout teams and the remainder of the group were returned to their units.

Eight classes were thus completed and from them came ten capable scout teams. Not only did the idea of an Army reconnaissance unit prove sound and valuable, but the thoroughness with which the idea was put into practice, the careful selection, the conscientious training—and luck—held the cost in lives to zero. Not a single scout was killed on any of the missions.

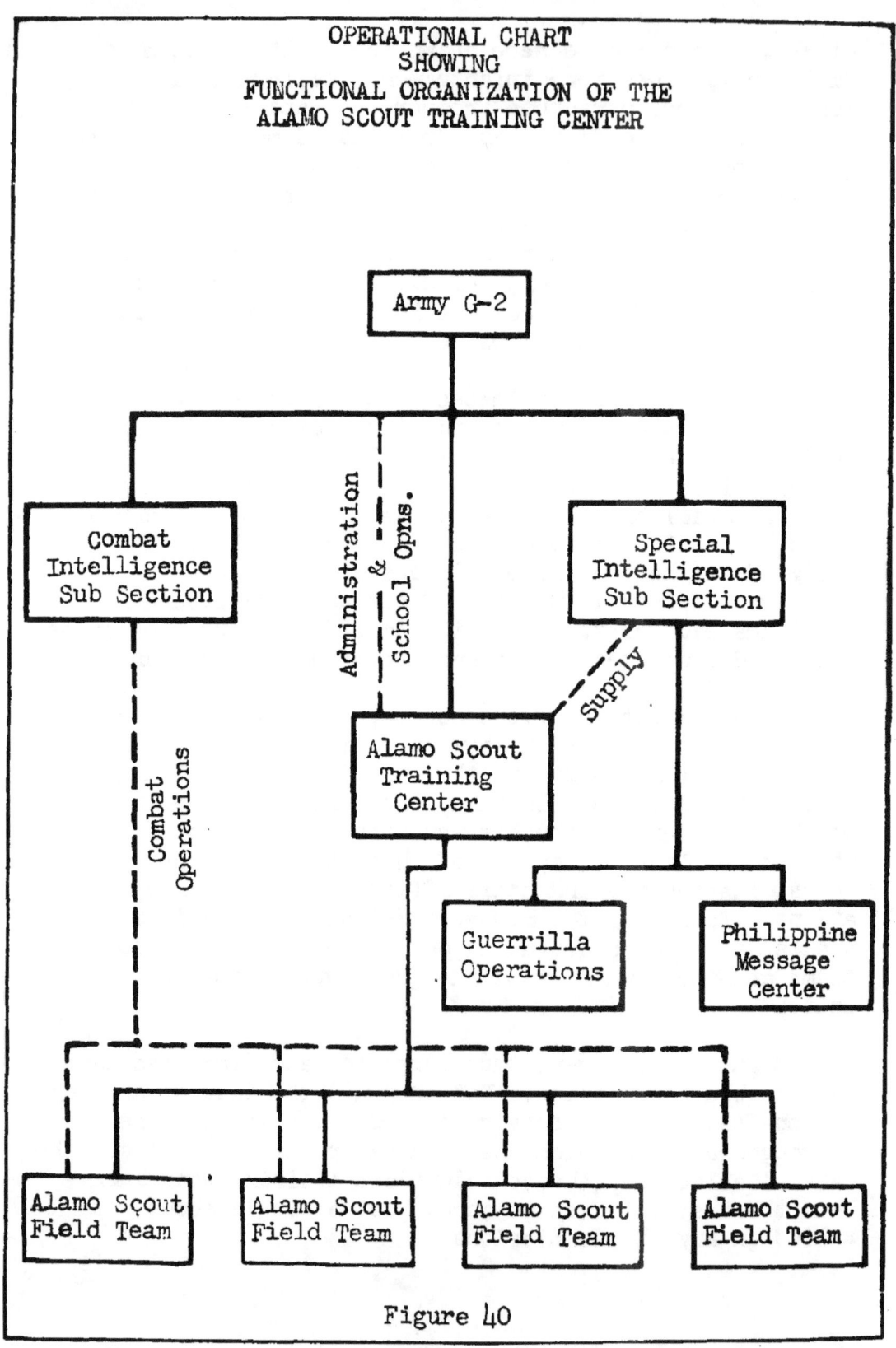

Figure 40

CHAPTER V

PHOTOGRAPHIC AND TOPOGRAPHIC INTELLIGENCE

STATISTICS:

The Luzon campaign was a final proving ground for the G-2 Topographic sub-section. The eight officers and 20 enlisted men who began to work as a team in the Leyte campaign had profited by their experience and were now capable of performing a maximum amount of the highest quality photographic and topographic intelligence work. It was fortunate that such was the case because the sub-section was called upon to perform a far greater amount of manhours work than in any previous campaign. In the first few weeks it became apparent that a 24-hour work schedule would have to be set up in order to process the volume of photography being received from the photo squadron laboratory. Two round trips a day were made over the 16-mile route from Calasiao to Dagupan by one of the file clerks. Normally, the first photos were received between 1100 and 1130; the second trip was completed about midnight. This schedule was in effect until the headquarters moved to San Fernando, Pampanga, at which time cub plane service was initiated and two trips were made during daylight hours. From S-Day until 1 July when Eighth Army assumed control, the sub-section processed a total of a little more than 708,000 photo prints.

The bulk of photographs were supplied to subordinate units in answer to their specific requests. Weather was an uncontrollable factor which prevented an absolute maximum in quality and timeliness of this type of intelligence, but a very large percentage of mission requests were successfully accomplished (see chart). A total of 577 requests were submitted to Army and relayed to the squadron designated for photographic support in this operation; twenty-four of these requests were cancelled because of change in situation, delays due to weather, etc.. The remaining 553 were successfully accomplished.

Copies of all photographs were checked by Army photo interpreters in order to obtain a maximum amount of intelligence value. Copies of reports were distributed not only to Army staff sections but also to corps and division intelligence officers in order that they might be compared with similar reports being prepared in those headquarters. A total of 255 reports were issued. Seventeen weekly third phase (consolidated) reports were also prepared and distributed.

Much praise was received from all headquarters for the high quality reports prepared during this campaign.

In order to determine just how much real value was being derived from photo intelligence reports, weekly liaison trips were made by officer and enlisted photo interpreters of the Topographic sub-section to the lower echelons down to platoons. Ground checks were made and valuable information obtained for constant improvement in the preparation of future reports. Usually, these trips were of a four or five day duration and were confined to methodical research in one division sector.

In the preparation of 2nd and 3rd phase reports, it was found that illustrated annexes did much to add to the value of these documents and several experienced draftsmen were kept busy assisting the interpreters. Over 750 job orders were registered by the draftsmen. Most of these were in connection with photo interpretation reports; the remainder were prepared for G-2 periodic reports.

From a statistical viewpoint all previous records were broken and it was readily apparent that the topographic subsection played a vital part in the overall search for information on the enemy situation during the campaign. Most important, however, was the experience gained. The subsection felt that after the Luzon campaign it was capable of executing the highest quality performance under almost any conditions.

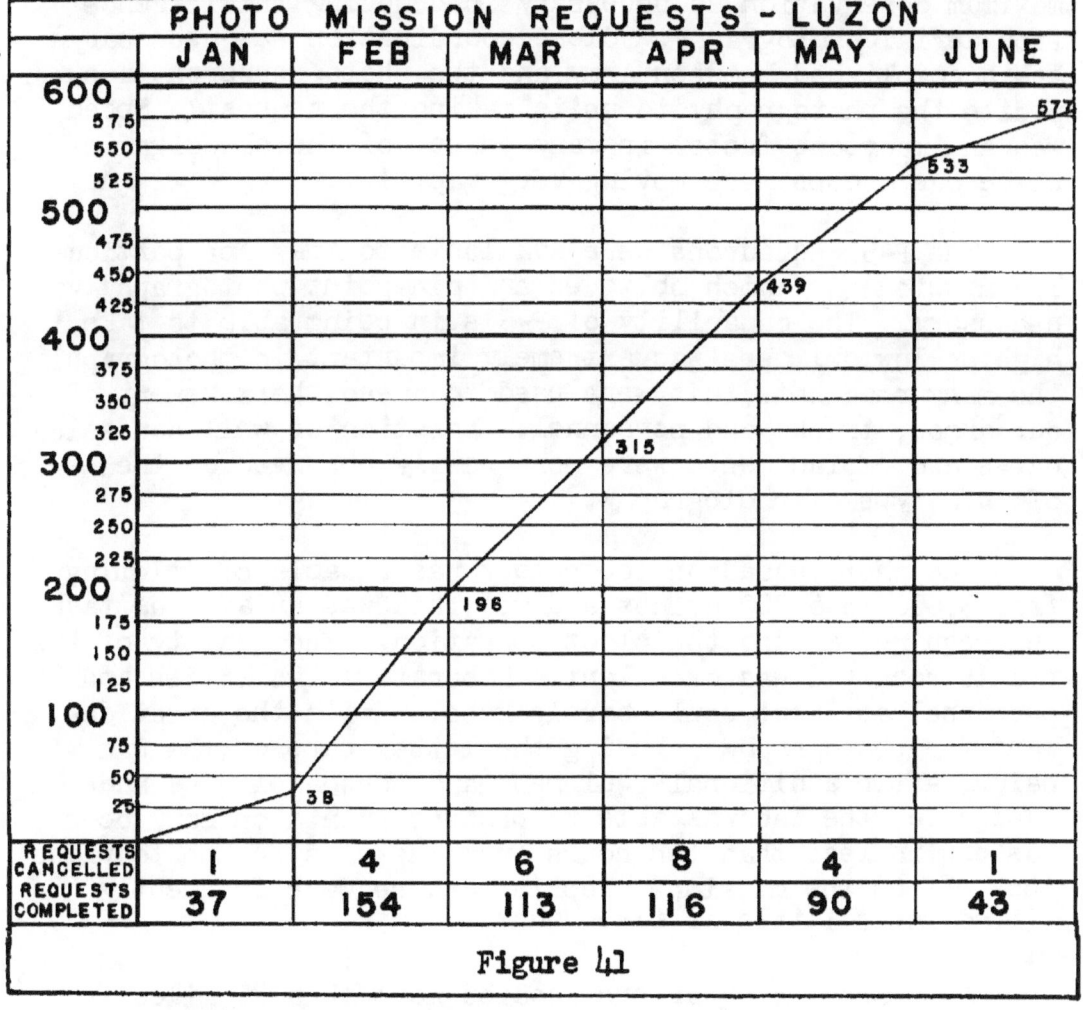

Figure 41

PHOTOGRAPHIC FACILITIES:

Due to the increasing demand for aerial photography during the Luzon campaign, it was possible for Army to use many facilities not available in previous operations. In many instances, improvised equipment was used to facilitate and expedite the demand for photography.

The P-38 squadron, which was used continuously as direct support for Army and its subordinate units to fulfil the photo requests, gained much respect from all concerned for the efficiency and success in its part of the campaign. Frequent requests required that the pilots fly dangerous missions over treacherous terrain in order to attain the maximum observation so necessary in deducing intelligence from aerial photography. Close coordination was necessary and accomplished between Army and the photo squadron to expedite the photography to units making the request. Speed was an important factor in many phases of the campaign in which our troops were moving very rapidly.

The P-51 squadrons were available to Army for particular missions in which obliques and pin-point photography was necessary. The capability of P-51s in being able to take high or low obliques was extremely important in photographing the many road nets that were used to speed the movement of our armor, trucks and personnel. Location of well concealed caves and emplacements were more easily observed by the use of this type of photography.

The photo squadron laboratory was capable of printing from 3,000 to 6,000 prints a day. This was an arduous task and required around the clock operation. The quality of the prints received was excellent. Laboratory facilities and personnel at first could barely keep up with the great demand for photography. During the latter part of the campaign, after additional equipment and personnel were made available, the lab was able to produce prints on many occasions in less than ten hours from the time the photo plane took off on the mission. Reprint orders were frequently filled in as little as five hours.

With Army Headquarters located more than 75 miles from the photo laboratory, an effort was made to facilitate the delivering of photography with the use of L-5 planes. Where cub strips were not available, air drops were accomplished to units requesting the photography. This method of rapid delivery was very successful (see section on delivery of photographs).

A great deal of credit for the success of the procurement and distribution of aerial photography had to be given to the Ground Liaison Officers attached to the photo units. Working directly under the Army G-2, these GLO's received all requests and obtained approval for flights from the air task force commander. Status of missions, intents for the next day and numbers of planes operational were a few of the facts that the GLO's were required to furnish Army each day. In addition – and this was perhaps their most important work – they briefed pilots before a mission and checked for completeness and for visual sightings by the pilot on his return. Only on low obliques and off-shore missions were pilots able to do any real visual reconnaissance work. After the photo reproduction was completed, the GLO's arranged, in coordination with Army, for any special means of delivery which would expedite the distribution of prints.

PHOTO MISSION REQUESTS:

Photo mission requests, during the Luzon campaign, were initiated by any staff section in any echelon having a need for photography. However, Army SOP prescribed that they should be forwarded through intelligence channels in order that proper coordination be achieved.

All echelons were requested to anticipate photographic coverage as far in advance as possible. Continuous check was made to determine whether existing coverage would provide the desired topographic and/or intelligence information. The Army G-2 topographic sub-section maintained a complete file of available coverage in current and advanced operational areas from which emergency requests were frequently filled. Flight lines of all photography received were plotted on a 1/250,000 scale map. Every effort was made by Army to visualize conditions under which combat units were operating and their anticipated needs for photography. Frequent visits were made to lower echelons to help coordinate methods by which the photography requests would be clearly understood by all concerned and help to eliminate any possible delay.

The following form for use in submitting a photo request was published in one of the weekly consolidated reports and all units were urged to use it as a check list:

UNIT DESIGNATION: Army, Corps, Division, Regiment or Battalion.

REQUEST NO.: Unit request number.

DATE: Date request is initiated (contained in regular message form).

MAP REFERENCE: For long runs or large areas use the 1/250,000 map. For short runs or pin-points where precision is necessary, use the 1/50,000 or 1/25,000 map. As a supplement to map reference, when existing maps do not furnish sufficient detail, use photo coordinates on previous coverage in the same area. Reference for atlas grid should include mission number and print numbers. Map reference should include title, scale and sheet numbers.

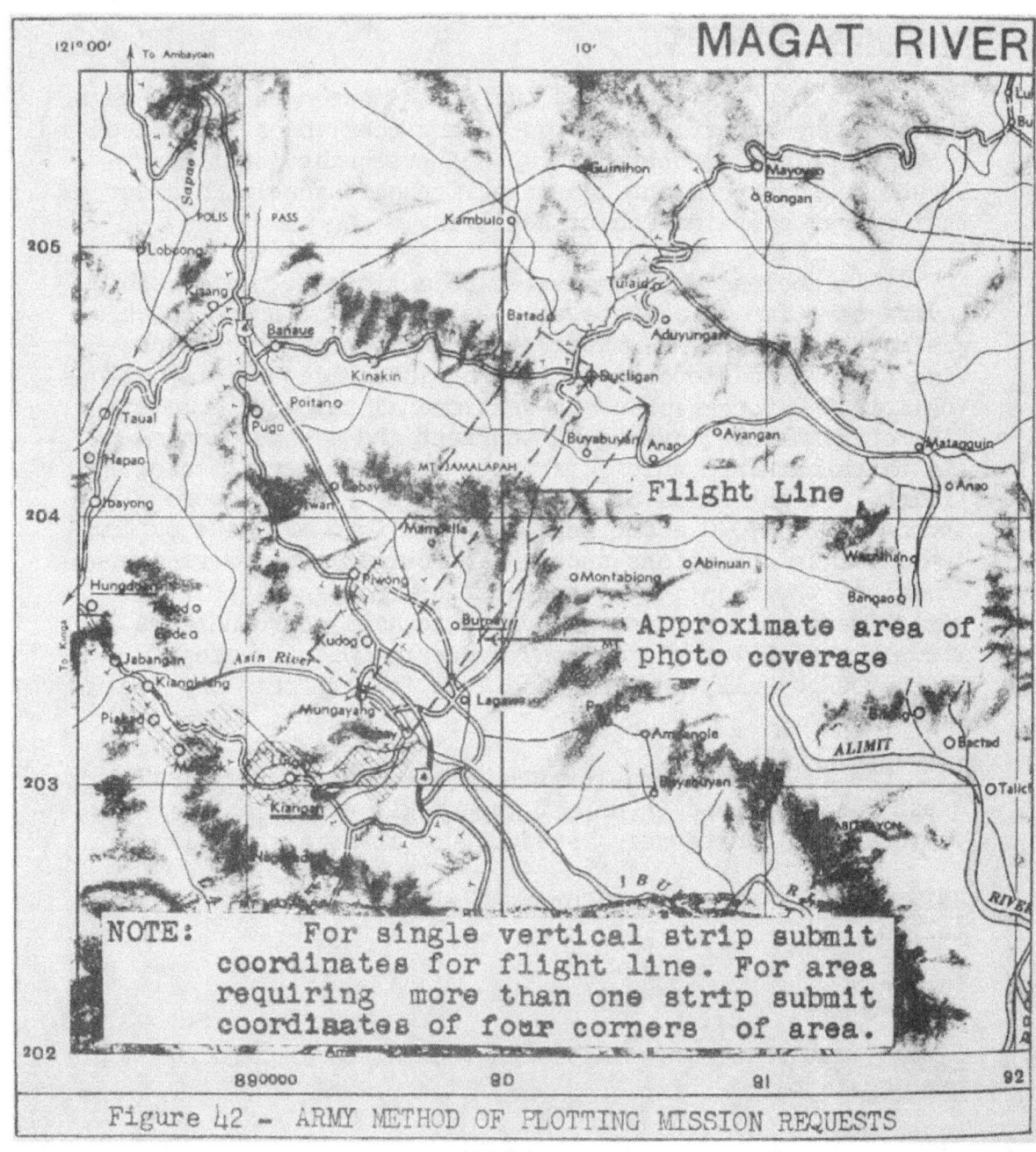

Figure 42 - ARMY METHOD OF PLOTTING MISSION REQUESTS

LOCATION: State general locality by reference to a well-known place name, then designate specific area, strip, pinpoint or large areas by map coordinates supplemented by photo coordinates if deemed necessary.

CAMERA & TYPE: K-17 wide-angle verticals, K-18 pin-point, K-17 low obliques.

FOCAL LENGTH: Expressed in millimeters or inches.

ALTITUDE: Expressed in feet; e.g., 20,000'.

SCALE: Expressed as representative fraction; e.g., 1/10,000.

OVERLAP: Five percent overlap is necessary as a minimum if continuous "tie-in" of all prints within a given strip is required. Sixty percent overlap is necessary for complete stereovision.

SIDELAP: Twenty percent sidelap is generally satisfactory for mapping and general use.

TIME OF FLIGHT: Time desired for photos to be taken. Shadow effects should be considered; also consider current weather conditions such as haze, clouds, etc., peculiar to certain areas during a particular season of the year. (Note: This information is normally deleted unless it will contribute to the intelligence value of the photography.)

PRIORITY: I, II, III, etc., according to urgency.

QUANTITY DESIRED: Number of sets of prints desired.

DEADLINE: Estimated date after which the photos requested will be of no operational value.

METHOD OF DELIVERY: If delivery by air drop is desired, request must be so stated.

PURPOSE: Purpose for which the photography is desired; e.g., tactical interpretation, operational planning, mapping, artillery targets, fire control charts, etc..

Requests for reprints were much more easily completed

since the supporting photo squadron retained the original negatives of all photography accomplished until they were of no further operational value as determined by Army, or until directed by higher headquarters to dispatch them to a central filing center. It was possible for all echelons to obtain reprints within a few hours by either air drop or jeep messenger.

DELIVERY OF PHOTOGRAPHS BY AIR DROP:

The Luzon operation offered the Topographic sub-section the first opportunity to make extensive use of L-4's and L-5's for the purpose of delivery of photographs. In the majority of cases where this method of delivery was used, there was a cub strip in proximity to the requesting unit and the plane landed to make delivery. However, there were occasions when a drop was necessary. When it became apparent that air drops would have to be made, experiments were conducted at Army in order to determine the best methods to adopt. The following tests were conducted and results noted:

Test #1:

Contents: Package contained 500 photographs, 9" x 9", K-12, 12" verticals. Weight - approximately 25 pounds.

Wrapping: Double thickness of heavy brown paper, outside wrapper of heavy waterproof paper and securely bound by several strands of small rope.

Conditions of drop: The package was dropped from a height of 150' on firm flat terrain and at a speed of 75 miles per hour.

Results: Unsatisfactory - package burst upon impact scattering photography over a wide area.

Test #2:

Contents: Package #1 contained 100 photos, K-18 verticals rolled the narrow width, wrapped with two thicknesses of heavy brown paper, placed in a sandbag with excess burlap rolled smoothly around the package and secured by several strands of wire.

Package #2 contained 250 photos, K-18 vertical photographs. These were placed flat, wrapped in two thicknesses of heavy brown paper, inserted in a sandbag, and secured with several strands of wire.

Package #3 contained 500 photos, K-17 verticals, 9" x 9". The photos were placed in two piles, wrapped in two thicknesses of heavy brown paper, protected by two sandbags and secured with several strands of wire.

Conditions of drop: All three packages were dropped from an L-4 plane, speed 40 miles per hour, at an altitude of approximately 12'. Terrain was level, firm and covered with short grass.

Results: Satisfactory - all packages were intact and photographs were not damaged.

Conclusions: Method of wrapping and conditions of drop were practical.

Test #3:

Conditions of drop: Identical packages and drop areas were used as in preceding experiment. Package #1 (same as in Test #2) was dropped from an altitude of 500' at a speed of 75 miles per hour.

Results: Satisfactory - package was intact and photography undamaged.

Conclusions: Method of wrapping and drop conditions were excellent. Photographs wrapped in this manner could be dropped at even higher altitudes with little or no damage.

Test #4:

Conditions of drop: Package #2 was dropped from an altitude of 250', speed approximately 60 miles per hour. Contents of this package was the same as in Test #2.

Results: Package was intact. However, the 12" photos

should be placed in a single stack since the shock forces the photos together with some damage to the edge of the photography.

Conclusions: Method of wrapping was satisfactory. K-17 photos should be placed in single stack for wrapping, limiting quantity to approximately 300 prints to permit use of sandbag as outside cover. Altitude of 250' and probably up to 500' would be very satisfactory.

The adopted procedure for drops, as a result of these tests, was 200 prints which would permit the use of a sandbag as the outside cover; wire was used to secure all packages; the speed of the plane was held from 60 to 75 miles per hour; and an altitude maintained as low as practical and not more than 500 feet. Air drops were found to be practical and were used with excellent results.

Figure 43 - "...occasions when a drop was necessary..."

CHAPTER VI

TRANSLATION AND INTERROGATION

LANGUAGE DETACHMENTS IN THE LUZON CAMPAIGN:

In preparing for the Luzon operation, Language Detachments had the advantage of experience gained in previous operations. Problems in procedure for handling captured enemy documents and prisoners of war, which had previously hindered the flow of information to other G-2 sub-sections, had been for the most part solved by the beginning of the Luzon Operation. In addition, the fact that all Language Detachments were attached to experienced G-2 Sections, fully cognizant of the value of information obtained from documents and prisoners, contributed greatly to the smooth operation of these detachments.

Figure 44 - "...fully cognizant of the value of information..."

The most significant contribution made by Language Detachments in the overall planning for the Luzon Operation was in gaining information from documents and prisoners captured on Leyte which could shed light on the situation on Luzon. In this way, information of considerable importance concerning order of battle, disposition of enemy units, strengths and weapons on Luzon was obtained. Since Luzon was used as a staging area for many major Japanese units reinforcing Leyte, information gained from documents and prisoners belonging to these units was of value to G-2 and had a direct bearing on the planning for the Luzon Operation.

Figure 45 - SEARCHING FOR DOCUMENTS IN THE FIELD

In the Luzon Operation, the Sixth Army had under its command three corps, under which were ten divisions, two regimental combat teams and two major guerrilla combat units. Each of these units had a Language Detachment. The basic procedure under which all Language Detachments functioned was set forth in GHQ SOPI No. 23, dated 8 September 1944, and this was adhered to by all Language Detachments throughout the Luzon Operation. The procedure was further defined at both Army and corps levels to meet the more detailed requirements of lower units.

Captured enemy documents were classified as follows:

"A"--Those documents containing information of any tactical value to any theater engaged in the war against Japan.

"B"--Those documents containing information of any strategic value to any theater.

"C"--Those documents of no military value.

All "A" documents were sent from division to corps, from corps to Army and from Army to ADVATIS. In the latter stages of the operation, when ATIS, GHQ superseded ADVATIS in the Philippines, they were sent from Army to ATIS, GHQ. "B" documents were routed from division to corps and directly from corps to ADVATIS/ATIS. "B" documents were re-scanned at corps in order to insure that no "A" documents had been overlooked. By sending the "B" documents directly from corps to ADVATIS/ATIS, duplication of work at Army was eliminated and transportation methods were simplified. As a rule, "C" documents were destroyed in the operational area at corps level, although many of them were released as souvenirs. The main volume of documents followed this prescribed channel. However, each Language Detachment, at whatever echelon of command, received "A", "B", and "C" documents directly from units adjacent to its headquarters.

The number of documents per batch varied at different echelons of command, and the size of individual batches ranged from a manila envelope at division level to a sandbag at Army level. This variation in size is accounted for by the fact that corps rebatched division documents and Army rebatched corps documents, the tendency at each higher level was to make one batch from several individual batches received from the lower unit. Documents of extreme value to the next higher headquarters were sent immediately, and the Language Detachment at the next higher headquarters was notified by telephone of their impending arrival. All documents containing cryptographic material were sent directly by each detachment to a designated representative of the Chief Signal Officer, GHQ.

Prisoners of war were evaluated at Division, and those possessing information of tactical value to the division were interrogated. Those of further intelligence value to higher headquarters were dispatched without delay to corps, while those of no intelligence value were sent to the main base stockade from the division. Prisoners of further intelligence value were sent by corps without delay to Sixth Army Headquarters. Those prisoners possessing information of strategic value were so classified at Corps and Army levels, and the Army Language Detachment was held responsible for sending them to ADVATIS/ATIS.

In all operations, the problem of the transportation of prisoners from lower to higher echelons was serious. In order to eliminate some of the difficulties, corps detachments recommended directly to ATIS, GHQ, prisoners of strategic value who at the same time were of no further tactical value at Army Headquarters. In this way, the necessity for sending such prisoners to Army was eliminated and the problem of transporting prisoners facilitated.

During the most active portion of the operation, Army Headquarters was situated close to the base stockade, and this made all prisoners readily available to Army interrogators in the event that a recheck or verification of information obtained from any individual prisoner was desired. However, during the later stages of the operation, the Army Headquarters was located at such a distance from the base stockade that in order to minimize transportation difficulties, selectivity in prisoner of war evaluation at corps level became increasingly important. All movement of prisoners of war was carried out through Provost Marshal channels.

In addition to the normal language functions, language personnel of this Detachment for the first time performed the duties of interpreters in the trial and execution of enemy spies.

STATISTICS:

The actual number of language personnel in all Sixth Army units was 36 officers and 153 enlisted men (144 linguists and 9 clerks). Within the officer group were 4 Naval language officers on liaison duty who were instructed to earmark any information from documents and prisoners of war of immediate importance to the Navy, and 4 Air Intelligence officers on liaison duty who were instructed to screen tactical air information of value to the Army and Allied Air Forces. One Naval language officer and one Air Intelligence officer were attached to each corps and Army Language Detachment. The average strength of each division Language Detachment was 2 officers and 10 enlisted men, and of corps and Army Language Detachments 4 officers and 15 EM. A number of Nisei enlisted men were given direct appointments as officers. Experience has shown that Caucasian and Nisei language officers work excellently together and complement each other to make an ideal combination.

On 23 April 1945, all language units within the command of Sixth Army were activated as detachments and assigned to their respective units in accordance with a War Department order. This did not make any significant change in the divisions, as their language personnel had already been assigned as individuals; however, the corps and Army language units had been on TDY from ATIS, GHQ. With the activation of these detachments, the Theater SOPI remained in effect.

For the period 9 January 45 to 1 July 45, all divisions and regimental combat teams under Sixth Army handled 8,031 batches of captured enemy documents, excluding those classified as "C". Of these, 4,961 were "A" batches and 3,070 were "B" batches. The "C" documents, which were at least three times as great in number, were not recorded because they were to be destroyed. The divisions issued 1,407

- 133 -

translation reports, an average of 117 per division and RCT. These reports comprised 8,484 separate translated items. An item is defined as a document partially or totally translated, or a series of identifications taken from postcards or identification discs. Irrespective of the number of personnel involved, this figure alone is quite impressive; and more so in view of the fact that the number of personnel involved in the translations was approximately 60 officers and enlisted men.

Out of a total of 7,297 prisoners of war captured during the entire Luzon Operation, the divisions evaluated 4,932 and actually interrogated 3,421. They issued 2,387 interrogation reports, an average of 199 per division and RCT. Here again, the personnel involved were approximately 60 officers and enlisted men. Of the 3,421 prisoners interrogated, 2,646 were Japanese, the rest being Formosans and Koreans. Ninety-four percent of the Japanese prisoners evaluated were interrogated, whereas thirty-six percent of the Formosans evaluated were interrogated.

The three corps handled 4,302 batches of "A" and "B" documents, of which 2,122 were "A" type and 2,180 were "B" type. They issued 484 translation reports, involving 4,663 separate items. This was an average of 161 translation reports per corps.

The corps evaluated 4,166 prisoners of war, of which 1,984 were interrogated; and 604 interrogation reports were issued. This was an average of 201 interrogation reports per corps. It is to be noted that most of these prisoners came directly from the divisions and were further interrogated.

The Army Language Detachment handled 836 batches of "A" and "B" documents, of which 746 were "A" type and 90 were "B" type. Translation reports issued numbered 279, involving 1,504 separate items.

The Army Language Detachment evaluated 1,166 prisoners of war, of which 207 were interrogated; and 165 interrogation reports were issued.

To summarize, all Language Detachments under Sixth Army issued 2,170 translation reports, involving 14,651 items. A total of 5,612 interrogations were made, and 3,156 formal interrogation reports were issued.

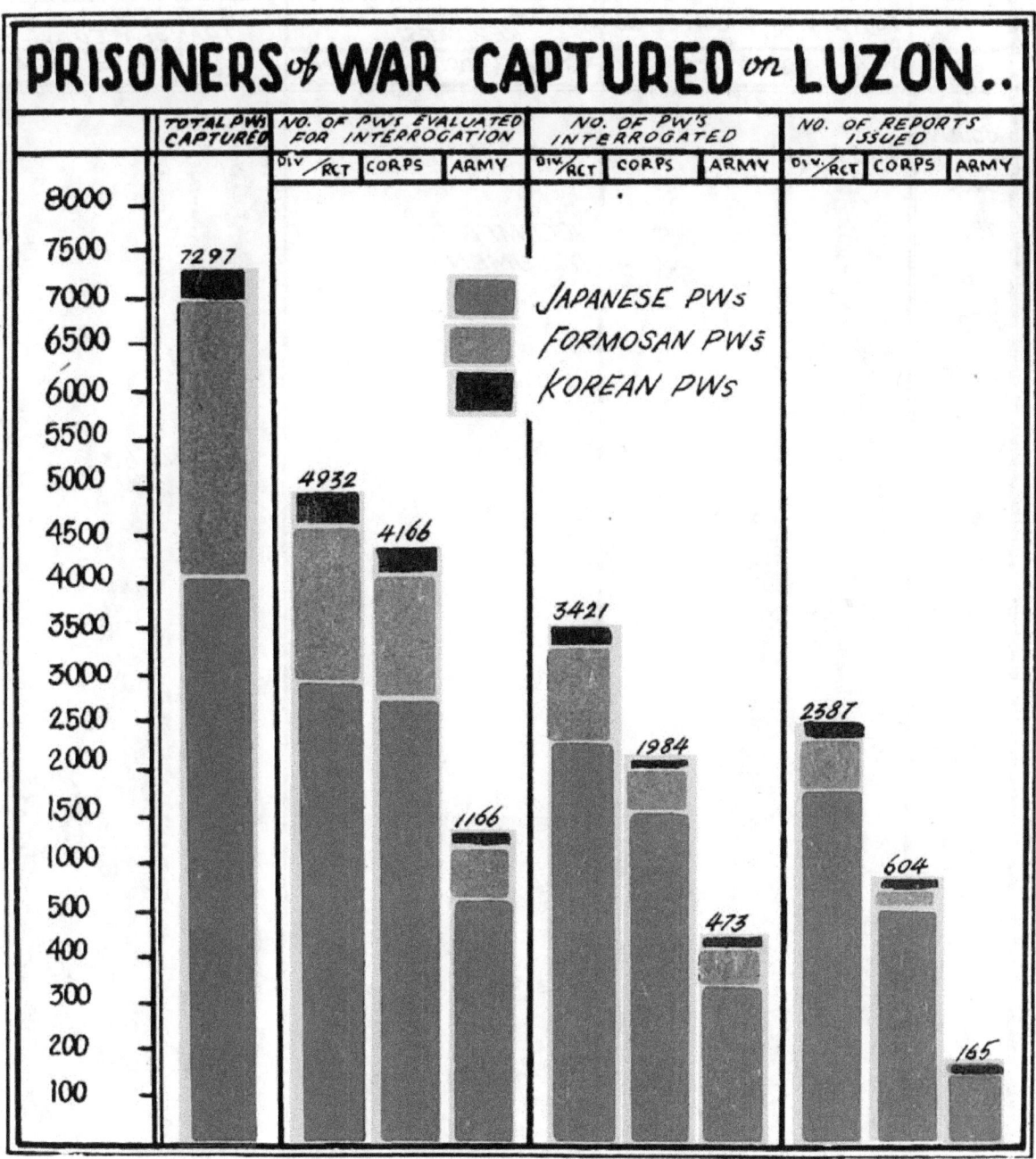

Figure 46

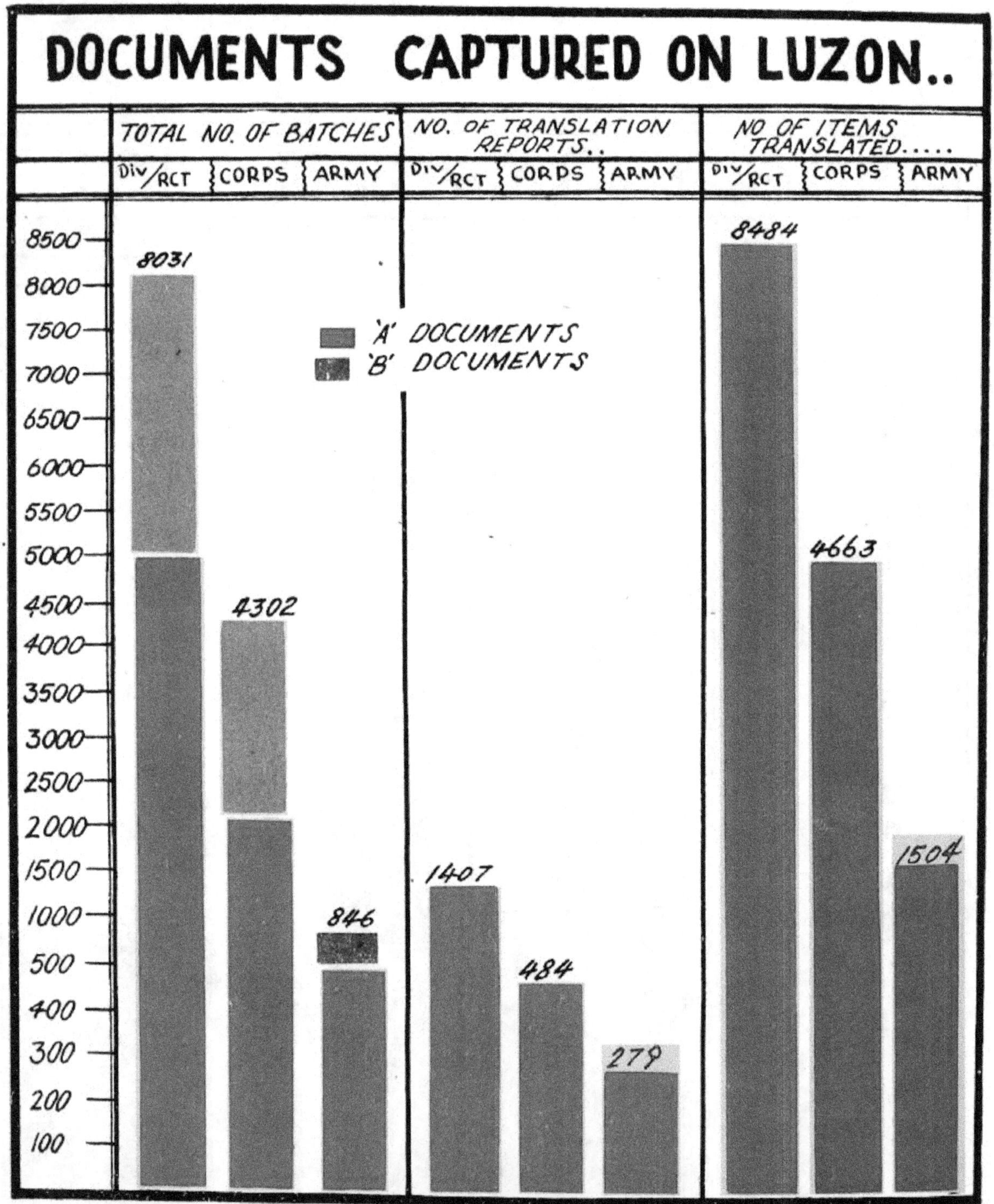

DOCUMENTS CAPTURED ON LUZON..

TOTAL NO. OF BATCHES			NO. OF TRANSLATION REPORTS..			NO OF ITEMS TRANSLATED.....		
DIV/RCT	CORPS	ARMY	DIV/RCT	CORPS	ARMY	DIV/RCT	CORPS	ARMY
8031	4302	846	1407	484	279	8484	4663	1504

'A' DOCUMENTS
'B' DOCUMENTS

Figure 47

CHAPTER VII

PSYCHOLOGICAL WARFARE METHODS

PSYCHOLOGICAL WARFARE ON LUZON:

When hostilities broke out between Japan and the United States, it was the common belief that no Japanese would ever fall into our hands, much less that he would surrender to our forces. Past events have shown, however, that such belief was erroneous. Japanese prisoners were captured, and more than half of those taken on Luzon voluntarily surrendered.

The objective of Psychological Warfare in Sixth Army was to hasten victory and to lessen the cost to our troops. To this end, it was utilized more effectively on the island of Luzon than in any previous campaign conducted by Sixth Army. The effectiveness can be measured by the fact that in the closing month of the Luzon campaign, nearly 15 enemy were surrendering to every 100 enemy casualties. Eighty percent of all prisoners taken had seen our leaflets, and seventy percent of all who surrendered made use of surrender passes. A total of 7,297 prisoners of war were taken during the Luzon Operation; of these, approximately 5,100 were voluntary surrenders.

MEANS OF DISTRIBUTION:

The strategic dropping of leaflets on the target was begun by PWB, GHQ, in mid-November 1944. From S-Day on, the tempo of leaflet-dropping increased and continued to increase as the campaign progressed; 8,500,000, for example, being dropped during the month of May, and a total of 29,500,000 being dropped throughout the period from 9 January to 30 June (see accompanying chart).

Of all leaflets distributed, 92% were dropped by supporting units of the Fifth Air Force, and 8% were dropped by Artillery Liaison planes. Artillery shells were employed to distribute leaflets on only a few occasions because of the difficulties of transporting the ammunition.

Voice broadcasting through the use of public address systems were found a most effective propaganda means. Every unit of the Sixth Army made use of this means of influencing the enemy, and speakers were used from jeeps, liaison planes, and from LCM's.

REACTIONS TO PROPAGANDA:

The strongest and most effective of the forces which reduced the Japanese morale was hunger brought on by the disruption of enemy supply lines. This factor was exploited, as well as other motivating forces, by Psychological Warfare. Among these were the cruelty of his officers, the hopelessness of the situation--accentuated by the devastating effectiveness of our bombing and shelling. The extreme hardships they were experiencing bore out what our newspapers and bulletins, general attacks on morale, good treatment, surrender leaflets, and broadcasts were dinning into the enemy's mind.

The Japanese soldier was so well trained that it was not until the second half of the campaign that these forces began to have effect.

Among the deterrents to the enemy's surrender was his rigid indoctrination, credence attached to the stories of American cruelty, ill treatment accorded to Japanese prisoners of war by Filipinos, prevention by officers, and the disgrace to themselves and their families.

These obstacles were nullified largely by aforementioned methods. Specifically, one means of effecting surrender is illustrated by the story of Rin and Ko.

Rin Sei Su and Ko Mei Seki were Formosans. Their surrender had been effected when our propaganda leaflets began to prey on their minds as food became scarce.

Thereafter, Rin and Ko went upon missions behind the

Japanese lines, telling their friends of their treatment and persuading them to surrender. It can be safely said that the majority of the 684 Formosans, Japanese, and Chinese taken by the 7th Cavalry Regiment should be directly credited to the influence of Rin and Ko.

Undoubtedly, the "Rakkasan News" played a prominent role in many surrenders; it convinced the Japanese of Japan's precarious position. Credibility of the paper was increasingly enhanced as more and more Japanese officers tended to confirm in their troops the authenticity of the publication's pictures and statements. This corroboration of the news was accentuated by the actual experiences of the troops themselves, and since, to the Japanese soldier, it was practically the only source of news of the outside world, it was eagerly received by the majority of the enemy troops.

That our program caused concern to the enemy command is shown by the following extracts from captured documents, the first of which was captured by the 25th Division and entitled "The General Attitude of the Soldier":

"The enemy is planning constantly to crumble our Army by means of skillful psychological warfare which is ordinarily difficult to detect. Therefore, the soldier must depend wholeheartedly upon his officers and endeavor to fulfill his obligations."

The second document (a notification from C/S Kobayashi Group) captured in the San Mateo area on 11 March stated:

"The enemy has recently been widely scattering propaganda leaflets stating that the Luzon operation has been favorable to him and that anti-war feeling is rising among our troops. Therefore, each unit will have its officers and men recognize that in actuality the Luzon operation has been favorable to us and at the same time will make particular effort to raise morale of troops. Furthermore, when leaflets are found, they will be handled over to superiors at once, and it is prohibited for officers and men in general to keep them."

(Note: The leaflets referred to apparently include the weekly Japanese newspaper.)

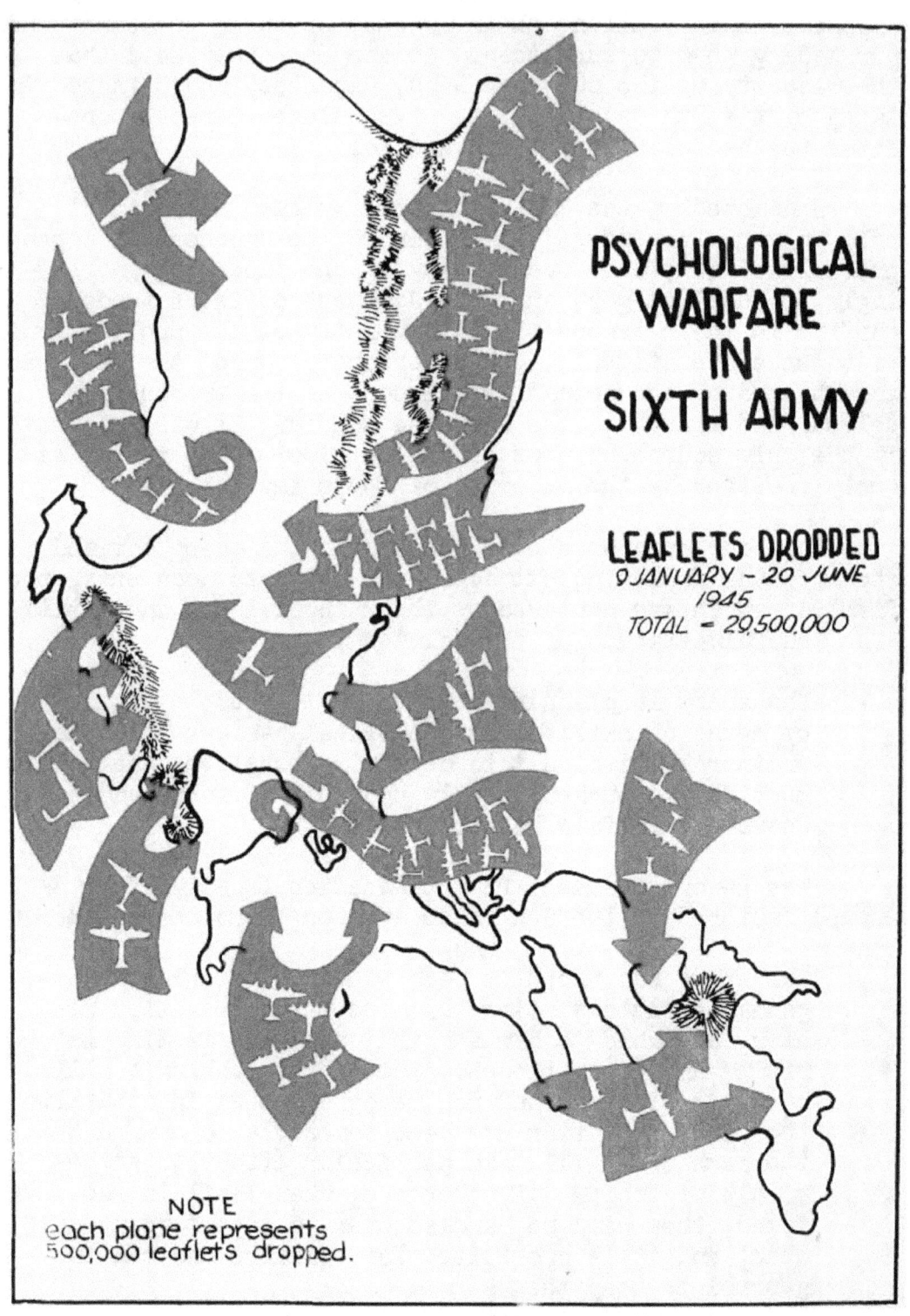

Figure 48

CHAPTER VIII

ENEMY ORDER OF BATTLE

JAPANESE MILITARY UNITS ENCOUNTERED ON LUZON:

Unit	Place Last Located	Date Last Contacted	Strength
MOBILE COMBAT			
2nd Armored Div	E central Luzon	6/45	9,500
8th Div (-5th Inf)	E of Manila-Batangas	6/45	10,000
10th Div	Balete Pass-Bataan	6/45	14,000
19th Div (-) (Less three Inf Bns)	Cervantes-Bontoc	6/45	11,500
23rd Div	Ambuclao area	6/45	13,750
103rd Div	N Luzon	6/45	11,750
105th Div	E of Manila-Kiangan	6/45	12,500
Elms, 11th Div	N Luzon	2/45	300
Elms, 16th Div	N Luzon	6/45	2,000
Elms, 26th Div	Balete Pass area	5/45	2,900
Elms, 49th Div	Montalban	2/45	100
Elms, 53rd Div	Bosoboso	4/45	550
Elms, 102nd Div	E of Manila	4/45	800
Elms, 37th Army (Incl elms 56th IMB)	E of Manila	5/45	1,500
Misc "Remaining Units"	E of Manila-N Luzon	5/45	1,500
58th IMB	Mountain Trail	6/45	5,300
61st IMB (Small elms in Cagayan Valley)	Batan & Babuyan I	5/45	4,400

Unit	Place Last Located	Date Last Contacted	Strength
1st Raiding Group	W of Clark- N Luzon	5/45	3,900
26th Ind Mixed Regt (-) (Elms on Samar)	Luzon	6/45	2,500
Yebiko Bn (PW Camp Guards) (Same as Ebisu Bn)	E of Manila	6/45	250
6th Prov Inf Bn	Mountain Trail	6/45	500
9th Prov Inf Bn (Hidaka Bn)	Mountain Trail	5/45	800
Naval Arty Units	Batangas	4/45	300
4th Ind Hvy Arty Bn	Mountain Trail- Batangas	6/45	575
4th Prov Med FA Btry	Bamban	1/45	125
6th Ind FA Bn	Mountain Trail	5/45	550
12th Med Arty Regt	Mountain Trail	6/45	1,100
20th Ind Hvy Arty Bn	Luzon	5/45	600
22nd Med Arty Regt (-)	Antipolo	6/45	700
14th Area Army SP Gun Co	Baguio	4/45	100
3rd Rocket Bn	E of Manila	6/45	800
4th Med Mortar Bn	E of Manila	6/45	550
5th Med Mortar Bn	E of Manila	6/45	550
6th Med Mortar Bn	Old Spanish Trail	6/45	550
7th Med Mortar Bn	Balete Pass	6/45	550
21st Ind Mortar Bn (-) (Elms on Leyte)	Antipolo	5/45	400
18th Ind AT Bn	Cagayan Valley	6/45	450
19th Ind AT Bn	Kiangan?	6/45	450
21st Ind AT Co	Balete Pass	5/45	140
23rd Ind AT Bn	Ipo	6/45	340
24th Ind AT Bn	Pangasinan	1/45	450
25th Ind AT Bn	Bamban-Salinas	6/45	450
26th Ind AT Bn	Balete Pass	5/45	450
37th Ind AT Co	Manila - SW Luzon	3/45	140
8th Ind Tank Co	Bagabag	6/45	130
9th Ind Tank Co	Ilagan	6/45	130
10th Ind Tank Co	Ilagan	6/45	60
11th Ind Tank Co	Cagayan Valley	6/45	130
12th Ind Tank Co	C Luzon	4/45	130
1st Fd Replacement Unit	E of Manila	5/45	4,000
1st-3rd Prov MG Cos	Villa Verde Trail	5/45	360

Unit	Place Last Located	Date Last Contacted	Strength
4th Prov MG Co	Gapan	2/45	120
13th Ind MG Bn	Ipo	6/45	290
25th Ind MG Bn	Ipo	5/45	290
26th Ind MG Bn	Bontoc	4/45	400
Elms, Gigo Force (See Note 1)	Lipa	4/45	100
Total Mobile Combat			**126,760**

BASE DEFENSE

Unit	Place Last Located	Date Last Contacted	Strength
Manila Naval Defense Force (Incl 31st Spec Base)	Manila-Infanta	6/45	13,000
Corregidor Defense Force	Manila Bay	5/45	6,700
Elms, 31st Naval Guard Force (Incl small dets)	Mariveles-Bicol	5/45	800
Elms, 33rd Spec Base Force	Camalig	3/45	200
35th Naval Guard Force (Incl Legaspi Naval Air Depot)	Camalig	5/45	1,500
Elms, Takao Naval Guard Force (Identified enroute)	Batan & Babuyan Is	10/44	
Poro Ca Unit	Mankayan	5/45	200
Olongapo Naval Unit	Olongapo	2/45	100
13th Naval Combat Sector	W of Clark	4/45	1,000
14th Naval Combat Sector	W of Clark	4/45	1,000
15th Naval Combat Sector	W of Clark	4/45	1,000
16th Naval Combat Sector	W of Clark	4/45	1,000
17th Naval Combat Sector	W of Clark	4/45	1,000
Elms, 1st Ship AA Regt (Bulk in Japan)	N Luzon	1/45	200
2nd Ship AA Regt (-)	NE of Baguio	6/45	1,500
Manila AA Hq	Cagayan Valley	6/45	600
2nd Searchlight Bn	Bagabag	6/45	350
76th Fd AA Bn (-)	E of Manila-Imugan	4/45	400
77th Fd AA Bn	N Luzon-E of Manila	6/45	550
78th Fd AA Bn	E of Manila	5/45	550
84th Fd AA Bn	W of Clark	6/45	550
89th Fd AA Bn	Mountain Trail	4/45	550

Unit	Place Last Located	Date Last Contacted	Strength
207th Naval Air Defense Unit	La Union	4/45	150
134th Fd Searchlight Unit (See Note 2)	Cagayan Valley	5/45	175
135th Fd Searchlight Unit (See Note 2)	Cagayan Valley	5/45	175
1st Spec Mach Cn Unit	Ipo	4/45	115
3rd Mach Cn Unit	E of Manila	3/45	100
7th Spec Mach Cn Unit	W of Clark	1/45	30
8th Mach Cn Unit	E of Manila-Salangbato	5/45	105
10th Spec Mach Cn Unit	E of Manila	4/45	100
11th Spec Mach Cn Unit	Mt Malepunyo	5/45	100
12th Mach Cn Unit	W of Clark	1/45	100
12th Spec Mach Cn Unit	W of Clark	3/45	85
13th Mach Cn Unit	W of Clark	1/45	100
13th Spec Mach Cn Unit	Kiangan	4/45	90
15th Spec Mach Cn Unit	Kiangan	4/45	100
26th Ind Mach Cn Bn	Bontoc	2/45	350
51st Spec Mach Cn Unit	N of Baguio	3/45	100
52nd Mach Cn Unit	Ipo	5/45	130
52nd Spec Mach Cn Unit	N of Baguio	6/45	100
53rd Mach Cn Unit	Bontoc	6/45	105
53rd Spec Mach Cn Unit	N of Baguio	3/45	100
54th Mach Cn Unit	Bagabag	5/45	105
54th Spec Mach Cn Unit	Bontoc	5/45	100
Elms, 64th Mach Cn Unit	N of Baguio	3/45	60
65th Spec Mach Cn Unit (Identified enroute)	Manila	10/44	
Elms, 66th Mach Cn Unit	N of Baguio	2/45	35
Elms, 68th Mach Cn Unit	N of Baguio	2/45	20
Elms, 69th Mach Cn Unit	N of Baguio	2/45	30
Elms, 71st Spec Mach Cn Unit	Manila	3/45	30
Elms, 72nd Spec Mach Cn Unit	N of Baguio	5/45	40
Total Base Defense			35,580

SERVICE TROOPS

Unit	Place Last Located	Date Last Contacted	Strength
14th Area Army Hq	Kiangan	5/45	2,000
41st Army (Corps) Hq (See Note 3)	E of Manila	6/45	

Unit	Place Last Located	Date Last Contacted	Strength
4th Air Army Hq	Echague	6/45	1,200
Southern Army Spec Intelligence Section	Kiangan	4/45	380
Baguio Defense Force	Mountain Trail	4/45	2,000
Engr Reserve Offr's Candidate Unit	E of Manila	2/45	150
Elms, 15th Ind Engr Regt (Identified enroute; bulk in New Guinea)	Unlocated	12/44	
Misc Army Flying Personnel	Throughout Luzon	6/45	5,000
Misc Naval Flying Personnel	W of Clark	4/45	2,500
Misc Ship Crews (Naval)	Zambales-Bontoc	5/45	500
Southern Air Route Dept	Yangiran	4/45	320
Elms, 1st Air Photo Unit (Bulk in Burma)	Bayombong	1/45	100
Elms, 1st Air Route Dept	Luzon	5/45	50
Elms, 1st Navigation aid Regt (Bulk in Japan)	Luzon	5/45	50
2nd Navigation Aid Regt (-)	W of Clark	3/45	300
7th Spec Airfield Cons Unit?	Lucban	2/45	100
8th Airfield Co	W of Clark	5/45	230
9th Air Intelligence Regt (-)	Luzon	6/45	400
10th Air Intelligence Regt (-)	Luzon	6/45	800
10th Air Sector Hq	W of Clark	4/45	100
11th Air Sector Hq	E of Manila	6/45	100
13th Airfield Co (-) (Elms on Lubang)	E of Manila	6/45	150
22nd Airfield Cons Unit	E of Manila	6/45	100
24th Fd Airfield Cons Unit	W of Clark	5/45	100
Elms, 30th Airfield Bn (Bulk in Manchuria?)	Pingkian	6/45	30
31st Airfield Bn	W of Clark	5/45	400
Elms, 32nd Airfield Bn (Bulk on Mindanao)	W of Clark	4/45	50
Elms, 32nd Airfield Co (Bulk on Negros)	E of Manila	1/45	70
33rd Air Sector Hq	Cagayan Valley	1/45	100
35th Air Sector Hq	Mt Isarog	5/45	100
36th Air Sector Hq	Balete Pass	5/45	100

Unit	Place Last Located	Date Last Contacted	Strength
36th Airfield Bn? (Possibly in Manchuria)	Tuguegarao	10/44	400
47th Airfield Co	E of Manila	4/45	200
50th Airfield Co	Cagayan Valley	5/45	200
51st Airfield Co	Cagayan Valley	3/45	200
52nd Airfield Co	W of Clark	3/45	200
86th Airfield Bn	Mt Banahao	5/45	400
99th Airfield Bn	W of Clark	5/45	400
125th Airfield Bn	Cagayan Valley	5/45	400
127th Airfield Bn	La Union	1/45	400
132nd Airfield Bn	W of Clark	4/45	400
133rd Airfield Bn	Cagayan Valley	4/45	400
134th Airfield Bn	E of Manila	4/45	400
136th Airfield Bn	Echague-Baguio	5/45	400
136th Airfield Cons Unit	E of Manila	5/45	100
137th Airfield Bn	W of Clark	4/45	400
137th Airfield Cons Unit	E of Manila	6/45	100
138th Airfield Cons Unit	W of Clark	6/45	100
146th Airfield Cons Unit (Identified enroute)	Unlocated	8/44	
147th Airfield Bn	Mt Isarog	5/45	400
148th Airfield Bn	E of Manila	6/45	400
149th Airfield Bn	E of Manila	6/45	415
150th Airfield Bn	W of Clark	3/45	400
151st Airfield Bn	W of Clark	5/45	400
152nd Airfield Bn	W of Clark	5/45	400
154th Airfield Bn	Echague	6/45	500
180th Airfield Bn	E of Manila	4/45	400
Prov Trk Bn	Pingkian	2/45	400?
3rd Fd Tpt Hq	N Luzon	4/45	100
6th Fd Tpt Hq	Kiangan	4/45	65
6th Rwy Tpt Command (Incl Guard Bn)	W of Aritao	5/45	600
8th Rwy Regt	Balete Pass-E of Manila	6/45	1,300
22nd Spec Trk Co	E of Manila	6/45	175
52nd Ind Trk Bn (Identified enroute)	Unlocated	12/44	
62nd Ind Trk Bn	W of Aritao	4/45	850
63rd Ind Trk Bn (-)	W of Aritao	6/45	450
130th Ind Trk Co	Villa Verde Trail	5/45	150

Unit	Place Last Located	Date Last Contacted	Strength
210th Ind Trk Co	E of Bayombong	4/45	200
260th Ind Trk Co	Kiangan	6/45	200
297th Ind Trk Co	E of Manila	3/45	175
320th Ind Trk Co	N of Baguio	2/45	130
321st Ind Trk Co	E of Baguio	4/45	175
322nd Ind Trk Co	W of Clark	2/45	175
326th Ind Trk Co	E of Manila	6/45	175
327th Ind Trk Co	W of Aritao	3/45	175
328th Ind Trk Co?	N Luzon	10/44	175
330th Ind Trk Co	Bagabag	6/45	175
Morishita Anchorage	Manila-Aparri	4/45	1,100
Submarine Tpt Exped Unit (Army Unit)	W of Aritao	6/45	300
1st Ship Tpt Command Br	Zambales	3/45	100
Elms, 1st High-Speed Tpt Bn (Bulk in Japan)	Zambales	2/45	300
1st Launching Unit?	Zambales	4/45	100
1st Amphibious Tpt Bn	Manila-Bolinao	3/45	500
2nd Amphibious Tpt Bn	Mountain Trail	6/45	700
3rd Ship Tpt Command (-)	Manila-Cagayan Valley	5/45	400
5th Ship Tpt Command Br	N Luzon	2/45	100
9th Sea Tpt Bn	Cagayan Valley	5/45	600
Elms, 9th Ship Engr Regt (Bulk in New Guinea)	W Luzon	3/45	100
10th Sea Tpt Bn	Cagayan Valley	6/45	600
12th Land Duty Co?	N of Baguio	2/45	100
Elms, 15th Debarkation Unit	Zambales	3/45	50
Elms, 21st Ship Engr Regt (Bulk in Visayas)	Manila	3/45	100
Elms, 23rd Ship Engr Regt (Bulk on Okinawa)	N of Baguio	12/44	100
24th Ship Engr Regt	E of Manila	6/45	1,200
25th Ship Engr Regt	Cagayan Valley	6/45	1,200
32nd Ship Engr Regt	Cagayan Valley	5/45	1,200
Elms, 34th Ship Engr Regt	La Union	12/44	200
Elms, 48th Anchorage Unit (Bulk in NEI)	N Luzon	2/45	150
63rd Anchorage Unit	Aparri	2/45	100
Elms, 76th Land Duty Co (Bulk in New Guinea)	La Union	12/44	80

Unit	Place Last Located	Date Last Contacted	Strength
111th Land Duty Co	E of Manila-W of Clark	5/45	350
124th Land Duty Co	Manila-Bayombong	4/45	350
144th Spec Sea Duty Co	Cagayan Valley	2/45	350
145th Spec Sea Duty Co	Cagayan Valley	2/45	350
146th Spec Sea Duty Co	Cagayan Valley	2/45	350
147th Spec Sea Duty Co	Cagayan Valley	2/45	350
148th Spec Sea Duty Co	Cagayan Valley	2/45	350
149th Spec Sea Duty Co	Cagayan Valley	2/45	150
150th Spec Sea Duty Co	Cagayan Valley	2/45	350
151st Spec Sea Duty Co	Cagayan Valley	2/45	350
1st Gyoro Base Unit	Salangbato	5/45	100
2nd Gyoro Base Unit	Mt Malepunyo	4/45	100
3rd Gyoro Base Unit	Obando	2/45	100
5th Gyoro Squadron	Legaspi	5/45	100
6th Gyoro Squadron	Batangas	3/45	100
7th Gyoro Squadron	Obando-Infanta	2/45	100
8th Gyoro Squadron	Mauban	11/44	100
9th Gyoro Squadron	Salangbato	4/45	100
10th Gyoro Squadron	Salangbato	4/45	100
11th Gyoro Squadron	Ternate	5/45	100
12th Gyoro Squadron	Sual	1/45	100
13th Gyoro Squadron	Batangas	3/45	100
14th Gyoro Squadron	Batangas	3/45	100
15th Gyoro Squadron	Batangas	3/45	100
16th Gyoro Squadron	Batangas	3/45	100
17th Gyoro Squadron	Obando	2/45	100
18th Gyoro Squadron	Manila Bay	2/45	100
19th Gyoro Squadron	Batangas	2/45	100
20th Gyoro Squadron	Obando	2/45	100
105th Gyoro Cons Bn	Mt Isarog	4/45	750
106th Gyoro Cons Bn	SW Luzon	4/45	780
107th Gyoro Cons Bn	E of Manila	6/45	850
108th Gyoro Cons Bn	E of Manila	5/45	850
109th Gyoro Cons Bn	SW of Infanta	6/45	850
110th Gyoro Cons Bn	E of Manila	5/45	850
111th Gyoro Cons Bn	Cavite Prov	5/45	850
112th Gyoro Cons Bn	Sual-Zambales	3/45	850
113th Gyoro Cons Bn	SW Luzon	4/45	850
114th Gyoro Cons Bn	Batangas	4/45	850

Unit	Place Last Located	Date Last Contacted	Strength
115th Gyoro Cons Bn	Batangas	4/45	480
116th Gyoro Cons Bn	SW Luzon	4/45	860
117th Gyoro Cons Bn	Obando	2/45	850
118th Gyoro Cons Bn	E of Manila	6/45	700
119th Gyoro Cons Bn	SW Luzon	5/45	800
120th Gyoro Cons Bn	Obando	2/45	750
Elms, Ship Signal Regt	Luzon	5/45	500
1st Sig Unit, Southern Army Sig Unit	E of Manila	5/45	300
2nd Signal Regt	Luzon	5/45	1,200
2nd Air Signal Group Hq	Ipo-W of Clark	4/45	400
3rd Ind Army Signal Co	Cagayan Valley	4/45	150
4th Spec Air Signal Unit	Ipo	6/45	200
5th Air-Ground Radio Unit	Ipo	5/45	160
Elms, 7th Signal Regt	N of Baguio	5/45	220
7th Ind Wire Co	W of Clark	1/45	150
9th Air-Ground Radio Unit	W of Clark	4/45	200
10th Air Signal Unit (Regt?)	Ipo-W of Clark	5/45	525
12th Air Signal Regt	Ipo	5/45	950
14th Fixed Radio Unit	Manila	10/44	50
17th Air Signal Regt (Possibly only elms)	W of Aritao-W of Clark	3/45	330
22nd Air Signal Regt	W of Clark Cagayan Valley	5/45	700
Elms, 25th Air-Ground Radio Unit (Part on Negros)	Cagayan Valley	6/45	150
27th Signal Regt (-) (Elms on Leyte)	N of Baguio (?)	5/45	1,300
Elms, 30th Signal Regt	Baguio-E of Manila	2/45	200
41st Fixed Radio Unit	Manila	10/44	50
61st Air-Ground Radio Unit	W of Clark-Ipo	5/45	180
96th Ind Wire Co	W of Clark	5/45	200
98th Ind Radio Plat	SW Luzon	6/45	60
101st Ind Wire Plat	W of Clark	1/45	50
107th Ind Wire Co	W of Clark	6/45	200
111th Ind Radio Plat	W of Clark	4/45	50
112th Ind Radio Plat (Identified enroute)	Unlocated	10/44	
117th Ind Radio Plat	N of Baguio	1/45	50
118th Ind Radio Plat	Manila	11/44	50

Unit	Place Last Located	Date Last Contacted	Strength
123rd Air-Ground Radio Unit (Terminology obscure)	W of Clark	4/45	100
124th Ind Radio Plat	Ipo	4/45	60
Southern Army Water Purification Section	Baguio	2/45	103
7th Area Army Vet Section (Identified enroute)	Unlocated	12/44	
12th Southern Army Hospital	S of Bontoc	4/45	600
14th Area Army L of C Vet Depot	Pingkian	6/45	160
16th Casualty Clearing Plat	Bayombong	6/45	110
30th Fd Water Purification Unit	Ipo-N Luzon	5/45	190
63rd L of C Hospital	E of Manila-Calauag	6/45	350
74th L of C Hospital	W of Bambang	4/45	300
78th L of C Hospital	E of Manila	4/45	300
92nd Casualty Clearing Plat	Baguio	2/45	75
93rd Casualty Clearing Plat	Aritao	2/45	55
129th L of C Hospital	S of Kiangan	6/45	300
134th L of C Hospital	W of Bambang	6/45	300
137th L of C Hospital	W of Clark-Ipo	3/45	300
Elms, 138th L of C Hospital (Bulk on Leyte)	Aritao	6/45	200
139th L of C Hospital	Bagabag	6/45	300
141st L of C Hospital	S Luzon	4/45	300
Naval Meteorological Stations	Bicol-Baguio	4/45	50
2nd Fd Meteorological Unit (-)	Luzon	4/45	300
22nd Fd Meteorological Unit (-)	Luzon	4/45	600
3rd Mobile Ordnance Repair Unit	Baguio	2/45	100
14th Area Army MP Unit	Luzon	5/45	660
2nd L of C Sector Unit	Tababas coast	5/45	500
14th Area Army L of C Inspectorate	Kiangan	5/45	220
61st L of C Sector Unit	N Luzon?	4/45	500
85th L of C Sector Unit	N Luzon-Tayabas	5/45	1,000
88th L of C Sector Unit	N Luzon	5/45	1,000
Manila Army Air Depot and Brs (Incl Fd Air Repair Depots)	Throughout Luzon	6/45	6,000

Unit	Place Last Located	Date Last Contacted	Strength
Fd Ship Main Depot Br (Main Depot in Japan)	E of Manila-Aparri	5/45	500
Southern Army Air Tpt Depot	Baguio	2/45	90
5th Fd Ship Depot	Cagayan Valley	5/45	1,500
14th Area Army Fd Ordnance Depot	Bambang	5/45	1,500
14th Area Army Fd Trk Depot	Cagayan Valley-Ipo	5/45	1,500
14th Area Army Fd Freight Depot	Cagayan Valley-E of Manila	6/45	2,000
16th Ship Air Depot	Baguio	2/45	160
18th Ship Air Depot	Ipo	5/45	150
22nd Fd Ordnance Depot	S of Kiangan	6/45	200
22nd Fd Freight Depot	Cauayan-Manila	6/45	500
27th Fd Freight Depot Br (Bulk in New Guinea)	Manila	2/45	100
Misc Exploitation Duty Units	Luzon	5/45	1,000
Construction Group	Cagayan Valley	2/45	400
1st Prov Duty Co	Baguio	2/45	300
2nd Survey Unit, Southern Army	W of Bambang	1/45	100
2nd Prov Duty Co	Baguio	2/45	300
3rd Prov Duty Co	Baguio	2/45	300
12th Fd Duty Unit	Pingkian	6/45	300
13th Fd Survey Unit	Bayombong	6/45	100
37th Cons Duty Co (-) (Elms on Mindanao)	N Luzon	12/44	200
49th Fd Road Cons Unit	N Luzon	2/45	100
Elms, 56th Cons Duty Unit (-) (Elms Negros & Mindanao)	W of Clark-Manila	2/45	100
57th Fd Road Cons Unit (-) (Elms on Mindanao)	Kiangan-E of Manila	6/45	100
Elms, 69th Spec Cons Co (Bulk on Biak)	Mountain Trail	4/45	150
103rd Naval Cons Unit	Luzon	6/45	700
16th, 320th-325th Fd POs	Luzon	5/45	500

Total Service Troops   95,550

Recapitulation:

Total Mobile Combat	126,760
Total Base Defense	35,580
Total Service Troops	95,550
Total Identified Units, 30 June	257,890

(Casualties not assessed)

These figures exclude laborers, although labor troops were usually included in counted casualties. However, the majority of these troops were unarmed and their inclusion in the above strength figures would have presented a distorted picture. For example, some of the units which contained only Formosans are not listed above. It is estimated that 13,000 laborers were located on Luzon.

Note 1 — The Gigo Force was formed at Lipa in the summer of 1944, and was a 350-man special suicide attack unit. In December 44, some personnel of this unit were used in the paratroops operation on Leyte; these were the men who attempted to land on U.S.-held airstrips, jump out of their transports, and destroy as much equipment as possible before being killed. About 100 men of this unit remained behind at Lipa, and they were apparently absorbed into the Fuji Heidan. The meaning of the term Gigo is unclear; the commander of the Force was Major Kanda, Yasuo, and the code number 1781 (1st Diversionary or Commando Unit) has been slightly connected with the Gigo Force.

Note 2 — Possibly a mistake for the 134th and 135th Airfield Cons Units.

Note 3 — This Hq was formed by drawing personnel from the 8th and 105th Division Headquarters and from the Kobayashi Heidan hence no strength can be carried.

All but a few of the foregoing units were rendered ineffective by 30 June 1945. The exceptions were the 61st IMB in the Batan and Babuyan Islands, and a number of units in the Cordillera and Sierra Madre Ranges. A list of these units follows:

Mountain Trail—Bontoc—Kiangan—Macdo area (Cordilleras):

	Est remaining strength on 30 June
Remnants, 2nd Armd Div & attachments	350
19th Div	3,300
Remnants, 23rd Div & attachments	700
Remnants, 58th IMB & attachments	700
Elms, 103rd Div	900
Elms, 105th Div	1,700
Elms, 77th Fd AA Bn	100
13th & 15th Spec Machine Cannon Cos	150
14th Area Army Hq and attached signal units	900
Remnants of air force units	400
Prov Truck Bn (-)	150
Remnants, 63rd Ind Truck Bn & Ind Truck Cos	350
Remnants, 25th Shipping Engr Regt (Ito Bn)	50
Remnants, N Luzon L of C Hospitals	350
Remnants, 14th Area Army Fd Freight Depot	300
Remnants, 14th Area Army Fd Ord Depot	300
Remnants, 14th Area Army Fd Truck Depot	200
Remnants, 22nd Fd Ord Depot	50
12th Fd Duty Unit & Exploitation Duty Cos	300
57th Fd Road Constr Unit	100
Elms, 85th and 88th L of C Sector Units	150
Remnants, 10th Div, 11th Ind Inf Regt & attachments	500*
	12,000

* A portion of these units remained E of Old Spanish Trail (vicinity of Dupax).

Northeast Luzon (Sierra Madres):

103rd Div (-)	3,500
Remnants, 3rd Bn, 26th IMR	100
Elms, 18th Ind AT Bn	100
Remnants 9th, 10th, 11th Ind Tank Cos	150
Elms, 2nd Shipping Arty Regt	100
134th & 135th Fd Searchlight Units	250
4th Air Army Hq and remnants of air force units	1,000

36th Air Sector Hq	50
36th Airfield Bn ?	200
Morishita Anchorage (-)	100
2nd Amphib Tpt Bn (-)	300
9th Sea Tpt Bn (-)	300
10th Sea Tpt Bn (-)	300
Elms, 24th Shipping Engr Regt	100
25th Shipping Engr Regt (-)	350
32nd Shipping Engr Regt	500
63rd Anchorage Unit	100
145th-151st (incl) Spec Sea Duty Cos	2,100
Elms, 27th Signal Regt	100
Elms, 88th L of C Sector Unit	150
Elms, 5th Fd Shipping Depot & Main Fd Shipping Depot	300
Elms, Manila Army Air Depot	600
Elms, 103rd Naval Constr Unit	250
	11,000
Total	23,000

ORGANIZATION OF THE 2ND ARMORED DIVISION:

The 2nd Armored Division was activated in August 1942 in Manchuria, under the Armored Army (Corps). Originally this division contained the 6th and 7th Tank Regiments under the 3rd Tank Brigade and the 10th and 11th Tank Regiments under the 4th Tank Brigade. However, the division was triangularized in January 1944, when the 11th Tank Regiment was detached and sent to the northern Kuriles. The 4th Tank Brigade Headquarters was dropped soon afterwards, so that the three remaining tank regiments were under the 3rd Tank Brigade. In November 1943 the Armored Army (Corps) was dissolved, and the 2nd Armored Division was transferred to the 1st Area Army. It is significant to note that General Tomoyuki Yamashita commanded the 1st Area Army before he went to Luzon to take over the 14th Area Army. The 2nd Armored Division was one of several major units of his Manchurian command which were later under him in the Philippines.

Before the 2nd Armored Division moved to Luzon in August 1944, two other organic components were dropped.

The divisional reconnaissance unit was sent to Okinawa where it was absorbed by the 27th Tank Regiment, and the divisional anti-aircraft defense unit was diverted to Central China. After the Division's arrival on Luzon in early September, small elements were sent to Leyte Island with the 1st Division to reinforce the garrison there.

Captured documents, materiel, and prisoners of war information disclosed that the 2nd Armored Division differed substantially from standard armored divisions' T/O and E in strength, equipment, and several organizational details. Although this divergence from the norm may to some extent be attributed to shipping and replacement difficulties, the most important variances appear to have been premeditated T/O and E changes. The overwhelming preponderance of medium tanks, the inclusion of self-propelled artillery pieces, and the absence of the divisional reconnaissance and anti-aircraft defense units are pertinent examples of such apparently purposeful changes. From several captured records it is evident that the division indulged in several organization and equipment experiments prior to its commitment. Products of such experiments were special artillery batteries and three independent anti-tank combat companies. Of these units only the anti-tank companies are mentioned in the appended charts; the special artillery units were presumably lost at sea enroute to Leyte Island The anti-tank combat companies did not fulfil their intended function during the campaign; they apparently had no anti-tank guns and were used as infantry units.

On the succeeding page is a summary of the division strength and major equipment, reconstructed from documents and prisoner of war statements. Further details will be found on the organization charts which follow. It will be remembered that this summary and the charts show actual, operational strength of the 2nd Armored Division while on Luzon and do not constitute a T/O and E. Note that great stress was placed on anti-tank guns. Each rifle company in the mobile infantry regiment had three 47-mm anti-tank guns. If the three independent anti-tank combat companies had contained their quota of guns, the divisional total would have been 70.

Unit	Strength	Medium Tanks	Light Tanks	Armored Cars	Arty	AT Guns
Div Hq	300	7	2			
3rd Tank Brig Hq	110	6	5	2		
6th Tank Regt	685	57	9	1		
7th Tank Regt	810	55	17			
10th Tank Regt	695	55	4	1		
Mob Inf Regt	1,965			9	6	27
Mob Arty Regt	1,260			2	35	2
Engr Regt	680			24		1
AT Unit	310					18
1st-3rd (incl) Ind AT Combat Cos	510					
Maint Unit	460	17				4
Tpt Unit	650					
Sig Unit	200					
Med Unit	800					
Total	9,435	197	37	39	41	52

By way of comparison, the following figures are presented for a U.S. Armored Division. These figures, as opposed to those of the Japanese 2nd Armored Division above, are T/O and E authorizations and not operational reports.

Unit	Strength	Medium Tanks*	Light Tanks	Armored Cars	Arty	AT Guns
Tank Bn	700	59	17			
Tank Bn	700	59	17			
Tank Bn	700	59	17			
Three Armd Inf Bns (total)	2,985	9				27
Div Arty	1,625	9		1	54(SP)	
Cav Rcn Sqdn	894		17	52		
Engr Bn	660					
All other components	1,463		9	2		3
Total	9,727	195	77	55	54	30

* Figure includes medium tanks 105-mm artillery pieces.

ORGANIZATION OF THE 2ND ARMORED DIVISION AT THE BEGINNING OF JANUARY 1945

Figure 49

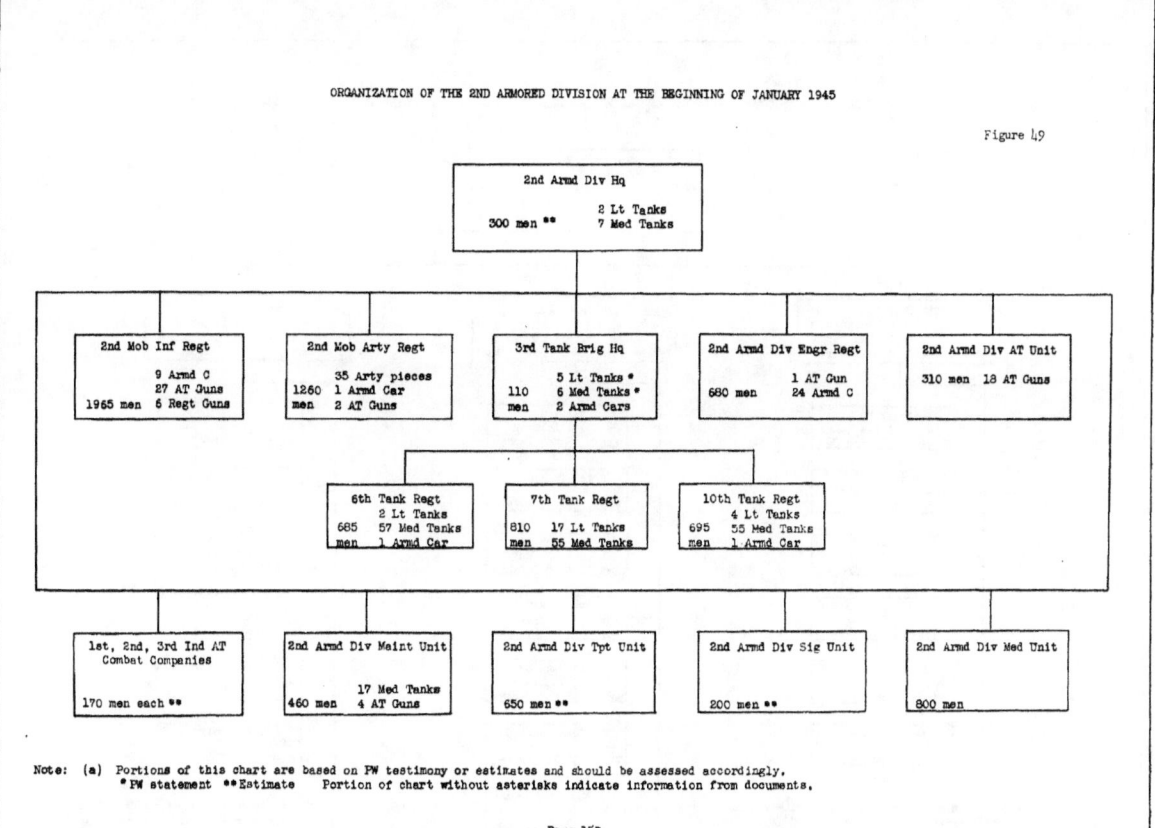

Note: (a) Portions of this chart are based on PW testimony or estimates and should be assessed accordingly.
* PW statement ** Estimate   Portion of chart without asterisks indicate information from documents.

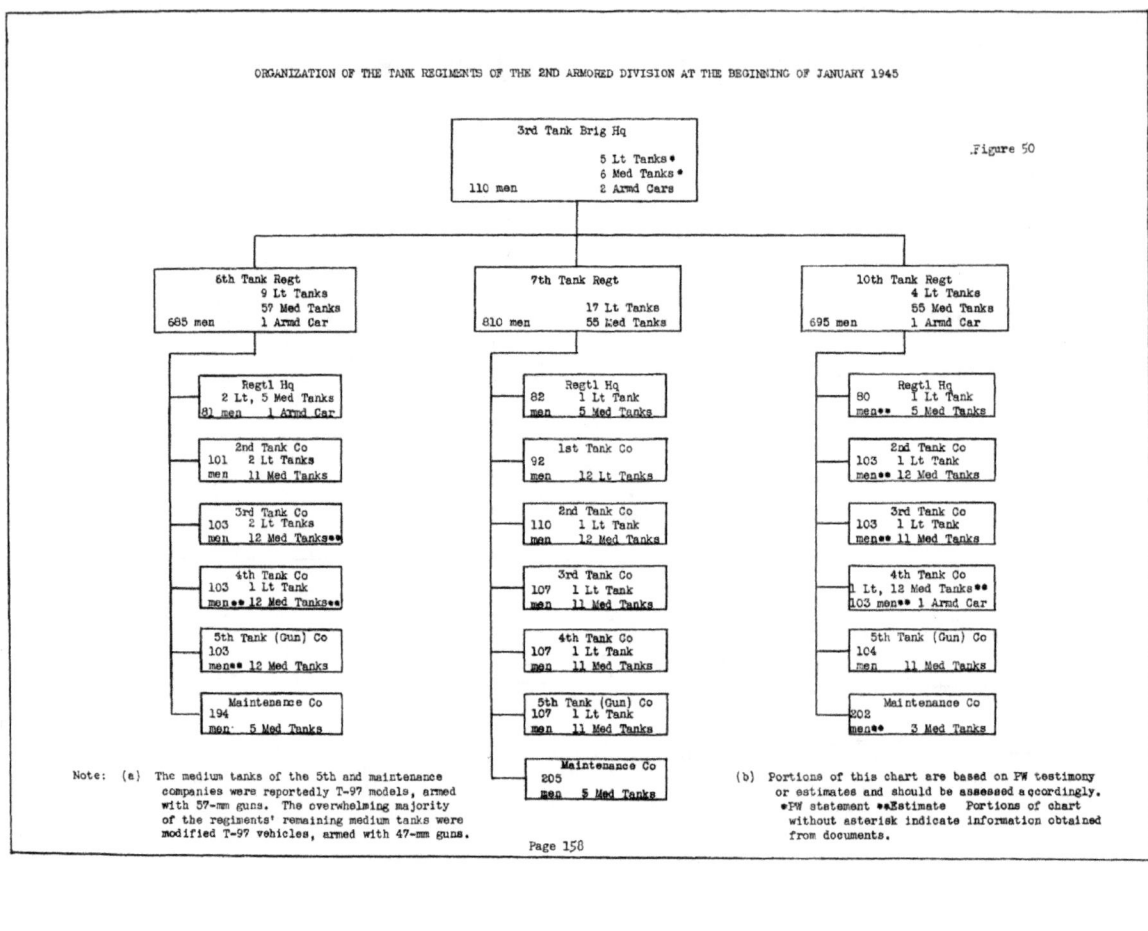

Figure 50. Organization of the Tank Regiments of the 2nd Armored Division at the Beginning of January 1945

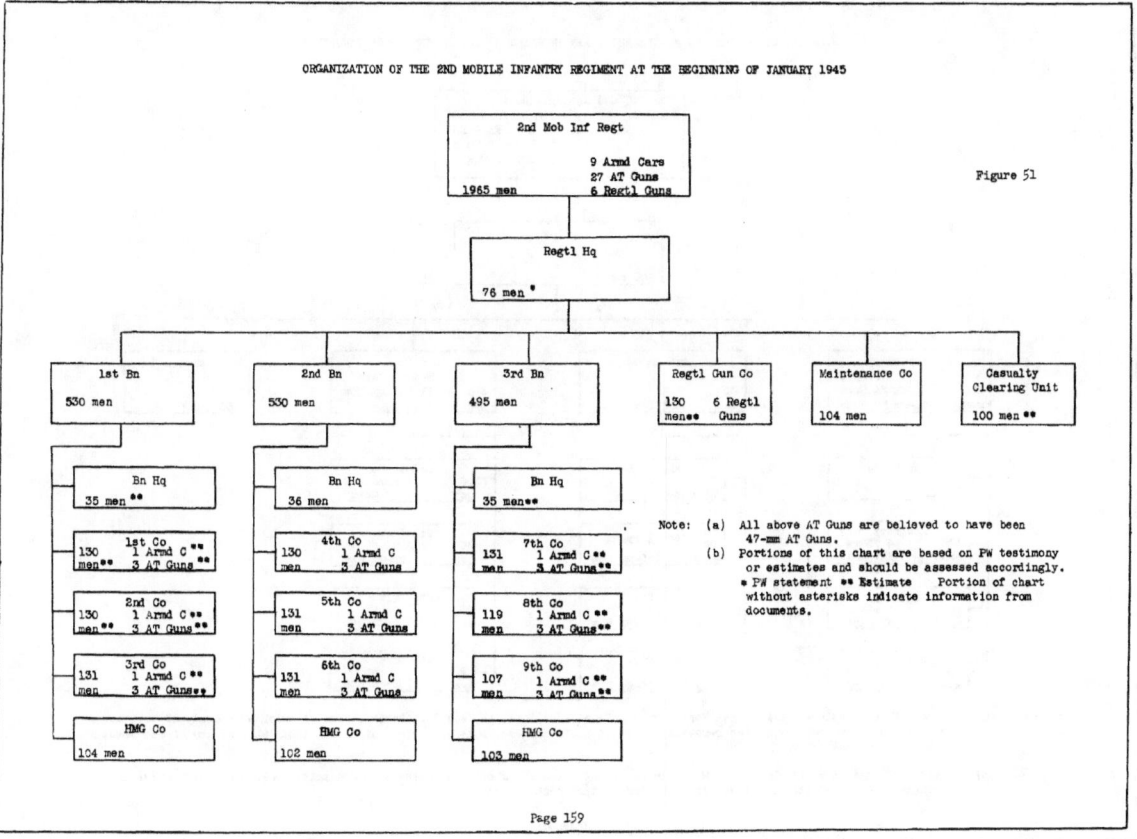

Figure 51. Organization of the 2nd Mobile Infantry Regiment at the beginning of January 1945.

ORGANIZATION OF THE 2ND MOBILE ARTILLERY REGIMENT AT THE BEGINNING OF JANUARY 1945

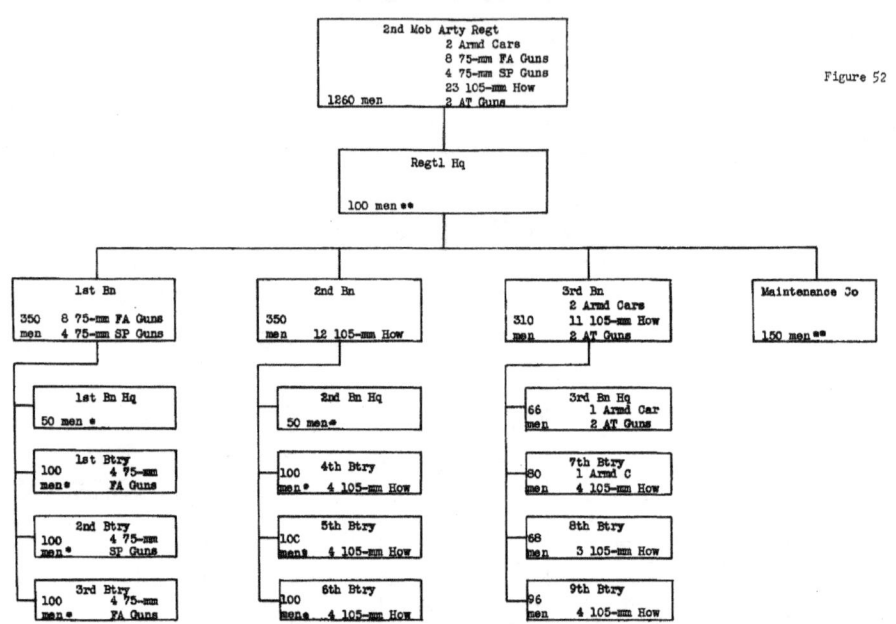

Figure 52

Note: (a) During Fall of 1944 the 2nd Mob Arty Regt formed several additional "special" batteries, some of which were equipped with 105-mm SP Guns. Some of these batteries reputedly moved to LEYTE and were sunk en route. It is not known whether any of the special batteries remained on LUZON.

(b) Portions of this chart are based on PW testimony or estimates and should be assessed accordingly. *PW statement **Estimate
Portions of chart without asterisks indicate information from documents.

ORGANIZATION OF THE SUPPORT AND SERVICE ELEMENTS OF THE 2ND ARMORED DIVISION AT THE BEGINNING OF JANUARY 1945

Figure 53

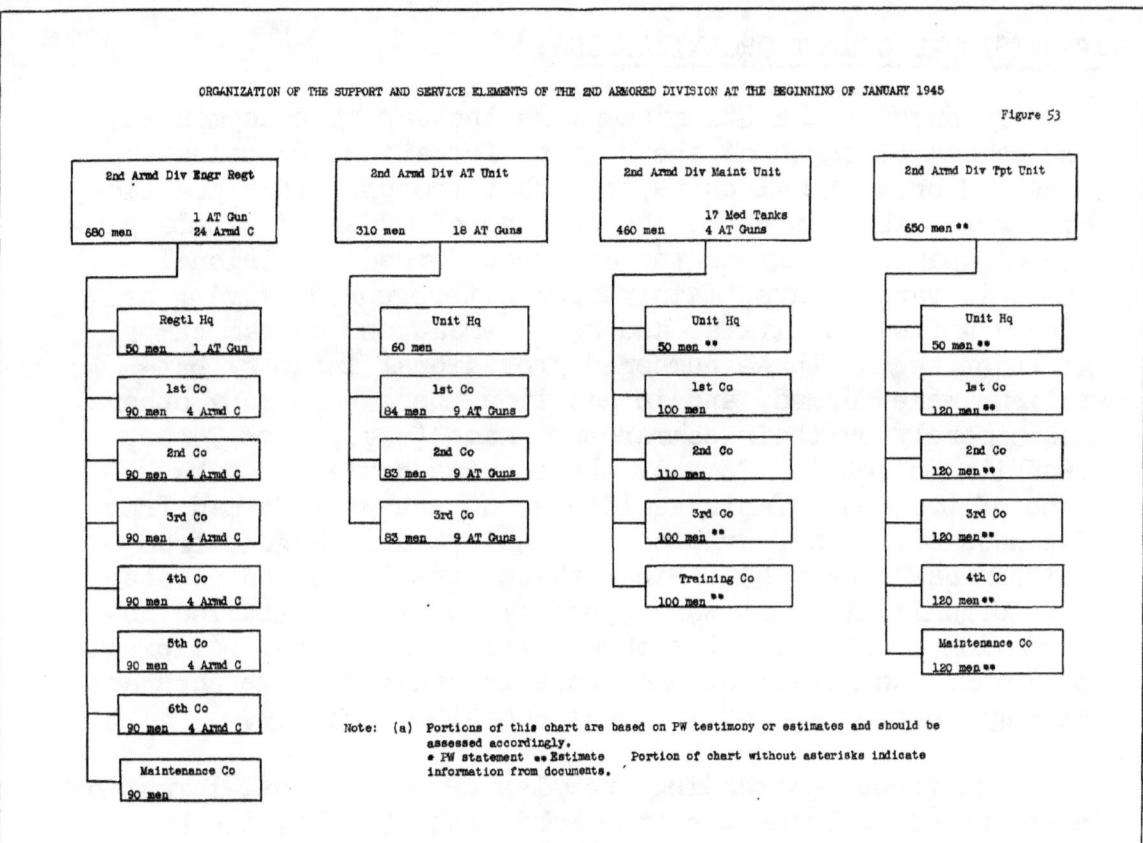

Note: (a) Portions of this chart are based on PW testimony or estimates and should be assessed accordingly.
* PW statement ** Estimate   Portion of chart without asterisks indicate information from documents.

PROVISIONAL COMBAT ORGANIZATIONS:

Throughout the Luzon campaign the Japanese augmented the combat strength of their major formations by using service and provisional units as combat troops. This practice, of course, added much to the worries of Order of Battle personnel, particularly as the Japanese formed provisional units in varied ways, mainly from heterogeneous flying and ground units, hospitals, and replacement and casual camps. At least twenty-three numbered provisional infantry battalions were formed, and in addition there were many others known merely by their commander's name (e.g., Mine Force, Iwashita Bn, etc). Some of these units contained a backbone of trained infantry soldiers, others were formed from Japanese civilians, drafted in Manila and in Baguio from October 44-January 45. Since these battalions had no standard organization, it was necessary to gather detailed information, concerning the organization, strength, equipment, training, and morale of each unit in order to make accurate strength estimates and to gauge combat efficiency.

The three outstanding examples of provisional formations encountered on Luzon were the Kobasyashi Heidan, the Ran Group, and the 1st Provisional Infantry Group (also known as Take Group or Ceyama Heidan). The Kobayashi Heidan is an almost near-perfect example of a provisional division, and the majority of its component organizations were newly-formed, purely provisional units. The Ran Group (later redesignated the Kembu Group), on the other hand, had only a provisional command structure, and as a rule the service and other elements comprising the group maintained their original entity. The 1st Provisional Infantry Group was merely a collection of hastily formed and never-integrated provisional infantry battalions. The source of men for these battalions was largely air personnel (both ground and flight).

From an historical standpoint, these Japanese methods of forming service troops into provisional organizations for combat, as used in the Luzon campaign, should be of considerable interest in the future training of Order of Battle and Combat Intelligence personnel. Therefore, although there is no norm for the formations of such units and although the examples discussed may be completely anomalous, the following detailed examination of both the Kobayashi Heidan and the Ran Group is made.

The outstanding provisional combat formation encountered on Luzon was the Kobayashi Group (Heidan). Under this organization were provisional units totalling almost divisional strength.

In Manila, prior to November 1944, Major General Kawashima, Osamu, commanded an organization known as the Manila Defense Force (code I-17661), in addition to his normal duties as Commanding General of the 82nd Infantry Brigade, 105th Division. This command was extremely fluid, and apparently included most of the army service troops in Manila as well as some combat forces. Its Commanding General, concurrently with the commander of the 31st Naval Base Force, was responsible for the defense of the city of Manila. In late November 1944, the 82nd Brigade moved its headquarters to Lucban (Tayabas), where it garrisoned the coast of Lamon Bay, and was not replaced in Manila by any combat formation of note. Major General Kobayashi, Takashi, formerly (1940) Commanding General of the Guards Division Infantry Group and (1942) Commanding General of the 6th Border Garrison in Manchuria, arrived in Manila to take charge of the Manila Defense Force.

Personnel of the Manila Defense Force which later, when the Force moved from Manila, became known as the Kobayashi Heidan, were derived from many sources. During the period October 44-January 45, all able-bodied Japanese civilians living in Manila were called into the Army. There was a total of eight drafts in Manila, each of about 200 men. The newly-inducted men received little or no training, although some were in the Army four months. The new units were partially equipped from the Manila supply dumps, and this issue was supplemented with bamboo spears. Other provisional units were formed from replacements headed for southern areas, from casual camps, and from miscellaneous service units. There follows a list of the original components of the Manila Defense Force (Kobayashi Heidan), and, where known, the source of the personnel:

Headquarters:

    Hq, Manila Defense Force   100

Hq, 1st Fd Replacement Unit — 100

Infantry:

- 1st Provisional Infantry Bn -- from drafted civilians (this unit was immediately transferred to Naval command on Corregidor) — ---

- 2nd Provisional Infantry Bn -- from drafted civilians (four rifle companies, one MG company) — 750

- 3rd Provisional Infantry Bn -- from drafted civilians (two rifle companies, one MG company) — 450

- 4th Provisional Infantry Bn -- from miscellaneous stragglers, and elements of the Manila Army Air Depot (two rifle companies, one MG company, one Bn Gun Plat) — 500

- 5th Provisional Infantry Co — 125

- 7th Provisional Infantry Bn -- from elements of the 368th and 370th Ind Inf Bns (56th Ind Mixed Brig) which were unable to reach their unit in Borneo; also from replacements for the 55th Ind Mixed Brig (Philippines), and the 1st Div "Remaining Unit" (Zanryu Tai) (four rifle companies, one MG company, Bn Gun Plat) — 550

- 8th Provisional Infantry Bn -- from personnel intended for 37th Army (Corps) Hq in Borneo (two rifle companies, later reinforced by attachments) — 325

- 10th Provisional Infantry Bn -- from drafted civilians, stevedores of the 3rd Shipping Tpt Command (then in Manila), and miscellaneous service troops (two rifle companies, one MG company, one Bn Gun Plat) — 500

3rd, 4th, Weapons, and Labor Companies, 355th
Ind Inf Bn (102nd Div) -- These companies
were unable to reach the rest of the bat-
talion on Negros   575

Abe Infantry Bn -- from infantry and engineer
replacements from the 57th Depot Division,
unassigned to an active unit (four rifle
companies, one MG company)   950

Iwashita Infantry Bn -- from Southern Army
Repl Pool, and infantry replacements
from the 57th Depot Division, unassigned
to an active unit (four rifle companies)   535

Goto Bn -- from the Morishita Anchorage Unit
of the 3rd Shipping Tpt Command. Lt Col
Morishita fled to N Luzon, leaving Major
Goto in command   1,100

Yebiko (or Ebisu) Bn -- from the guards at
the various PW camps in the Manila area
(three rifle companies)   250

Yokogawa Co, 14th Area Army Provisional Fd
Repl Unit -- from hospital patients   200

Total Infantry Troops   6,810

Artillery, Mortar, and Rocket:

2nd Btry (less one plat), 8th FA Regt --
normal combat unit   70

5th Provisional Arty Btry, 6th Provisional
Arty Btry, 7th Provisional Arty Btry --
origin of personnel unknown. Total of
eight 75-mm guns, 100 men per battery   300

Remaining Unit, 2nd Shipping Arty Regt --
normal unit   200

4th Medium Mortar Bn -- normal combat unit

(three companies, each with four 150-mm mortars)	560
5th Medium Mortar Bn -- same as 4th	510
3rd Rocket Bn -- normal combat unit (Hq, three companies, ammo company, 36 8-inch rocket launchers)	1,000
21st Ind Mortar Bn (-) -- originally this battalion had three mortar companies. 2nd and 3rd Cos were sent to Leyte; 4th Co formed from replacement pool; 1st and 4th Btrys then equipped with a total of 24 8-inch rockets, and placed under Kobayashi Heidan	400
<u>Total Arty Troops, etc.</u>	3,040

Machine Gun and Machine Cannon:

1st Provisional MG Co, 3rd Provisional MG Co, 5th Provisional MG Co -- from personnel sent to Luzon by the 86th Div (Japan); 1st and 3rd Cos later moved to N Luzon; strength 80 apiece	240
7th Provisional MG Co -- from hospital patients evacuated from New Guinea	100
12th Provisional MG Co -- from personnel intended for 37th Army (Corps) in Borneo	110
2nd Provisional Machine Cannon Co -- origin unknown	100
<u>Total MG and Machine Cannon Troops</u>	550

Anti-tank:

4th Provisional AT Co, 5th Provisional AT Co, 6th Provisional AT Co -- from hospital

patients; each company had 80 men and four
　　　47-mm AT guns   240

　　37th Ind AT Co -- normal combat unit   140

　　Total Anti-tank Troops   380

Engineer:

　　7th Co, 105th Div Engr Unit (less 2nd Plat) --
　　　normal unit   140

　　1st Provisional Engr Co, 2nd Provisional
　　　Engr Co -- origin unknown, strength 150 each   300

　　Engr Reserve Officers Candidate Unit   100

　　Total Engr Troops   540

Signal:

　　Manila Defense Hq Signal Unit   200

　　One Section, 30th Signal Regt -- normal unit   40

　　Yoshitoku Provisional Signal Co -- formed
　　　from signal casuals   160

　　Total Signal Troops   400

Transport:

　　1st Provisional Truck Co -- formed from re-
　　　placements for 8th Tpt Regt (8th Div)   150

　　One Horse Plat, 8th Tpt Regt, 8th Div; one
　　　Plat, 24th Shipping Engr Regt; Montalban
　　　Branch Fd Freight Depot; Montalban Branch
　　　Truck Depot -- all normal units   400

　　Total Transport Troops   550

Suicide Boat (Gyoro):

- 167 -

```
    3rd Suicide Boat Hq              ) -- all
    11th Suicide Boat Squadron       ) normal
    17th Suicide Boat Squadron       ) units
    20th Suicide Boat Squadron       )
    111th Suicide Boat Base Bn       )
    117th Suicide Boat Base Bn       )
    120th Suicide Boat Base Bn       )
      Elms, 7th Suicide Boat Squadron   )
      Elms, 105th Suicide Boat Base Bn  )
      Elms, 107th Suicide Boat Base Bn  )        3,200
```

Miscellaneous:

```
    Montalban Branch Ordnance Depot )
    1st Half, 63rd L of C Hospital  )
    Veterinary Collection Station,  )
      85th L of C Sector Unit       )
    Elms, 5th Fd Shipping Depot     )             600
```

Recapitulation:

Hq	200
Infantry	6,810
Artillery, Mortar, and Rocket	3,040
Machine Gun and Machine Cannon	550
Anti-tank	380
Engineer	540
Signal	400
Transport	550
Suicide Boat	3,200
Miscellaneous	600
Total Strength, Kobayashi Heidan	**16,270**

It is interesting to note that this Force, excluding the suicide boat elements, contains very nearly the same components as a normal triangular division on a slightly smaller scale. The presence of the 4th and 5th Med Mortar and the 3rd Rocket Battalions added numerical strength to the normal artillery component of a division, but the absence of heavy artillery weakened the Force. In the terrain over which the Kobayashi Heidan fought, the presence of these mortars and rockets bolstered their positions greatly.

In early January, plans for the defense of Manila and of the rugged Marikina Watershed to the east were made. The defense of the city was left largely to Naval troops, with elements of the Kobayashi Heidan attached. The major naval unit in Manila was the 31st Special Base Force. This unit was reorganized in early January to include all the naval base troops in the Manila area and became known as the Manila Naval Defense Force, under Rear Admiral Iwabuchi, Mitsuji. On 3 January the Commanding General of the 8th Division, Lieutenant General Yokoyama, Shizuo, was given command of the 105th Division, the Kobayashi Heidan, and all other troops in south Luzon. He was in command of all enemy activity generally south and southwest of the Pampanga River. The exact boundary paralleled the Pampanga River from its mouth to the confluence of the Pampanga and Bamban Rivers, then north along the latter to Licab and Guimba, and then west to the Baler Bay area. This combination of troops became known as the Shimbu Group (Shudan), which on 1 April was redesignated the 41st Army (Corps).

The 8th Division had formerly been garrisoning southwest Luzon, and the 105th Division had been in the Lamon Bay--Bicol Peninsula area. On 8 January the Shimbu Shudan was ordered to send elements of the 105th Division, including the Commanding General, north out of the Shimbu Shudan area. The Commanding General and the equivalent of three battalions managed to reach north Luzon before the all-important north-south road, Highway #5, was cut by our troops. The severance of Highway #5 completely separated the Shimbu Shudan from the rest of the enemy garrison in north Luzon.

Lieutenant General Yokoyama then prepared for battle. The Navy had previously been entrusted with the defense of Manila. Comparatively small forces were left in southwest Luzon and in the Bicol, while the bulk of General Yokoyama's command concentrated in the rugged hills of the Marikina Watershed. That area was then divided in three commands assigned as follows with the numbers keyed to the map shown on the following page.

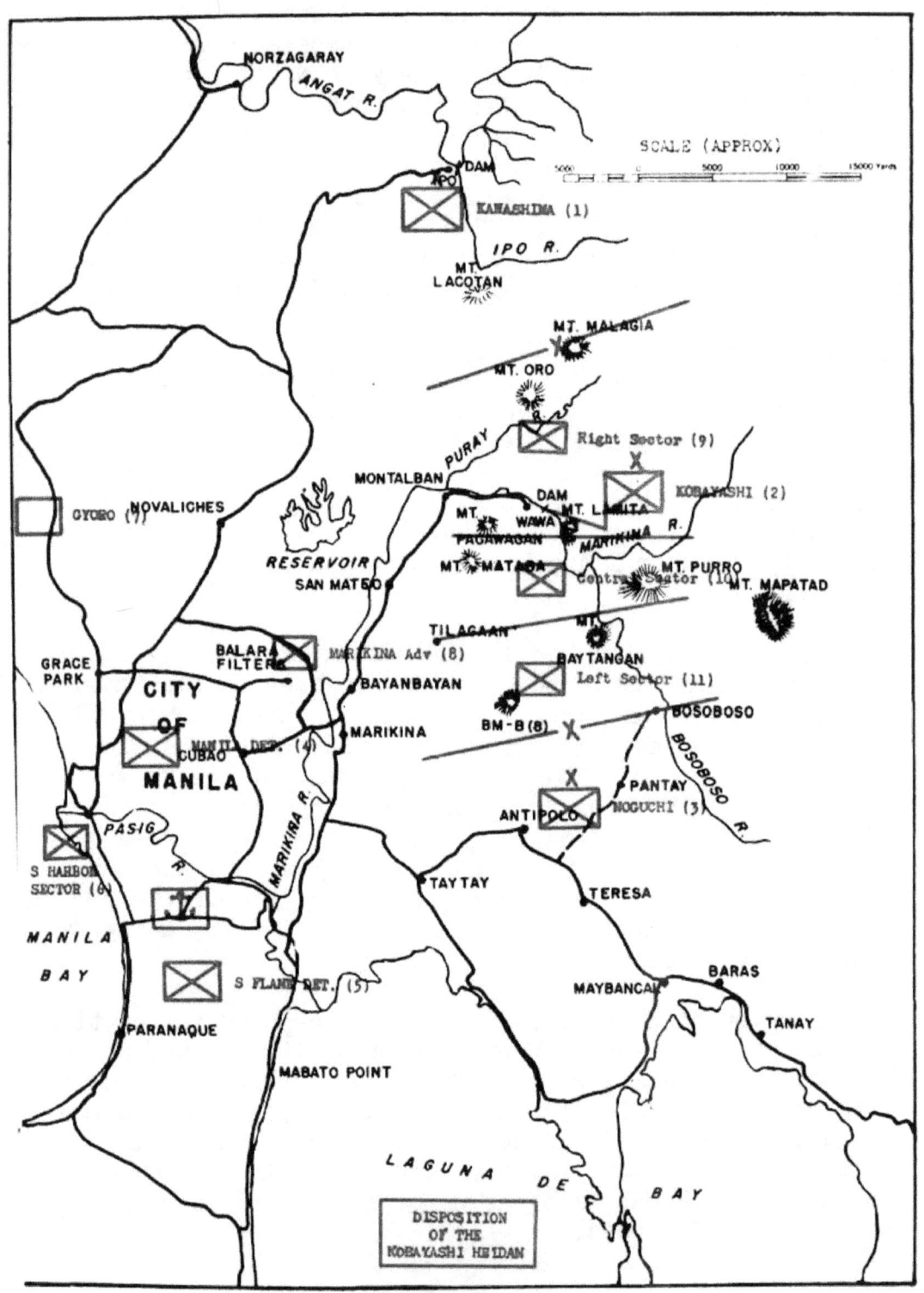

Figure 54

(1) North flank, centered at the Ipo Dam - Major General Kawashima, Osamu, Commanding General of the 82nd Infantry Brigade, 105th Division.

(2) Center, or Montalban area - Major General Kobayashi, Takashi, Commanding General of the Kobayashi Heidan.

(3) South flank, centered at Antipolo - Major General Noguchi, Shikuo, Commanding General of the 81st Infantry Brigade, 105th Division

In turn, Major General Kobayashi formed the troops under his command into separate task units and assigned defense areas. The troops left in Manila were placed under the command of the Manila Naval Defense Force, a subordination which is very unusual in the Japanese armed forces.

Before the final dispositions were drawn up, one major and several minor changes were made. The addition of the 11th Air Sector Command to the Kobayashi Heidan was the major change. The 11th Air Sector Headquarters, which controlled all the Army air-ground troops in the Manila air center, comprised the equivalent of four airfield battalions, two airfield companies, a land duty company, and a few flying personnel. The estimated strength of the 11th Air Sector Command, prior to commitment, was 2,400. The minor changes were apparently designed only to complicate order of battle records. For example, for no apparent reason the 7th Provisional Machine Gun Company was redesignated the 11th Provisional Machine Gun Company.

The following list, except for 12 and 13, is keyed to the map and contains dispositions of the Kobayashi Heidan, as outlined in an operational order, dated 2 February. This was the second in a series of such operations orders, but the final one before our forces necessitated further changes:

(4) Manila Detachment, Kobayashi Heidan (under command of Manila Naval Defense Force):

    CO — Colonel Noguchi, Katsuji

2nd Provisional Infantry Bn (less 6th Co, on Bataan)
3rd Provisional Infantry Bn
3rd, Weapons, and Labor Cos, 355th Ind Inf Bn
7th Co, 105th Div Engr Unit
Yoshitoku Provisional Signal Co
Yokogawa Co, 14th Area Army Provisional Fd Replacement Unit
37th Ind AT Co

Estimated Strength - 3,100

(This force was assigned to the defense of Manila, north of the Pasig River, but withdrew under orders to Intramuros, where it fought until annihilated)

(5) South Flank Detachment (under the command of the Southern Force, Manila Naval Defense Force):

CO -- Captain Abe, Saburo

Abe Infantry Bn
2nd Co, 5th Medium Mortar Bn
4th Provisional AT Co
One platoon, 5th Provisional Arty Btry
2nd Provisional Machine Cannon Co (less 2nd Plat)

Estimated Strength - 1,300

(The South Flank Detachment was assigned the mission to defend the southern approach to Manila. It was surrounded and annihilated at Mabato Point, despite abortive efforts to evacuate elements to Tanay by barge)

(6) South Harbor Sector Unit (under command of the Manila Naval Defense Force):

CO -- Major Goto, formerly of 3rd Shipping Tpt Command Hq

Goto Bn
Miscellaneous shipping troops

Estimated Strength – 1,100

(This force was charged with the destruction of the Manila docks, and blocking of the mouth of the Pasig River, jobs which they accomplished with only mediocre success. The unit was annihilated in Intramuros)

(7) Gyoro ("Fishing" or Suicide Boat) Unit:

CO — Lt. Col. Kawagoshi, Naonori

(This unit contained all the Suicide Boat elements listed in paragraph 2, except the 11th Suicide Boat Squadron and 111th Suicide Boat Base Battalion, which were detached from the Kobayashi Heidan. Unit also commanded one platoon, 24th Shipping Engineer Regiment)

Estimated Strength – 2,300

(The Gyoro Unit was committed north of Manila in the Obando area, and had the mission of harassing our L of C along Highway #3. It was destroyed in place with the exception of a few stragglers that reached Bataan and Montalban)

(8) Marikina Advanced Force:

CO — Captain Bando, Yasuo

7th Provisional Infantry Bn (less 3rd Co)
2nd Plat, 2nd Provisional Machine Cannon Co

Estimated Strength – 460

(This force was placed as a reconnaissance screen for the main strength of the Kobayashi Heidan, in position on the high ground northwest of Marikina. The Force wasted much of its strength in unsuccessful infiltrations to destroy the Balara Water Filters. When our forces started to drive east of Manila, the remnants of the Force withdrew under orders and joined the Right Sector Unit.

This Force was interesting from an Order of Battle standpoint as it had many code designations in addition to its name, e.g. I-17661, I-422 Force; "Ma Zen"; Bando Force; and "2nd Paratroop Annihilating Unit")

The following Sector Units comprised the main strength of the Kobayashi Heidan, and were responsible for holding the central (or Kobayashi Heidan) part of the Shimbu Line east of Manila.

(9) Right Sector Unit:

CO -- Colonel Hara, Kazuo

Hq, 1st Fd Replacement Unit
4th Provisional Infantry Bn
3rd Co, 7th Provisional Infantry Bn
5th and 12th Provisional MG Cos
6th Provisional AT Co
2nd Btry (less one Plat), 8th FA Regt (8th Div)
5th (less one plat) and 7th Provisional Arty Btrys
5th Medium Mortar Bn (less 2nd Co)
Remaining unit, 2nd Shipping Depot
Elements, 5th Fd Shipping Depot

Estimated Strength - 1,980

(The Right Sector Unit was assigned the defense of the area from Mt Malagia to the southern slopes of Mt Pacawagan; its major strongpoints were on Mt Oro, Mt Pacawagan, and Mt Lamita. As our attacks hit hardest south of this area at first, a large proportion of the Right Sector was moved to reinforce the Central and Left Sectors)

(10) Central Sector Unit:

CO -- Major Idekura, Toshinobu

10th Provisional Infantry Bn
4th Medium Mortar Bn
Yebiko (or Ebisu) Bn

Estimated Strength - 1,310

(The Central Sector Unit was responsible for the defense of the area from Mt Pacawagan south to Tilagaan; its major strongpoint was Mt Mataba, and the Mango and Ampid River gorges north and south of Mt Mataba respectively. It was destroyed in place)

(11) Left Sector Unit:

CO — Colonel Nambu, Yoshinori

8th Provisional Infantry Bn
Main strength, 11th Air Sector Command
3rd Rocket Bn
7th Provisional MG Co
5th Provisional AT Co
6th Provisional Arty Btry

Estimated Strength - 3,800

(The Left Sector Unit was to defend a line from Tilagaan to a point south of BM-B. After the death of Colonel Nambu, Lt. Col. Fushimi (commanding officer of the 11th Air Sector Command) became commander of the unit. Major resistance developed on Mt Baytangan and the hills to the southeast. Mt Baytangan was to be held to the last man, and the Left Sector was reinforced with the Hq and 2nd Battalion of the 26th Independent Mixed Regiment, and the 185th Independent Infantry Battalion (105th Division), both of which units came north from the Bicol Peninsula. Colonel Takanami, Kinji, commander of the 26th Independent Mixed Regiment was the man charged with the defense of Mt Baytangan)

(12) Forces under direct command of the Kobayashi Heidan:

Hq, Kobayashi Heidan
5th Provisional Infantry Co (designated as reserve unit, but committed under the Central

           Sector Unit)
      Signal Unit   CO -- Captain Miyoshi, Makitaro
        Manila Defense Hq Signal Unit
        One section, 30th Signal Regt
      1st Provisional Engineer Co (less one platoon)
      2nd Provisional Engineer Co
      Engr Reserve Officers Candidate Unit
      1st Provisional Truck Co
      Veterinary Section, 85th L of C Sector Unit
      1st Half, 63rd L of C Hospital
      Montalban Branch Ordnance, Fd Freight and Truck
        Depots

      Estimated Strength, direct control units - 1,075

(13) Antipolo Sector Unit (This Force was originally under the Kobayashi Heidan, but in mid-January was transferred to the Noguchi Heidan; the components listed here are those as of the date of transfer).

      CO -- Major Iwashita, Yanosuke

      Iwashita Infantry Bn
      21st Ind Mortar Bn (less 2nd and 3rd Cos on Leyte)
      4th Co, 355th Ind Inf Bn (102nd Div)
      One platoon, 1st Provisional Engr Co

      Estimated Strength - 1,135

Recapitulation:

Manila Detachment	3,100
South Flank Detachment	1,300
South Harbor Sector Unit	1,100
Gyoro Unit	2,300
Marikina Advanced Force	460
Right Sector Unit	1,980
Central Sector Unit	1,310
Left Sector Unit (including 11th Air Sector Command)	3,800
Forces under Direct Command	1,075
Antipolo Sector Unit	1,135

    Units transferred (11th and 111th Suicide
      Boat, 1st and 3rd Provisional MG Cos)   1,110

    <u>Total, Kobayashi Heidan</u>   <u>18,670</u>

      Our plan of attack against the Shimbu Line east of Manila was to turn the south (or enemy left) flank. The Noguchi Group (Heidan) in the Antipolo area was first to feel our offensive might and was pushed back, the bulk of the Group being destroyed. Then our troops turned north and came into contact with the left Sector Unit of the Kobayashi Heidan. The Left Sector Unit was depleted and then reinforced so that it could hold Mt Baytangan. Several companies from various suicide boat base battalions from Infanta first and then later the Headquarters and 2nd Battalion, 26th Independent Mixed Regiment, and the 185th Independent Infantry Battalion, 105th Division, were employed to reinforce the Left Sector Unit. As our troops pressed forward from the south and east, more reinforcements were called in, including strong elements of the Kawashima Group in the Ipo area. The 3rd Battalion of the 17th Infantry Regiment, the 31st Infantry Regiment (less 3rd Battalion), the 8th Reconnaissance Regiment, and others were used to reinforce the Kobayashi Heidan.

      The employment of these regular combat troops in the same area as provisional units afforded an interesting comparison. As long as the provisional units remained in their well prepared cave positions situated in precipitous terrain, they proved fully as capable as regular combat troops. Some hills largely held by provisional troops, for example, Mt Mataba, were more stoutly defended than others held by roughly the same number of regular combat troops, for instance Mt Purro, where elements of the 31st Infantry Regiment were committed. In general the Kobayashi Heidan proved very capable on the defensive. However, their mid-February attempt at a major counterattack was completely abortive. Our intelligence reports noted increased patrol activity during this period, but not until after the attack was meant to have taken place did our forces know they had been undergoing a major operation to drive us from the city of Manila, and then was known only through captured documents. This failure was due in large measure to the break-down of the improvised command structure and to the complete failure of signal communications. It is felt that had the provisional battalions of the Group been formed into provisional regiments, and with a more closely knit command structure, it would have been a much more efficient fighting force.

Another excellent example of provisional combat organization is afforded by the Japanese Kembu Group (initially known as the Ran Group), which was encountered in the heavily fortified section of the Zambales Mountains west of Clark Field and Fort Stotsenburg. The commander of the Kembu Group was the Commanding General of the 1st Raiding Group, Major General (later Lieutenant General) Tsukada, Rikichi. The 14th Area Army (supreme headquarters in the Philippines) and 1st Raiding Group operational orders dated 8-10 January 1945 stated that General Tsukada would command all units of the 4th Air Army in the Clark Field sector, and small elements of the 2nd Armored, 10th, 103rd, and 105th Divisions, and would be responsible for the area northeast of the Pampanga River to include Tarlac Province and Bataan, excluding the Mariveles area. This order stressed that General Tsukada would not try to defend Clark Field proper, as it is in open terrain, but would prevent our use of the area as long as possible by interdicting it with fire from the hills to the east. The code name for the Group was Ran which was the code name of the 1st Raiding Group, but later, because the 1st Raiding Group was expanded by the absorption of other units, a new code (Kembu) was assigned.

The principal difference between the Kembu Group and the Kobayashi Heidan was that under Kembu service organizations were incorporated intact, retained their original entity, and were loosely coordinated by an improvised command structure. There was some effort made to keep the same types of service organizations under one command, but it did not follow throughout the Group. Combat troops were kept somewhat separate. In addition to the Kembu Shudan, whose total strength was 15,600, there were a great many naval air-ground troops in the area west of Clark Field and miscellaneous shipping personnel in Zambales, bringing the total for the Clark Field—Zambales—Bataan area to approximately 30,000.

It is next to impossible to gauge the combat efficiency

of the Kembu Group or of its components, as virtually all the fighting was done from well-prepared cave positions situated in extremely difficult terrain, and in this type of fighting service personnel can perform as well as veteran infantrymen.

The following table gives the breakdown of the Kembu Group:

<u>Kembu Group Headquarters</u>:

    CG -- Lieutenant General Tsukada, Rikichi

    Estimated Strength - 200

<u>Eguchi Detachment</u>:

    CO -- Lt. Col. Eguchi, Kiyosuke, formerly CO, 10th Air Sector Command

    10th Air Sector Hq
    31st Airfield Bn
    99th Airfield Bn
    150th Airfield Bn
    151st Airfield Bn
    152nd Airfield Bn
    8th Airfield Co
    52nd Airfield Co
    Elements, 60th Flying Regt
    Shibazaki Composite Bn (less two companies), 4th Air Army Hq
    84th Fd AA Bn
    Special AAA Unit
    7th Special Machine Cannon Unit
    12th Special Machine Cannon Unit
    13th Machine Cannon Unit
    322nd Independent Truck Co
    Elements, 26th Transport Regt, 26th Division
    Elements, Southern Air Route Dept
    Elements, 56th Construction Duty Co
    Elements, 111th Land Duty Co
    "Other transient forces"

    Estimated Strength - 4,600

Takayama Detachment:

    CO -- Lt. Col. Takayama, Yoshinobu, formerly CO of the 2nd Mobile Infantry Regiment, 2nd Armored Division

    2nd Bn, 2nd Mobile Infantry Regt
    Regtl Gun and Maint Cos, 2nd Mobile Infantry Regt
    3rd and 4th Cos, 178th Ind Inf Bn, 103rd Division
    25th Ind AT Bn (less 1st Co)
    6th Btry, 2nd Mobile Arty Regt, 2nd Armored Div
    4th Provisional Medium Arty Btry
    Oishi Provisional Labor Unit
    132nd Airfield Bn
    137th Airfield Bn
    12th Machine Cannon Unit
    Two companies, Shibazaki Composite Bn, 4th Air Army Hq
    "Others"

    Estimated Strength - 3,600

Yanagimoto Detachment:

    CO -- Captain Yanagimoto, Takanori, formerly CO, 3rd Bn, 2nd Mobile Infantry Regt, 2nd Armored Division

    3rd Bn, 2nd Mobile Infantry Regt
    8th Independent Tank Co

    Estimated Strength - 650

Takaya Detachment:

    CO -- Major Takaya, Saburo, CO, 2nd Glider Infantry Regt, 1st Raiding Brigade

    2nd Glider Infantry Regt, 1st Raiding Brigade

    Estimated Strength - 750

Bataan Detachment:

CO -- Colonel Nagayoshi, Sanehira, CO of the 39th
   Infantry Regt, 10th Division

39th Infantry Regt (less 1st Bn), 10th Division
Small elements, 10th FA and Engr Regts, 10th Division
2nd Co, 359th Ind Inf Bn, 105th Division
1st Provisional Bn
6th Co, 2nd Provisional Infantry Bn
Tank Platoon, 4th Co, 10th Tank Regt

Estimated Strength - 3,000

(Although under the Kembu Group, the Bataan Detachment operated independently in Zigzag Pass.)

Composite Signal Unit:

CO -- Colonel Ogasawara, Shozo, formerly CO, 2nd
   Navigational Aid Regt

Elements, 2nd Navigational Aid Regt
1st Raiding Signal Unit
4th Co, 10th Air Signal Regt
Main strength, 22nd Air Signal Regt
Main strength, 96th Independent Wire Co
Main strength, 107th Independent Wire Co
101st Independent Radio Platoon
"Others"

Estimated Strength - 1,300

(Elements of the Composite Signal Unit were early committed as infantry troops, as this force obviously contained many more signal men than were required to maintain the Kembu Group's limited signal net)

Forces under direct command of the Kembu Group:

1st Raiding Machine Cannon Unit
Naga Working Unit (24th Fd Airfield Construction Unit)
San Fernando Garrison Force

        1st Sub-Depot, Manila Air Depot
        138th Fd Airfield Construction
        "All flying personnel"

    Estimated total, forces under direct control -
                                        1,500

    <u>Total Strength, Kembu Group - 15,600</u>

<u>THE IPO AREA - AN ORDER OF BATTLE STUDY:</u>

    Throughout the Luzon operation, Order of Battle was able, with few exceptions to provide accurate strength estimates and to furnish many detailed reports concerning enemy location and dispositions. Perhaps the best example of the latter is the Ipo area, the north flank of the Shimbu line in the area east of Manila. Our forces sweeping into Manila left a screening force in front of (west of) the Ipo area, and the situation remained fairly static from 3 February until 7 May when the U.S. 43rd Division started its attack.

    During this three month period many patrol clashes afforded opportunities to capture important documents and prisoners. This enabled Order of Battle personnel to piece together the command structure, the dispositions, and the strengths of the Japanese forces present. However, unlike the case of the Kobayashi Heidan, no comprehensive documents were captured until after the offensive began, and the necessary intelligence information had to be secured by gleaning the maximum from seemingly unproductive sources.

    The first documents taken in the Ipo area revealed, through a study of personalities, that the area was garrisoned by the 358th Independent Infantry Battalion, the 31st Infantry Regiment (less 3rd Battalion), and a large number of signal troops. Documents captured elsewhere indicated that control of the area was vested in Major General Kawashima, Osamu, formerly Commanding General of the 82nd Brigade, 105th Division. This force, known as the Kawashima Group (Heidan), was apparently assigned the code name Shinshu (Assault). General Kawashima had only one battalion, the 358th Independent Infantry Battalion, of his original brigade. Prisoner of war statements revealed the presence of elements of the 8th Field Artillery Regiment. This was not clarified until another prisoner of war, taken in Batangas in late April, revealed that the bulk of the 2nd and 3rd Battalions, 8th Field Artillery Regiment, and elements of the 4th Battalion had moved to Ipo in January. One map of the Ipo area showed an unidentified Osako Force; personnel lists captured later in southwest Luzon showed that a Captain Osako commanded the 118th Suicide Boat Base Battalion, which had been in Batangas in January. Since no contact identifications of that battalion had been made in southwest Luzon, this strongly indicated that the Osako Force was the 118th Suicide Bat Base Battalion.

Prisoners of war captured prior to our attack on Ipo revealed that the signal troops, the 9th Provisional Infantry Battalion, and remnants of the Uno Force (which was composed of four companies, each from a different major formation) had been formed into two provisional regiments, the 1st and 2nd Shinshu Regiments. These regiments were referred to as the Tomono and Hanabusa Forces respectively, after the commanders, Lt. Col. Tomono, Ikuji, (formerly CO, 12th Air Signal Regt), and Major Hanabusa, Kanemaru (formerly CO, 9th Air Intelligence Regiment). A close comparison of personalities of the miscellaneous signal units and other service troops believed to be in the area with the company commanders of these new formations proved to be of interest. This comparison revealed that the miscellaneous signal and service units had been absorbed into the Shinshu regiments; thus enough information to warrant strength estimates. The Tomono (1st Shinshu) Regiment was estimated to have 1800 men, which later proved slightly low; the Hanabusa (2nd Shinshu) Regiment was estimated at 1500 men, an estimate which proved to be almost exact. The only large unit known to exist in the Kawashima Heidan but still unidentified was the Narukami Force, which was later found to be the 1st Shinshu Independent Battalion.

One major change in the order of battle of the Kawashima Heidan occurred when, in March, the 31st Infantry Regiment (-) and the 118th Suicide Boat Base Battalion moved into the Kobayashi Heidan area. This was discovered when contact identifications of these units were picked up in the Kobayashi sector, and was substantiated by captured diaries.

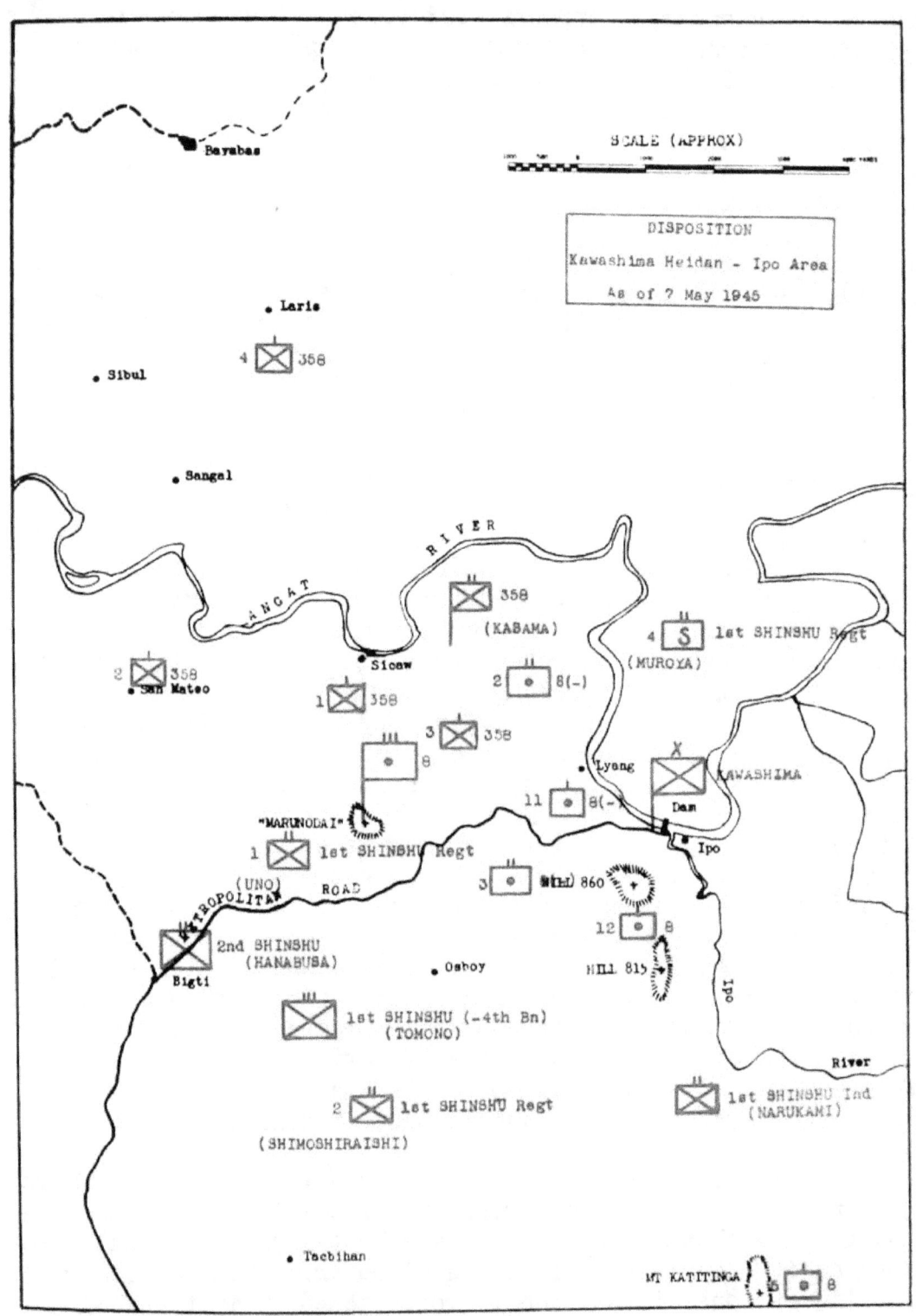

Figure 55

- 184 -

This move took the heart out of the Kawashima Heidan, as the 31st Infantry (-) was the strongest unit in the Ipo area. The only other basic combat unit in the Heidan was the 358th Independent Infantry Battalion which was, until April, disposed south of Bayabas and north of the Angat River.

The dispositions of the Kawashima Heidan (see map), as estimated in April, showed that the Group was poised to defend in great strength the axis of the Metropolitan Road, the best approach to the Ipo Dam. Even without the 31st Infantry Regiment, which had been disposed between Osboy and the road to the northwest, this approach was strongly defended. Until April, the Kasama Force (358th Independent Infantry Battalion and attachments) had been dug-in along the line Bayabas--Sangal--Angat River. In April, according to reliable prisoner of war information, the whole force, except the 4th Company near Laris, moved south across the river. This, of course, opened the north flank. Patrols previously determined that the south flank was uncovered and that no continuous line existed joining the Kawashima Group to the north flank of the Kobayashi Heidan farther south. Thus obviously the easiest way to our objective, Ipo Dam, was not along the Metropolitan Road, but from the north or the south. On the basis of this information a double envelopment was ordered.

Starting on 7 May a guerrilla force left Bayabas, flanked the 4th Company, 358th Independent Infantry Battalion, and advanced well down into the Angat River bend before it met any opposition. The Muroya Battalion (or 4th Battalion of the 1st Shinshu Regiment) had been previously determined to be a small, poorly equipped force; thus the guerrillas were able to seize quickly the high ground 1,000-3,000 yards north of the dam. The southern pincer reached Mt Katitinga with scattered opposition, and quickly advanced towards Hill 815 (2,000 yards south of Ipo). As soon as our flanking maneuver had been detected, the 1st and 2nd Shinshu Regiments and the bulk of the Kasama Force (minus 2 companies placed under Captain Takahashi, Adjutant of the Kawashima Group, and which later fled north from Laris and escaped) started moving east along the Metropolitan Road to hold open the gap at Ipo. The 8th Field Artillery Regiment, leaving their guns behind, did the same. By 12 May all these units, though slightly disorganized, had reached Hills 860 and 815, which they attempted to hold at all cost. During the period 12-15 May they launched several counterattacks against our forces south of Hill 815. They also dispatched one force across the Angat River to contain the guerrilla elements north of the dam.

When virtually all components of the Kasama Force (less the companies left under Captain Takahashi), the 1st and 2nd Shinshu Regiments, and part of the 8th Field Artillery Regiment had been identified in the fighting on the two hills south and southwest of Ipo, it became obvious that the heretofore strongly-held Bigti road junction and the Metropolitan Road had been abandoned. As a result our holding force in that area was ordered forward and advanced virtually unopposed through the maze of prepared positions which were described as virtually impenetrable. By the time this force reached Ipo, opposition both north and south of the dam had been overcome. The Japanese, however, had managed to hold open the gap at Ipo long enough for the Kawashima Group Headquarters and several hundred disorganized troops to escape eastward. In the barren terrain to the east this force was never able to reorganize.

REPLACEMENTS FOR THE 23RD DIVISION AND 58TH INDEPENDENT MIXED BRIGADE:

For more than five months the 23rd Division and 58th Independent Mixed Brigade, entrenched along the approaches to Baguio, kept organized forces in the field despite protracted heavy casualties. Though more than 7,000 replacements were incorporated into the two units at varying intervals during the campaign, these thousands failed to produce opposition fully commensurate with their numbers. The deficiency may, in good measure, have been due to the insufficient training of replacements and to equipment shortages, but a study of intelligence records disclosed that a variety of ill-coordinated replacement systems, aggravated by contradictory orders and dilatory execution of instructions, contributed greatly to this state of affairs. A brief discussion of the replacement methods involved may well parallel the action taken in the case of these two units.

The initial wave of approximately 1,000 replacements reached the 23rd Division, which had suffered grave losses due to ship sinkings, almost as the Division landed in the Lingayen Gulf ports in December 1944. These replacements were trained infantry men and were assimilated into the various understrength units in an efficient manner. They were members of a Southern Area Army Replacement Pool, formed when Manila was the seat of Southern Area Army Headquarters. The pool must have been originally of imposing size; for more than five thousand men remained on Luzon after the bulk of the pool, together with the Southern Area Army Headquarters, evacuated to Saigon. Captured documents indicate that the pool requisitioned personnel directly from Japan for reassignment at the discretion of the Southern Area Army Commanding General.

The 58th Independent Mixed Brigade, which had suffered heavy losses during the first days of our Luzon operation obtained its first replacements, approximately 300 men, from this pool, but soon had to draw on stranded replacements for the 30th and 100th Divisions, enroute to Mindanao from Japan. These and similar replacement groups had, contrary to the pool system, been assigned in Japan to the various Mindanao Units. Unable to proceed to their destination, they came under control of the 14th Area Army and through it were parcelled out to needy divisions.

It is interesting to note that, after these initial replacements, no efforts were made to keep personnel available in the pool or in the division groups to fill future requirements. What personnel remained unaffected by the initial transfers, were formed into provisional infantry units and committed as such. Consequently the 23rd Division and the 58th Independent Mixed Brigade were, for several months, forced to minimize their losses through consolidation and reorganization of their own slender forces. They were soon reduced to near-impotency and found themselves dependent on temporarily attached provisional infantry units, which proved a poor substitute for regular replacements as they were subject to conflicting sources of authority. The 6th, 9th, and 10th Provisional Infantry Battalions, for instance, were not able to reach their designated positions in sufficient force because of contrary orders issued by different headquarters. Only after our April breakthrough into Baguio amplified the deficiency did the Japanese commanders rectify the situation. The 9th Provisional Infantry Battalion was soon converted into a new 545th Independent Infantry Battalion (58th Independent Mixed Brigade), the 10th and 11th Provisional Infantry Battalions became reconstituted battalions of the 64th and 71st Infantry Regiments (23rd Division), and the 6th Provisional Infantry Battalion was subsequently used to revitalize the 544th Independent Infantry Battalion (58th Independent Mixed Brigade).

At irregular intervals throughout the campaign the 23rd Division and, on a smaller scale, the 58th Independent Mixed Brigade received additional reinforcements from 14th Area Army Headquarters and the Baguio Defense Force. These largely individual replacements were either members of defunct units, such as the 2nd Shipping Artillery Regiment, the 1st Raiding Group Engineer Unit, and miscellaneous service units, or ex-patients of the Baguio hospitals. Though the number of such replacements was large, they represented but a fraction of the manpower available at Baguio. According to civilian and prisoner of war observations, many of the potential replacements at Baguio were farmed out to various line of communications units for temporary duty. Subsequent breakdown of communications and lack of central authority caused these organizations to disintegrate.

ORDER OF BATTLE TECHNIQUE - LESSONS LEARNED:

During the campaign it was learned that Army and corps headquarters should maintain adequate files on air (flying) units, especially their location and commanders. Prior to the Luzon operation this subsection kept very sketchy records of flying units, as they were normally evacuated to safety prior to our landings. On Luzon, however, an estimated total of 8,700 flying and air administrative personnel were trapped on the island and committed as ground troops. As these men were formed into provisional infantry battalions and were very often commanded by flight officers, knowledge of these officers became of paramount importance because in most cases the provisional battalions were known only by the commander's name. This did not mean that files on air units had to include all of the flight officers; but only commanding officers of the squadrons and higher units. It was not necessary to keep detailed information on the location of individual flying units, but enough information should have been kept so that an estimate could be given for the number of air personnel available for use in provisional ground formations. One of the principal difficulties that arose on Luzon concerning air formations was that no record of the Luzon air units had been kept, making it nearly impossible to estimate accurately the number available for use as ground troops.

One of the salient features of the Luzon campaign was the tremendous use of personality designations for units, as opposed to code names and numbers. It was very rare to find code references in operations orders or other official documents, and in some areas (notably east of Manila) the unit designations were hardly ever given; in every case these were replaced by the name of the commander. Thus, personalities assumed a much greater importance as compared with code names and numbers. This is not to say that code numbers were not used, for they made their appearance on identification discs, in paybooks and the like. However, the commanding officer's name was used almost exclusively in orders, and, where commanding officers were killed, this changed, sometimes from day to day. For example, the Sato Battalion might well become the Takahashi Battalion, because the battalion commander, Sato, had been killed and replaced by a former company commander, Takahashi. This necessitated complete checks of personalities, and great attention to detail, so that the Takahashi Battalion would not be picked up in strength estimates in addition to the Sato Battalion.

When the Japanese formed specific task forces from parts of many different units, they lacked a specific designation for the units thus formed and the commander's name was employed. This necessitated careful evaluation of units reported by personality only. For example, the 22nd Special Airfield Construction Unit under a Major Suzuki was combined with the 136th and 137th Field Airfield Construction Units to form the Suzuki Battalion.

However, when the Suzuki Force was mentioned in an operational order, it was often difficult to determine whether the unit in question was the 22nd Special Airfield Construction Unit (Major Suzuki's original command) or the entire composite force of the three airfield construction units (Major Suzuki's new and additional command). Usually when the commander of a specific unit took over additional forces, he retained both commands concurrently. However, occasionally a new commander for the individual unit was appointed.

In addition to the increased use of personalities, it was noted that the Japanese developed new code systems. The Japanese used encoded place names, for security, for convenience, and as supplements to far from adequate maps. However, on Luzon encoded place names were not exceptions, but rather the rule. It was obviously essential to break these codes, as no documents could be correctly interpreted without the knowledge of the locations. Very often map keys were captured showing these place names, but where this did not occur, it was found necessary to question all prisoners of war very carefully as soon as encoded place names appeared.

Another method encountered on a large scale on Luzon was the use of internal company codes inside of regiments or independent units. These codes usually appeared on identification discs, either as numbers or as kana characters. Sometimes sequences could be detected, but they had to be verified by prisoners of war. In some of the suicide boat base battalions, the following number sequence was used:

Headquarters	1
1st Company	2
2nd Company	3
3rd Company	4
Maintenance Company	5

Some units employed kana sequences, others no sequence at all. An example of the complete lack of the system follows. This code was used by the 3rd Battalion,

2nd Mobile Artillery Regiment, 2nd Armored Division:

    3rd Battalion Headquarters — Ume Unit
    7th Battery — Na Unit
    8th Battery — Ha Unit
    9th Battery — Ku Unit

In general, each code sequence of this nature had to be determined individually; and it did not necessarily follow that two regiments in the same division used the same system.

The Kobayashi Heidan had what is believed to be a unique code system, involving three-digit numbers which were in no way connected with their corresponding Manshu numbers. The code for the Manila Defense Force (the same as the Kobayashi Heidan) was I-17661; when the Manila Defense Force formed its many provisional units and it became necessary to devise a system of interior designation, three-digit numbers (e.g., I-422) were allotted to these units. However, this code was not correct without the Manila Defense Force code number preceding it. For example, the interior code for the 3rd Provisional Infantry Battalion was I-388, but this designation in itself, although used in operational orders etc, was not complete. The complete designation was I-17661, I-388, or "I-388 Force of I-17661 Group." When the Kobayashi Heidan was divided into detachments and sector units (see discussion of Kobayashi Heidan), abbreviated codes were used; for example, the Marikina Advanced Force was known as "Ma Zen," a shortened form of "Marikina Zensen" (Marikina forward line). The Fuji Group (Heidan) in southwest Luzon derived its name from its commander, Colonel Fujishige.

During the Luzon campaign, in all tactical Order of Battle sections (including units as high as Army Headquarters), it was necessary to keep extremely detailed files, with cards on each company of all combat formations. Although this required a great deal of work, it enabled Order of Battle personnel to readily spot at any given time which elements of a regiment or of a battalion had been heavily committed, and which ones were still virtually intact. Also, it was a great aid in pin-pointed small formations in relation to each other as they opposed the U.S. forces.

CHAPTER IX

TECHNICAL INTELLIGENCE DATA

LATE TRENDS IN JAPANESE MATERIEL:

Desperately striving to offset Allied superiority in arms, the Japanese in the later campaigns of the war hastily revised weapons to meet his own particular needs. He increased fire-power by improved artillery, and by greater use of rockets and mortars. More efficient weapons were developed to threaten our tanks; and, conversely, better armor was being produced. Hampered by materiel inferiority, he further resorted to weapons designed to exploit his suicidal philosophy.

All these trends in enemy war materiel began coming to light during operations in the Philippines and adjacent areas.

Aware of deficiencies in his artillery, the enemy attempted to correct them, even at that late date. His aim was apparently to secure greater fire-power and greater mobility.

For the first time, 12-inch howitzers were encountered on Luzon. During the Luzon operation, the Naval 120-mm dual-purpose gun served both for anti-aircraft and coastal defense. Central Pacific reports stated that the enemy employed the 100-mm dual-purpose gun both in coastal defense and as a field piece. In general, increased use of heavy artillery was observed in all 1945 campaigns.

Self-propelled artillery was used on Luzon for the first time in the Pacific war. Two types of guns, the 75-mm and the 15-cm, were encountered, both mounted on Type 97 medium tank chassis. In addition to these weapons, a third self-propelled gun, the 10-cm, was in production. However, this gun was not encountered.

The 75-mm gun, Type 90, an extremely versatile and modern field piece, was first discovered on Leyte, and extensively employed on Luzon. Improvements in this weapon showed that the enemy was fully conscious of deficiencies in the bulk of his field artillery.

Enemy ground commanders placed increased reliance upon mortars for support of ground troops. The trend was towards an increase in both quantity and size of mortars employed.

In the Luzon campaign, the enemy made liberal use of 15-cm and 90-mm mortars as substitutes for field artillery. The 320-mm (spigot) mortar, encountered on Iwo Jima, was used as a coastal defense weapon. Reportedly, the enemy later developed a 240-mm mortar.

Although Japan lagged behind the United States, Russia, and Germany in rocket warfare, increased interest in this class of weapons developed in the late months of the war.

The Japanese Navy's 8-inch rocket, first introduced on Leyte, was extensively employed on Luzon. The Army matched this with the Type 4 rocket. Another weapon, the Navy's ponderous 18-inch rocket, came to light in Manila, but was never employed against our troops. Tests conducted on these rockets indicate that all three were probably designed for shock effect on troops, rather than for anti-personnel fragmentation. It was found that the accuracy of these weapons left much to be desired.

Attempting to compensate for deficiencies in air support, the enemy began developing rocket-bombs. Separate rocket motors were designed for attachment to aerial bombs for ground launching.

Prisoners of war first described the improvised launchers, to be attached to 63-kg bombs, which were later found in Manila. Again, subsequent tests revealed that the weapons were most inaccurate.

Extensive use by the enemy of "hollow charge" ammunition and high velocity anti-tank weapons showed the enemy's increasing concern about our armor.

All enemy field pieces could be classified as potential anti-tank weapons, since ammunition had been developed employing the Munro principle of controlled explosive force. Because the effectiveness of the "hollow charge" did not depend upon muzzle-velocity, even the 70-mm battalion howitzer could be termed an AT gun.

Widely employed on Luzon was the 47-mm anti-tank gun, Type 1 (1941). It was an excellent weapon, with mechanized carriage and a high muzzle-velocity (2750 f/s). It proved most effective in combat, and tests showed penetration of $4\frac{1}{2}$ inches of armor at close range and direct angle of impact. Even more formidable as an anti-tank weapon was the 75-mm gun, Type 90, using armor-piercing ammunition.

New weapons for dealing with tanks were provided the enemy infantryman. Lunge and shoulder-pack mines proved suicidal, but effective. Rifle and hand grenades using the hollow-charge principle were more conventional, but no less destructive weapons.

Belated modernization of enemy armor was indicated by late Japanese developments. One example was the armored personnel carrier found on Luzon. Another was the appearance of the medium tank, Type 97, armed with the 47-mm anti-tank gun, Type 1.

German sources confirmed the late Japanese attempt to modernize and improve their armor. These reports indicated that at least four new tanks were being developed.

1) Type 3 medium tank, a variation of the earlier Type 97 medium tank, armed with a short 75-mm gun, Type 99.
2) Another improved model of the Type 97 medium tank, with maximum armor-plate of 60-mm thickness, and armed with a short 75-mm gun, Type 99.
3) A new 7.2 ton tank about 11 feet along.
4) A Type 4 medium tank probably capable of engaging the U.S. M-4 on equal terms. It weighed about 30 tons,

had armor of 75-mm maximum thickness, and a top speed of 30 miles per hour. Its swivel turret was cast steel, and the tank was armed with a long 75-mm tank gun, Type 99.

A marked trend towards the use of suicide weapons appeared in the Philippines and adjacent areas. Capitalizing on a philosopy peculiar to the Japanese, these weapons were effectively employed, and proved a real menace.

On Leyte, Luzon, and particularly on Okinawa, the spotlight was thrown on the Kamikaze pilots, who crash-dived their explosive-laden planes into Allied shipping. Appearance of a piloted aerial-torpedo, the rocket-propelled "Baka" bomb, came as a shock to the Occidental mind.

The Japanese Navy developed two suicide weapons, both found on Luzon; the piloted torpedo and the suicide crash boat. The Army had its "shoulder-pack" and lunge" mines, first encountered on Leyte, but employed in greater quantity on Luzon. The latter campaign also brought to light the Army's "Gyoro" (fishing) battalions, whose weapon was the "Q" boat, equipped with depth charges and designed to crash Alled transports.

Death to the user is the common denominator of these varied weapons. Their appeal to the morbid imagination of the Japanese was great. Their development and use was another indication that the enemy had abandoned the offensive completely, and was desperately on the defensive.

JAPANESE IMPROVISED ORDNANCE IN THE PHILIPPINES:

A variety of improvised Japanese ordnance was recovered in the Philippines. These improvised weapons consisted of mines, hand grenades, mortars and mortar shells, and mounts that permitted the utilization of aircraft machine guns in ground defenses. Some were simple and evidently hurriedly constructed while others showed careful and detailed planning to adapt certain items to new and novel purposes.

Minefields had afforded the Japanese the greatest opportunity in the past for improvisation and no decrease of this tendency was noticed in the Philippines. Anything was grist for the mill when it was time to construct a minefield. Such things as aerial bombs, depth charges, artillery shells, and the like were used to such an extent as mines that the practice was looked upon as SOP for the Japanese. Although they had many standard mines designed for anti-tank and anti-personnel uses, these were rarely in quantity. For example, the minefield in Laloma Cemetery at the entrance to Manila was constructed almost entirely of Japanese depth charges.

Many types of hand grenades of local manufacture were recovered in the Philippines. In Manila 1st Cavalry Division troops captured a shop that had been used by the Japanese to manufacture hand grenades similar to their Type 97, differing mainly in the method of ignition, while on Mindanao Eighth Army troops recovered a well designed, chemically fuzed grenade. Other improvisations used 81-mm mortar shells and Type 89 Grenade Launcher shells.

Many improvised mortars and mortar shells were also captured. One 60-mm weapon was made from iron pipe and equipped with two $\frac{1}{2}$-inch steel rod legs and a wooden base plate. Two improvised stick mortars, similar in principle to the Type 98 50-mm Mortar, were found in Baguio. Although both mortars were of the same design, they were of different calibers, one being 3 inches, and the other 4.7 inches in diameter. Both mortars were crudely designed and constructed. Mild steel was used entirely but the larger mortar had a wooden base made of 4 x 8 inch timbers for the mortar to rest on. The most unusual mortar, however, was a 5-inch mortar found near Cebu City. This mortar was constructed of one airplane cylinder, complete with head, with other sections of a cylinder bolted together as a unit to form a complete weapon. The firing mechanism was a spring release plunger type, which was screwed into the spark plug hole of the cylinder head. There was no mount for the weapon and it appeared probable that it would be employed by placing it in a hole in the ground and bracing the upper barrel by means of short timbers or rocks.

Figure 56
AIRCRAFT 12.7-mm GUN ON MOBILE IMPROVISED MOUNT

Although aircraft guns have often been used in improvised mounts for ground defense, the mounts have either been very light and unstable or have been fixed. For the first time weapons were recovered in the Philippines which showed that careful attention had been given to providing stable, mobile mounts. Provision was made for traverse, elevation, crew protection, and recoil. The guns generally appeared to be well designed for their intended purpose.

The Japanese found it necessary to provide protection for troops traveling through guerrilla territory and did so by converting commercial trucks into armored cars. The vehicles used were Ford, 4 x 2, $1\frac{1}{2}$ ton trucks. One was armored by two sheets of $\frac{1}{4}$-inch steel plate, separated by an air space. No weapons or provisions for them were found on this vehicle. The other car was armored by 3/16-inch steel with an interior wall of $3\frac{1}{2}$ inches of concrete. Protection was good but the weight of the armor was excessive. This car was provided with a turret mounting a machine gun. Performance of these two cars would be poor due to overloading the original truck chassis.

The development of these weapons show that in later campaigns of the war, the Japanese were doing their somewhat awkward best to make up for their disadvantage in equipment and materiel. It can be considered likely that if the war had continued, these developments would have been further improved and at least partially effective.

NAVAL 20-CM SPIN STABILIZED ROCKET AND IMPROVISED LAUNCHERS:

The Japanese 20-cm Naval SS Rockets and Launchers were first recovered from coconut log emplacements facing out to sea near San Jose, Leyte. There were no indications that any of the rockets had been fired on our landing forces, although one rocket was found in place on the launcher, fully fuzed and ready for firing.

The overall length of this rocket was $37\frac{1}{4}$ inches. Right hand rotation stabilized the projectile in flight. It had a much higher charge weight ratio than any other known Naval ammunition (35.3%).

Two types of launchers were recovered. One launcher was a multiple type, capable of launching three rockets simultaneously. The other was a single-troughed launching rack with an adjustable bipod. Launchers on Leyte were constructed of metal, whereas those of similar design found on Luzon were made of wood.

This spin stabilized rocket was designed as a short range weapon for a blast rather than a fragmentation effect. Maximum range fired from the open launching racks was reported to be 1,800 meters. Targets fired upon could not have been seen from the pillbox emplacements found. Also, the lack of a traversing mechanism and a means of changing elevation without manually shifting the front bipod would have hindered making corrections on the target.

Figure 57
ARMY 20-CM SS ROCKET AND TYPE 4 LAUNCHER

Figure 58
ARMY 20-CM SS ROCKET AND TYPE 4 LAUNCHER (FIRING)

ARMY 20-CM SPIN STABILIZED ROCKET AND TYPE 4 LAUNCHER:

Several of these projectiles, the first Army rockets recovered, and the Type 4 launcher, were used against our troops in the Manila area and east of Manila. The date of manufacture, late 1944, emphasized the trend toward increased use of rockets by the enemy.

In general appearance the launcher was similar to a large trench mortar. It incorporated traversing mechanism in the bipod and employed standard mortar fire-control devices. The tube, 20.3-cm inside diameter and 75 and 5/8 inches long, was open at both ends and contained a hinged opening for insertion of the rocket. It was fired with a 25-foot lanyard attached to a pull igniter.

The explosive head was a thin-walled tube containing nose fuze, booster and filling of cast TNT. The motor threaded onto the explosive head and was equipped with six nozzles canted 25 degrees. The propellant was ballistite ignited by a black powder charge located just forward of the igniter, which screwed into the motor base plate. Projectile and motor had a combined weight of approximately 185 pounds.

The rocket was stable in flight, exploded high order, and had an approximate range of 3,200 yards at 800 mils.

Figure 59 - 447-MM SS ROCKET

447-MM SPIN STABILIZED ROCKET AND CART TYPE LAUNCHER:

The launcher and eighty-five rockets were recovered in the Manila area, where they reportedly were brought a month before our landing in Lingayen Gulf. It is not known whether the weapon was used against our troops.

The rocket was 447-mm in diameter, weighed roughly 1,500 pounds, and consisted of an explosive head $41\frac{1}{2}$ inches long and a motor 27 inches long. The head was a 3/4 inch steel barrel, filled with picric acid, to which was welded a nose containing a fuse, picric acid booster cylinder and an Army gaine. For the propellant charge the motor used 60 kg of ballistite sticks, ignited by a charge of black powder located forward of the central stick. The motor base plate was equipped with six canted nozzles, a propellant-restraining grill, a threaded recess for the primer and a light protective base cover. By flashing through the perforation in the central ballistite stick, the primer ignited the black powder.

With 4-foot wooden wheels and a 12-foot wooden launching platform, the launcher resembled a two-wheeled cart. The firing mechanism, wheel brakes, and general construction were very crude, suggesting that the design was a field expedient.

The rocket was stable in flight, had an approximate range of 2,150 yards at 800 mils elevation, exploded high order with good fragmentation, and produced a crater resembling that of a U.S. 1,000-pound bomb.

Figure 60 - TYPE 97 IMPROVED MED TANK WITH 47-MM GUN

TYPE 97 IMPROVED MEDIUM TANK WITH 47-MM GUN:

A number of modified Japanese medium tanks were encountered on Luzon. They were basically an improvement on the Type 97 Medium Tank. The tank studied was manufactured at the Tokyo Army Arsenal in 1944.

The tank was 18 feet 2 inches long, 7 feet 6 inches wide, and 7 feet high. It was equipped with a V-12, air-cooled, valve-in-head, diesel engine with Bosch fuel pumps. The transmission provided four speeds forward and one speed in reverse. Dual steering was employed, utilizing both clutch-brake and epicyclic gear steering systems. The turret had been changed from a circular type to a semi-rectangular over-hanging type that gave a long, low appearance. Racks were mounted on the turret sides for use with the Type 94 self-projecting smoke candles. Except for a portion of the turret, all armor was riveted. The track was the conventional Japanese center-guide all steel type, 13 inches in width.

The tank mounted two Type 97 (1937) 7.7-mm tank machine guns and one Type 1 (1941) 47-mm tank gun. One machine gun was mounted in the rear of the turret, the other forward in the hull. The ammunition racks hold 120 rounds of 47-mm and 2,500 rounds of 7.7-mm ammunition, the former being both APHE and HE. The Type 1, 47-mm tank gun was almost identical to the 47-mm anti-tank gun. It was 9 feet 7 inches long, allowing 15 degrees total traverse and an elevation from plus 10 to minus 10 degrees. The turret could be traversed 360 degrees.

FLAME-THROWING TANK:

The first Japanese flame-throwing tanks to be encountered by U.S. forces were captured in the vicinity of Aritao, Luzon, during June 1945. Eight tanks were recovered. Examination proved them to be one basic vehicle with two primary modifications. Nameplate data from the tanks disclosed the vehicles themselves were manufactured between 1940 and 1941. It is entirely possible that the chassis was manufactured for some other tactical purpose and was then redesigned to accommodate flame-throwing equipment.

Figure 61 - FLAME-THROWING TANK

The vehicle was full-tracked, armored, and powered by a 12-cylinder, air-cooled, in-line diesel engine, and was 19 feet 6 inches long, 7 feet wide, and 5 feet 4 inches high. Armor thickness was 1 inch on the front, $\frac{1}{2}$ inch on the sides and rear, and $\frac{1}{4}$ inch on the top. The suspension varied from the usual Japanese tank in that eight very large leaf springs were used instead of coil compression springs, and that there were eight bogie wheels per track. The tanks were equipped with forks that could be lowered in front of the tracks to remove obstacles. These forks were controlled by a cable leading inside. The vehicles were also equipped with a rear power winch, an electrical intercommunication system, and smoked glass vision slits for the flame-thrower operator.

The two modifications of the basic vehicle differed in the mounting of the armament and fuel tanks. One model had interior tanks only; the other was equipped with nine external fuel tanks. One large external cylindrical tank was mounted on a rack at the rear of this type, and four smaller tanks made of $\frac{1}{4}$-inch armor, were mounted on the side of the vehicle above the bogies.

Figure 62 - MODIFIED FLAME-THROWING TANK

Armament, consisting of flame-throwers, and type 99, 7.7-mm tank machine guns with telescopic sights, was varied on the eight vehicles recovered. The flame-throwers were of two types, a long nozzle and short nozzle type, both ignited by carbon arcs. Two methods of arrangement were found. The first used one flame-thrower and two machine guns forward and one flame-thrower in the rear (One vehicle had one of the forward machine guns replaced by a third flame-thrower). The second arrangement included one flame-thrower and one machine gun forward, and two flame-throwers on each side of the vehicle, with provision for a sixth flame-thrower in the rear. Mounts for guns and flame-throwers allowed a traverse of 20 degrees and permitted elevation from -5 to 10 degrees.

It appeared that these flame-throwing tanks were intended as assault weapons, to destroy entanglements and personnel in fortification. However, their light armor and limited armament left them vulnerable to all but small arms fire, and there were large dead spaces in their fields of fire. Maximum speed was estimated at 25 miles per hour, and maximum range of the flame-throwers was estimated at 100 to 150 feet, depending on the thickness of the fuel used. The vehicle was maneuverable, would turn 360 degrees in its own length, and flotation was good. Five men were apparently needed for the crew.

Figure 63 - FULL TRACK PERSONNEL CARRIER

PERSONNEL CARRIER, FULL TRACK:

Although not encountered before our return to the Philippines, several of these vehicles were captured there by U.S. forces. One was recovered on Leyte, and at least four were found on Luzon.

The vehicle was full tracked, armored, and powered by a six cylinder air-cooled Diesel engine. The bogie wheels and suspension were similar to those of the Type 95 Light Tank, but the track was both longer and wider than that of the tank. This carrier, 15 feet 9 inches long overall and 6 feet 8 inches wide, was protected with $\frac{1}{4}$-inch armor on all sides and rear, but was open at the top except for the driver's compartment. There were doors at the rear and one on each side to permit personnel to leave the carrier rapidly. The driver's compartment was on the left front of the body and was equipped with metal vision slits for driving under fire. The vehicle had four speeds forward in addition to high and low range transfer case and was equipped with a spring-mounted towing pintle.

Being much lighter than the Type 95 Light Tank, employing an engine of similar power, and having roughly the same track contact, the vehicle gave excellent cross-country performance. The addition of the transfer case increased the range and power as compared with a light tank. U.S. combat troops found these vehicles to be highly satisfactory artillery prime movers.

Figure 64
HALF-TRACK PERSONNEL CARRIER AND PRIME MOVER

HALF-TRACK PERSONNEL CARRIER AND PRIME MOVER:

A Japanese combination personnel carrier and prime mover was recovered near Manila, Luzon.

The vehicle was without armor or armament of any kind.

It had a folding canvas top and four wide seats providing seating capacity for approximately 16 persons. Storage compartments for equipment and luggage were provided under the seats. The vehicle was equipped with a large winch and towing pintle in the rear.

The engine, a 6-cylinder, in-line, water-cooled diesel type, was connected to a four-speed forward, one-speed reverse, spur-gear transmission. The chassis layout was similar to the German standard half-track, while the suspension and steering followed the Opel truck half-track conversion. The front transverse leaf spring, independent wheel suspension was an original and effective feature. The vehicle was 18 feet 3 inches long, 6 feet 4 inches wide, 7 feet 10 inches high, had a ground clearance of 13 inches, 110 horsepower, and weighed approximately 6 tons.

Performance tests indicated a maximum speed of 25 miles per hour, an estimated radius of action of 125 miles, and proved that the vehicle could manipulate a trench 3 feet wide, a vertical wall 18 inches high, a 50% slope, and a stream 3 feet deep. Ample power and cross-country mobility were provided to allow it to fulfill the functions of a prime mover and personnel carrier.

TYPE 1, SELF-PROPELLED 75-MM GUN:

Two Self-Propelled 75-mm Guns were recovered near Santa Fe, in northern Luzon, during June 1945. They had been identified as the self-propelled weapon; previously known only from a captured photograph.

The vehicle appeared to be identical to the chassis of the Type 97 improved Medium Tank, utilizing the same suspension and V-12 air-cooled diesel engine, and differing only in having the turret replaced by an armored fighting compartment.

The gun was the Type 90, 75-mm field gun, modified for vehicle mounting. The horizontal sliding breechblock was somewhat smaller than that of the field gun. A continuous pull firing mechanism was used. HE, APHE, WP, or illuminating shell ammunition could be used. The total traverse of the gun was estimated to be 20 degrees, elevation from minus 5 to plus 25 degrees, tube length 8 feet 9 inches, with a maximum recoil of 750-mm.

Figure 65 - TYPE 1 SELF-PROPELLED 75-MM GUN

The weapon was apparently designed for use as a tank destroyer or light assault gun. The use of the Type 97 Medium Tank chassis provided excellent mobility, was capable of speeds up to 25 miles per hour, and, had approximately half the ground pressure of the U.S. M A3 Medium Tank, and could maneuver well over rugged terrain. In contrast to the Japanese 15-cm Self-Propelled Gun, this weapon was provided with an interior mantlet and armored recoil mechanism. The fighting compartment, the front of which had 2 inches of armor plate and the sides $\frac{1}{2}$ inch, showed a decided trend on the part of the enemy toward heavier armor. This gun could probably have been operated safely under frontal small arms fire.

SELF-PROPELLED 15-CM HOWITZER:

A Japanese 15-cm Self-Propelled Howitzer was recovered

for the first time in the hills west of Ft Stotsenburg, Luzon. The weapon was manufactured at the Osaka Artillery Arsenal, and the chassis was made in January, 1942, at the Sugamo Army Arsenal.

Figure 66 - SELF-PROPELLED 15-CM HOWITZER

With certain variations, the vehicle on which the gun was mounted resembled the Type 97 Medium Tank chassis. It was powered by the same engine, and the performance was probably similar. Hull and turret plates were riveted. The vehicle weighed approximately 15 tons, was 18 feet long, 7 feet 8 inches wide, and 7 feet 9 inches in height.

The 15-cm gun was a Type 38, with hydro-pneumatic recoil, interrupted screw breechblock, and had an elevation from -5 degrees to 30 degrees with a 10 degree traverse. Only HE ammunition utilizing Type 88 instantaneous fuze was recovered with the gun.

A mount on the right of the gun may have been intended for a machine gun. It is estimated that a crew of 3 or 4 men were required to operate this weapon.

ARMY 30-CM ARMY HOWITZER, TYPE 7TH YEAR:

A battery of Japanese 30-cm Howitzers, Type 7th Year,

was captured near Rosario, Luzon. The battery consisted of two howitzers and one dummy position. The gun positions circular, measuring 33 feet in diameter and 8 feet in depth. One position was skillfully camouflaged by a house on rails, approximately 40 feet square and 6 feet high, which was rolled back before firing.

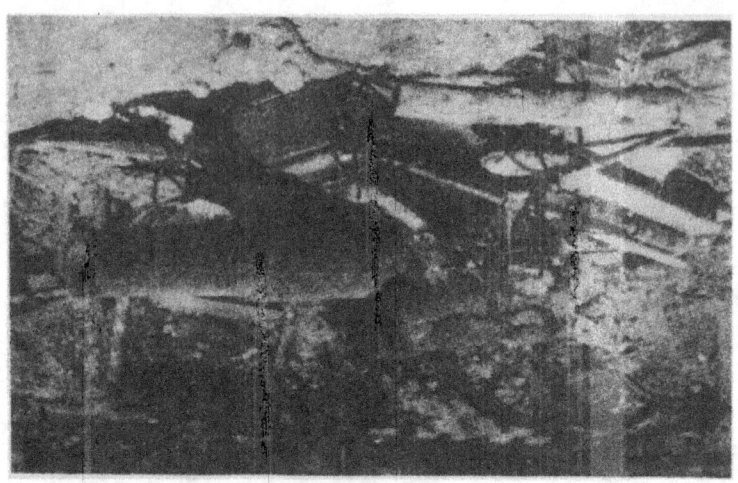

Figure 67
ARMY 30-CM HOWITZER, TYPE 7TH YEAR

The base mount was a truncated steel cone embedded in concrete 6 to 8 feet underground. The gun carriage was a rectangular steel frame 18 feet 9 inches long and 4 feet 8 inches wide. The carriage was rigidly attached to the base plate, and the gun, carriage, and base plate revolved as one piece.

The tube, believed to be of the built-up type, had an overall length of 16 feet 6 inches. The breech mechanism was an ordinary interrupted screw having eight segments of twenty threads. The percussion hammer firing mechanism was operated by a lanyard. A panoramic sight was mounted on the right side of the gun. Two air flasks were mounted on the carriage for blowing out the tube after firing. Additional pertinent gun data were as follows: diameter of tube 12 inches (approximate), elevation from 3 to 70 degrees, traverse 360 degrees, and maximum range 15,000 yards (estimated).

In loading the gun the shell was brought up by a

manually drawn cart to a four wheel tray at the rear of the carriage; this tray rolled on the carriage structure to the breech. The shell was then hoisted and transferred to the breech. It is estimated that 16 men were necessary to man this weapon.

Figure 68 - TYPE 11, 12-CM DUAL PURPOSE GUN

TYPE 11, 12-CM DUAL PURPOSE GUN:

Two Japanese Type 11, 12-cm dual purpose guns were recovered for the first time at Legaspi, Luzon, emplaced in log and earth pillboxes, covering beach and water approaches. These guns were manufactured in March 1944 by the Sasebo Naval Arsenal, and according to civilian reports were emplaced at Legaspi on 27 October 1944.

The gun tube, believed to be of the built-up type, had an overall length of 18 feet $3\frac{1}{4}$ inches. The breechblock was manually operated, horizontally sliding, equipped with a firing mechanism which could be operated by the gun crew member in charge of the elevating handwheel. The gun could also be fired by a lanyard. The traversing wheel was in a horizontal position with a shaft engaging the elevating arc gear. The base was made of steel and was imbedded in a rock foundation in the emplacements where the guns were found. Additional pertinent gun data follows: height of gun 6 feet 11 inches; elevation, from -10 degrees to 50 degrees; traverse, 360 degrees; ammunition, semi-fixed, nose time-fuzed.

It is possible that this weapon was a shipborne gun adapted for coast defense and anti-aircraft purposes. Two weapons of similar caliber had been previously captured, the Type 89, 12.7-cm dual purpose gun and the Type 10, 12-cm dual purpose gun.

Figure 69 - TYPE 97, 15-CM MORTAR

TYPE 97, 15-CM MORTAR:

The Japanese Type 97, 15-cm Mortar was recovered for the first time near Rosario, Luzon. This weapon was used extensively and effectively by the enemy during the Luzon operation.

This mortar was classified by the enemy as a medium mortar although it was approximately of 6-inch caliber. It had a heavy base plate and the usual design of bipod incorporating elevating and traversing mechanisms of the buttress screw type.

In extensive test firing over water, the Type 100 combination, instantaneous short delay mortar fuze was used. Fragmentation of the projectile appeared to be excellent, as indicated by splashes ranging out to approximately 100 feet of the point of impact. Fifty to 100 fragment splashes were observed for each of the thirty-five rounds fired. The maximum range obtained with a full complement of propelling increments was 4,650 yards; a minimum average range of 400 yards at 1,200 mils elevation was observed.

During the first 6 rounds fired it was noted that the base plate shifted to the rear; later the base plate settled firmly into the ground, and no further shifting was observed. The propelling powder used in the increments and propelling cartridge was almost smokeless; however, a muzzle flame from two or three inches to approximately three feet long, depending on the number of increments used, extended from the muzzle during the firing.

Figure 70 - TYPE 3, POTTERY LAND MINE

TYPE 3, POTTERY LAND MINE:

First encountered near Tacloban, Leyte, shortly after our initial landing there, this mine was the first Japanese non-metallic type mine recovered. On Luzon the mine was found in large quantities.

The case of the mine, made of earthen-color terra cotta, was circular in shape, and except for the springs, pins, and striker of the fuze, the mine was non-metallic. Manufactured in two sizes, the larger size was $10\frac{1}{2}$ inches in diameter, $3\frac{1}{2}$ inches thick, and contained $6\frac{1}{2}$ pounds of bursting charge, while the small size was $8\frac{1}{2}$ inches in diameter and contained $4\frac{1}{2}$ pounds of bursting charge. Ammonium nitrate-TNT and similar mixtures were the explosives used.

The fuze was largely constructed of bakelite and had a spring-loaded hammer type dual-action detonator, sensitive to a pressure of $4\frac{1}{2}$ pounds or a pull of 22 pounds. It was threaded to be interchangeable with standard artillery fuzes so that the mines could be improvised using ordinary mortar or howitzer ammunition.

Not detected by the usual type mine detector, the mine was also easy to camouflage. It was said to be effective against tank tracks and to have an effective anti-personnel radius of 33 feet for the large size and 26 feet for the small size.

SACK MINE:

Many mines of this type, sometimes known as "Burlap Bag Mines," "Burlap Bag Booby Traps," or "Demolition Sack Charges," were found during operations on Luzon. The exact purpose for which they were designed is not definitely known; in fact, a large proportion of the mines recovered appeared to be field improvisations.

These mines employed an ordinary pull type fuze igniter. Either one large blasting cap or three small blasting caps were used at the end of its fuze train as a booster. The fuze was inserted into a primer charge of TNT contained in a small silk bag. Sometimes the primer charge was used alone, but several types of bursting charges were employed, using TNT, picric acid, or even the heads of lunge mines. In some cases the main charge was contained in a 24-inch by 15-inch rubberized bag, shaped like a hot water bottle. This type was prepared by filling the rubberized bag with about ten or fifteen pounds of powder and placing the primer charge in the neck of the bag. Both were then placed in a burlap bag with the pull cord protruding. In some cases a burlap bag was used alone, filled with about twenty-five pounds of TNT.

These charges could be employed as mines, booby traps, or as demolitions, and the Japanese threw them at our tanks in unsuccessful attempts to knock them out. The mines deteriorated rapidly due to seepage of moisture into the fuze and primer charge. Most of the mines recovered were, for this reason, not in functioning condition.

LUNGE MINE:

This mine was first recovered during the operations on Leyte. The Japanese later used it in repeated attempts to knock out our tanks and other vehicles.

The mine consisted of $6\frac{1}{2}$ pounds of high explosive built in the shape of a hollow charge into a cone-shaped fougasse which was fastened at its apex to the end of a 59-inch carrying pole. It was a suicide anti-tank device which the operator employed by thrusting the short legs of the fougasse against a vehicle as he lunged toward it. The momentum of the lunge caused the carrying pole to shear a pin and penetrate the cylinder with which it was attached to the fougasse, thus driving a striker into the instantaneous type detonator located inside the apex of the fougasse. The resultant explosion killed the operator, but the main force of the explosion was directed against the vehicle according to the hollow-charge principle.

This weapon was capable of knocking out American medium tanks. A captured Japanese document stated that the mine "is quite effective" even against 3-inch armor, and that in tests it penetrated as much as 6 inches of steel plate. However, few of these lunge attempts proved successful in combat.

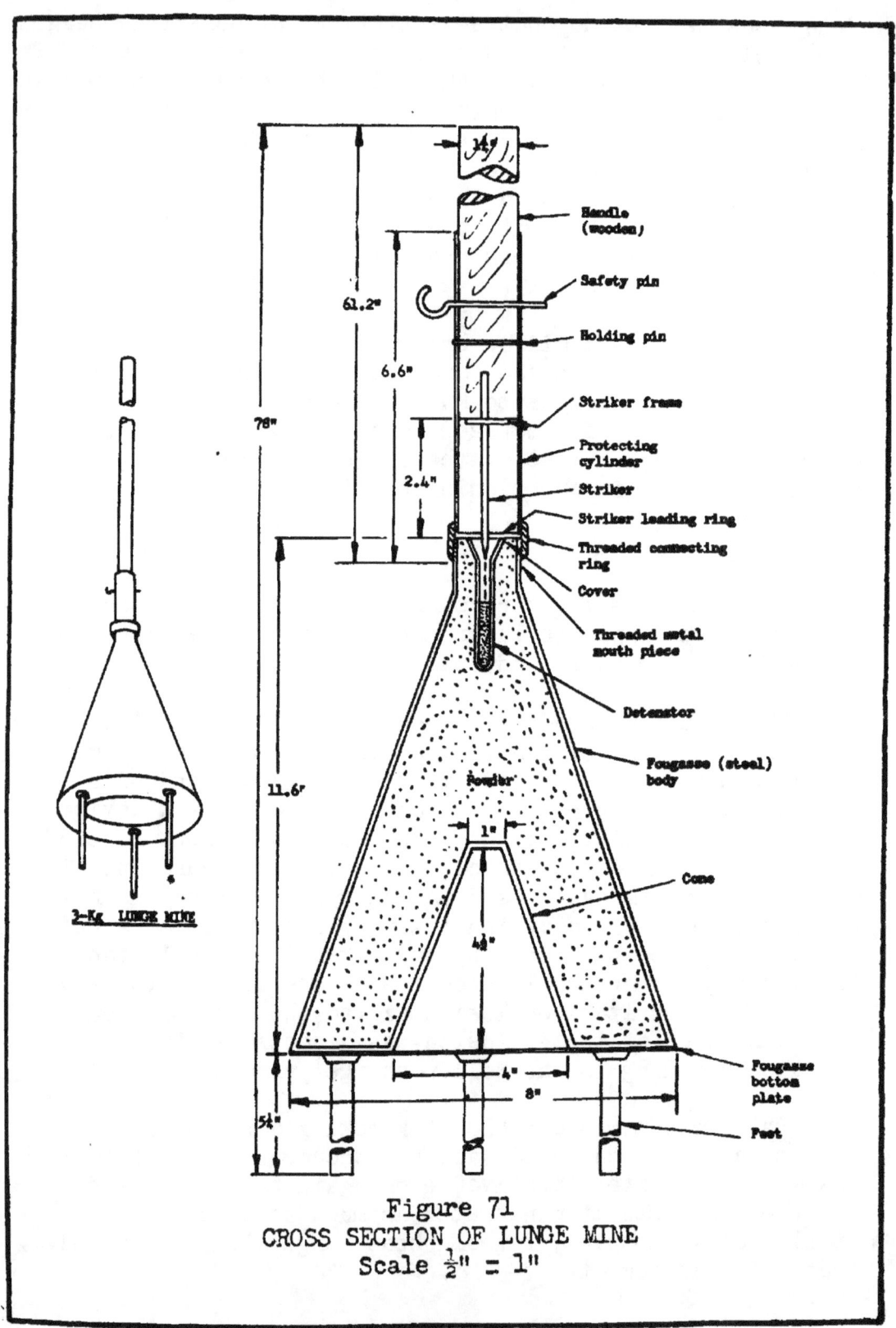

Figure 71
CROSS SECTION OF LUNGE MINE
Scale ½" = 1"

NAVY SUICIDE CRASH BOATS:

Japanese suicide crash boats manned by Naval personnel were found in a tunnel on Corregidor. The boats were loaded on small carts which were mounted on rails running from the tunnel to the beach where they were to be launched.

The Navy Suicide Crash Boat was 16 feet 8 inches long and had a beam of 5 feet 8 inches. The hull was plywood construction throughout and was powered by an automotive type, 6-cylinder, in-line, gasoline engine. The explosive charge was built into the hull of the boat. This last feature was the main difference between the Army and Navy suicide boats.

The Type 98 explosive charge weighed 640 pounds and was located below the deck forward of the cockpit. The charge could be fired by three methods: 1) electrically on impact; 2) electrically by closing a switch; and 3) by use of a pull igniter.

From the disposal point of view, the boat was dangerous to anyone unfamiliar with the circuit and switch details. It would also have been simple to rig this boat as a booby trap either electrically or through the pull igniter.

The boat carried a big charge that would be effective against ships. The only defense that a ship had was, as in the case of the suicide plane, accurate gunfire.

ARMY SUICIDE CRASH BOAT:

Japanese suicide boats, to be manned by Army personnel, were recovered at Lingayen Gulf, Luzon. These craft were the principal weapon of the Japanese Gyoro ("fishing") battalions.

The army suicide boat was made of plywood with a length of $18\frac{1}{2}$ feet and a beam of 5 feet 10 inches. It was decked with a forward hatch leading to the engine and has a cockpit aft. The boat was powered with a 6-cylinder Chevrolet automotive engine, about 85 horsepower. The maximum speed of the craft was estimated at 35 knots. The fuel capacity was about 56 gallons.

The two 120 kg depth charges were mounted on racks abreast of the cockpit. The charges could be either dropped close aboard or released when the boat crashed into the ship. At least one attack of the former type was made, resulting in damage to a merchant ship during the Luzon campaign.

Although parts of the release mechanism were not available, the operation is believed to have been as follows: the charges were fitted in the racks and held by an arrangement of slings and bars. Rods fitted to extend beyond the bow would be driven back releasing the charges during a collision with another ship. However, the coxwain could place a crossbar forward to release the charges.

Figure 72 - SPRING-DRIVEN DEMOLITION CLOCK

SPRING-DRIVEN DEMOLITION CLOCK:

This clock was first recovered from southern Luzon, where it was found unconcealed, set to explode a Japanese ammunition dump of 75-mm ammunition.

The clock and a firing assembly were contained in one brass and celluloid case 2-11/16 inches long, 2-3/8 inches wide, and 7/8 inches thick. It was a finely-made, 8-day, jewelled, spring-driven mechanism apparently of European design. The face was a disc graduated from 0 to 7 days 12 hours in 1 hour intervals. For setting the delay, an index line was engraved on the case and on a celluloid face plate. The edge of the disc had a raised lip in which a firing slot was filed. The firing assembly consisted of a firing pin, retainer, retainer arm, and release arm. When the set time had elapsed, the firing slot allowed a tit on the release arm to pass through the slot, causing the release arm to move out and free the retainer arm and firing pin. Under spring pressure, the firing pin was then driven against a primer, which detonated the demolition charge.

In using this clock, explosives such as picric acid blocks could be primed with a short length of safety fuze leading from the primer.

TYPE 99, ELECTRIC DEMOLITION CLOCK:

This demolition clock, first recovered on Luzon during March 1945, had often been referred to in captured enemy documents. It was contained in a sturdy wooden box $5\frac{1}{4}$ inches wide, 4-5/8 inches high, and 6-3/4 inches long. The box was in two sections fastened together by two spring clamps on each side. At one end were two brass threaded recesses for lead wires to the explosive charge, and there was a small knife switch to break the circuit while emplacing the clock. An electric winding, spring-driven clock, calibrated from 0 to 11 days in intervals of 2 hours, was contained in the lower portion of the box. The current for operating both clock and detonator was supplied by a battery located in a well next to the clock proper. To set the device, the calibrated clock face was rotated until the desired graduation was opposite a pin on a metal bar which was spring-held against the face. After the desired interval, this pin slid into a notch cut into the clock face at the 0 graduation, closing the circuit which applied the battery voltage to an electric detonator.

Tests indicated the clock was satisfactory and accurate in operation.

CHAPTER X
ENEMY MATERIAL CAPTURED OR DESTROYED

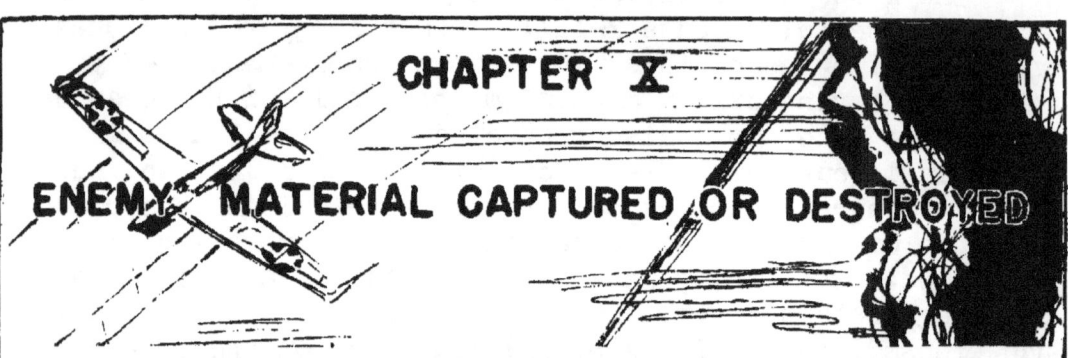

The following pages list the enemy materiel destroyed or captured during the Luzon campaign between 9 January 1945 and 30 June 1945 and will aid the reader in estimating the extent of the damage inflicted on the enemy during that period.

LIST OF ENEMY MATERIEL CAPTURED OR DESTROYED BY SIXTH ARMY ON LUZON FROM 9 JANUARY 1945 TO 30 JUNE 1945

ARTILLERY, ROCKETS AND MORTARS:

Guns	Amount	Anti-aircraft Guns	Amount
15-cm	49	120-mm	14
10-cm	6	90-mm	13
155-mm	26	40-mm	7
155-mm GPF	3		
150-mm	10	**Mortars**	
120-mm	80		
105-mm	54	15-cm	15
90-mm	10	150-mm	21
88-mm	1	120-mm	1
75-mm	246	105-mm	2
75-mm Mtn	5	90-mm	51
70-mm	12	81-mm	53
70-mm Bn	13	81-mm Barrage	14
57-mm	3	70-mm	3
47-mm	124	70-mm Barrage	7
40-mm	50	60-mm	21
37-mm	114	50-mm	230
25-mm	245	Knee Mortars	607
25-mm D/P	16	Stick Mortars	1
20-mm	391	U/I Caliber	170
8" C/D	2		
5"	3	**Grenade Dischargers**	
3"	7		
U/I Caliber	65	50-mm	
S/P, U/I Caliber	5	U/I Caliber (ea)	
		U/I Caliber (cases)	
Howitzers			
		Captured U.S. Guns	
30-cm	2		
15-cm	3	37-mm	1
10-cm	1	S/P, U/I Caliber	1
150-mm	21		
105-mm	27	**Rocket Launchers**	
70-mm	11		
		U/I Caliber	55
		70-mm Rocket Launchers	2

SMALL ARMS:

Machine Guns	Amount	Miscellaneous Arms	Amount
20-mm	5	Bayonets (many unreported)	446
.50-cal	62	Sabers and Swords	85
.50-cal 8-barrel	1		
7.7-mm AA (twin-mount)	1		
HMGs	1,240		
LMGs	982		
Lewis-Type	2		
Caliber U/I	356		
AA, Caliber U/I	8		
HMGs, Captured US	3		
LMGs, Captured US	4		
MGs, Captured US, Caliber U/I	2		

ORDNANCE VEHICLES:

	Amount
Tanks, Medium	230
Tanks, Light	35
Tankettes	14
Tanks, U/I Size	32
Tanks W/Flame Throwers	8
Tanks, Light, Captured US	3
Half-Tracks	3
Armored Cars	8
Armored Personnel Carriers	14
Armored Wagons	12
Tracked Semi-Trailers	5
Prime Movers	15
Heavy Wrecker	1
Trucks, Misc.	1,362
Personnel Carriers	2
Recon Cars	1
Staff Cars	17
Sedans	321
Station Wagons	1
Japanese Bantams	1
Vehicles, U/I Type	179
Motorcycles	7
SMP	1
Trailers	22
Tow Carts	59
Bicycles	41

Sub-Machine Guns & Pistols

	Amount
Thompson SMGs	13
SMGs	10
Bren Guns	2
Machine Rifles	10
Machine Pistols	15
BARs, Captured US	32

Rifles and Pistols

	Amount
7.7-mm Rifles	1,216
6.5-mm Rifles	63
.22-Cal. Rifles	4
Sniper's Rifle, Cal U/I	1
Rifles, U/I Cal (ea)	5,993
Rifles, U/I Cal (cases)	2
Carbines	59
Shot Guns	19
M-1 Rifles, Captured US	34
1903 Rifles, Captured US	59
Rifles, Captured US, Cal U/I	302
Pistols	74

Captured US Vehicles

	Amount
GMC, 2½-ton	1
C & R, ½-ton	2
Ambulances	2
Jeeps	1
Civilian Cars	103

ORDNANCE - - AMMUNITION AND EXPLOSIVES:

Artillery (in cases)	Amount
150-mm	2,020
120-mm	262
105-mm	3,307
90-mm	48
75-mm	9,101
70-mm	445
47-mm	1,872
40-mm	410
37-mm	888
25-mm	196
20-mm	1,635
3"	152
Mixed Artillery, U/I Cal.	1,506

Artillery (loose rounds)	
155-mm	168
150-mm	548
120-mm	1,215
105-mm	2,920
75-mm	20,358
70-mm	226
47-mm	4,142
40-mm	2,896
37-mm	308
25-mm	11,702
20-mm	210,012
15-cm	3,021
6"	3,000
5"	34
3"	850
Mixed Arty, U/I Caliber	34,000

Mortar (in cases)	
120-mm	31
90-mm	172
81-mm	1,100

Mortar (in cases) (Continued)	Amount
50-mm	113
15-cm	215
Type #2	17
Knee Mortar	434
Mortar, U/I Caliber	20

Mortar (loose rounds)	
150-mm	72
90-mm	50
81-mm	658
77-mm	165
70-mm	36
50-mm	840
15-cm	1,000
Knee Mortar	1,377
Mortar, U/I Caliber	1,124

Rockets (loose rounds)	
120-mm	60
20-mm	35
Rockets, U/I Caliber	25
Grenade Discharger (cases)	80

Fuses	
Type 88 (cases)	1
Howitzer (cases)	3
50-mm (cases)	2
Safety (cases)	2
Misc. Fuses, U/I Type (cases)	194

Small Arms & Machine Gun Ammunition	
.50-cal (cases)	163
.45-cal (cases)	1

Small Arms & MG Ammunition (Continued)

	Amount
12.7-mm (cases)	70
.303-cal (cases)	313
.30-cal (cases)	196
7.7-mm (cases)	113
6.5-mm (cases)	5
.25-cal (cases)	41
.22-cal (cases)	1
MG ammo, U/I Cal (cases)	1,046
Misc. Small Arms Ammo, U/I Cal. (cases)	5,328
Misc. Small Arms Ammo, U/I Cal. (rounds)	448,648
Dum Dum (cases)	2

Miscellaneous Demolitions and Explosives

	Amount
Grenades (cases)	504
Grenades (each)	402
TNT (cases)	158
Dynamite (cases)	59
Dynamite (lbs)	6,800
Black Powder (lbs)	1,200
Picric Acid (blocks)	171
Picric Acid (kegs)	240
Picric Acid (lbs)	500
Demolition Charges (cases)	4
Demolition Charges (lbs)	227
Satchel Charges (each)	109
Pole Charges (each)	35
Hollow Charges (each)	317
Booby Traps, Misc.	16
Bangalore Torpedoes (cases)	87
Bangalore Torpedoes (ea)	56
Naval Torpedoes (each)	12
Caps, Detonator. (cases)	2

Miscellaneous Demolitions and Explosives (Continued)

	Amount
Molotov Cocktails (cases)	4
Firecrackers (cases)	3

Mines

	Amount
Tape Measure (each)	69
Magnetic (each)	77
AT Mines (cases)	3
AT Mines (each)	50
AP Mines (cases)	12
AP Mines (each)	55
Lunge Mines (each)	54
Mines, U/I (cases)	40
Mines, U/I (each)	106

Bombs

	Amount
1000-lb (each)	4
500-lb (each)	81
250-lb (cases)	50
100-lb (each)	33
50-lb (each)	17
30-lb (each)	2,000
Screaming (cases)	326
Spigot (each)	5
Depth (each)	61
Bombs, U/I (each)	743
Bombs (used as land mines)	1,360

ORDNANCE – MISCELLANEOUS:

Optical & Fire Control

Field Glasses	27
Field Glasses Tripods	6
Telescopes	13
B.C. Scopes	15
Periscopes	16

Optical & Fire Control (Continued)	Amount
Sights, Telescopic	4
Mortar Sights w/case	2
Range Finders	19
Arty Sighting Equip (cases)	2
Gun Cameras	10
Bombsights	100
AA Fire Director w/Equip	1
Artillery Scope	1
Fire Control Instruments, Misc.	5
Sights, Panoramic	5

Machine Gun Parts	Amount
HMG, Sights	5
HMG, Spare Barrels, .303 cal	22
HMG, Springs, Recoil	16
HMG, Wheel, Hand Elevating	3
HMG, Piston, Operating Bolt	11
HMG, Pins, Firing	118
HMG, Bolts	14
HMG, Back-Plate	2
HMG, Knob, Elevating	4
LMG, Magazines	26
LMG, Magazine Accessories	13
LMG, Piston Operating Bolt	18
LMG, Bolts	19
LMG, Bipod	10
LMG, Magazine Loader	4
LMG, Grip, Hand	1
LMG, Spare Barrels	95
LMG, Springs, Magazine	9

Machine Gun Parts (Continued)	Amount
LMG, Hider, Flash	4
LMG, Rest, Shoulder	2
LMG, Handle, Bolt Operating	1
MG Links (cases)	1
MG Wrench, Combination	4
MG Ruptured Cartridge Extractor	3
MG, Spare Barrels, U/I Cal (cases)	3
MG, Spare Barrels, U/I Cal (each)	36

Small Arms Parts	Amount
Rifle, Stocks, (cases)	7
Rifle, Cal .25 Ariska, Hand Guard	10

Miscellaneous Weapons Parts	Amount
Searchlights	28
S/L Power Units	18
S/L Aiming Devices	11
Bomb Release	1
Caissons	99
Carriages, 15-cm Howitzer	4
Stationary Mortars	2
Magazines, AA Gun	4
Lanyard, Knee Mortar	9
Shank, Knee Mortar	1
Base Plate, 50-mm Mortar	1
Plate, Side, 20-mm Gun	2
Bags, Auto Clips	2
Aiming Circle	1
Aiming Posts	4

Miscellaneous Automotive Parts	Amount
Tires	1,193
Tubes	110
Ignition Wire (cases)	1
Battery Plates (cases)	1
Engine Parts (cases)	1
Auto Parts (cases)	48
Diesel Parts (cases)	20
Engines	5
Motor, Current Flow	2
Wheels, U/I	32
Gaskets, Head	71
Fan Belts	50
Radiators	2
Hoses, Radiator	25
Pump, Fuel, Auto	7
Distributors	12
Spark Plugs	24
Nuts, 9/16" SAE	24

Miscellaneous Automotive Tools	
Wrench, Socket	4
Compressor, Air	2
Drill, Electric	1
Cement, Gasket	4
Valve Grinding Compound (case)	1
Jacks, Auto	1
Machine Shop (complete)	1

Miscellaneous	
Batteries (cases)	4
Batteries (each)	73
Battery Terminals	4
Gas Pumps	4
Scales, Fairbanks	1
Spare Parts Kits, U/I	24
Springs, Assorted	85
Studs	10

Miscellaneous (Continued)	Amount
Cases, Canvas (box)	1
Box, Lead-Lined	1
Misc. Equipment (cases)	5

SIGNAL EQUIPMENT

Radios	
Radios, Sending	1
Radios, Sending & Receiving	1
Radios, Field	2
Radios, Tank Receiver	2
Radios, Misc. U/I	99
Radios, Commercial Sets	3
Radio Stations	2
Radios, Captured US	4
Short Wave Receivers	2
Transmitters	52
Receivers	57
Radars	7

Radio Parts & Equipment	
Radio Cases, W/Tubes	3
Radio Cabinet, W/Horn	1
Radio Batteries (cases)	1
Radio Tubes (cases)	6
Radio Tubes (each)	3,004
Oscillators	2
Radio Cord (bags)	2
Crystals	16
Generators, Radio Transformers	2
Condensors, Radio	4
Radio Equipment, Misc.	1
Boxes, Radio Equipment w/Case	2
Radio Repair Equipment (chests)	8

Radio Parts & Equipment (Continued)	Amount
Radio Parts	1
Tools, Radio (chests)	27

Telephones & Parts

Hand Phones	4
Field Phones	1
Telephones, Misc.	110
Headsets (cases)	1
Switchboards	15
Telephone Bells	18
Distribution Panels, Switchboard	3
Telephone Eliminators	7
Telephone Wire (reels)	1
Wire Pike	2

Telegraph Parts

Telegraph Keys	11
Telegraph Transmitter	2

Miscellaneous (Electric)

PA System	1
Microphones	2
Speakers	2
Switchbox	1
Sender, Signal, #32A	1
Signal Sets, U/I	3
Generators, Power	44
Generators, Hand	4
Batteries, 12-V	7
Batteries, 6-V	20
Batteries, U/I	3
Charger, Battery	2
Transformers	8
Transformer Tuning Units	4
Transformer Tubes (cases)	10

Miscellaneous (Electric) (Continued)	Amount
Coils	8
Rheostats	1
Relays	1
Ammeter	4
Voltmeter	5
Direction Finder	1
Antennae, Direction Finder	8
Electric Cable (coils)	16
Signal Wire (coils)	21
Electrical Equipment (chests)	2
Signal Equip, Misc. (cases)	47
Blinker Lights	15
Lantern, Signal	6
Lens, Set, Signal Lantern	1
Spotlights	3

Miscellaneous (non-electric)

Aerial Cameras	2
Signal Flags (sets)	6
Air Signals (boxes)	12
Flares (boxes)	12

ENGINEER EQUIPMENT:

Bulldozers	14
Carryalls	2
Cement Mixers	6
Rock Crushers	1
Steamrollers	12
Tractors, Misc.	47
Tractors, Caterpillar	8
Rollers, Misc.	8
Wheel Barrows	15
Ponton Bridge Sections	3
Boats, Collapsible	5

Engineer Equipment (Continued)	Amount
Topographic Sets	1
Seismograph	1
Surveyors Transit	2
Surveyors Tripod	1
Surveyors Stakes (set)	1
Power Plants	2
Electric Welding Set	2
Water Purification Unit	2
Water Pumps	2
Air Compressors	1
Picks	34
Sledges	40
Shovels	30
Wrenches	8
Hammers, Misc.	3
Hammers, Blacksmith	48
Blacksmith's Set	1
Saws, Misc.	16
Plane	1
Wood Chisels	12
Wood Bits	23
Drills, Diamond (cases)	5
Wire Cutters	4
Vises	5
Tools, Misc. (boxes)	4
Tool Chests, W/Tools	4
Wood Case, W/Tools	1
Blow Torch	1
Dies & Taps (sets)	2
Cant Hooks	12
Cruppers	5
Pulley Blocks (cases)	1
Wire (spools)	148
Bolts, Large (each)	13
Nails, 5" (cases)	3
Nails, Misc. (cases)	16
Pipe, ½" (feet)	580
Pipe, U/I Size (pieces)	695

Engineer Equipment (Continued)	Amount
Pipe Fittings (cases)	3
Drift Pins	42
Rivets (cases)	200
Strainers, Circular	40
Water Cans	3
Tar Paper (rolls)	13

MEDICAL EQUIPMENT:

Adhesive Tape (rolls)	500
Bicarbonate of Soda (cases)	9
Dental Supplies, Misc. (chests)	50
Field Hospital (complete)	1
Forceps	25
Hypo Needles	500
Iodine (quarts)	150
Medical Bandages (cases)	4
Medical Bandages (each)	5,000
Medical Chests	195
Medical Supplies, Misc. (cases)	211
Medical Supplies, Misc. (tons)	50
Novacain & Vitamins (bottles)	1,200
Oxygen Tents	3
Pulmotor	1
Rubber Tubing (feet)	200
Surgical Instruments (sets)	2
Sulpha Drugs (bottles)	1,000
Syringes	200

Medical Equipment (Continued)	Amount
Veterinary Set	1

CHEMICAL WARFARE EQUIPMENT:

	Amount
Chloropicrin (tanks)	20
Chloropicrin (cylinders)	25
Decontamination Agents (cases)	60
Gas Masks, Misc.	922
Gas Masks, Navy Type 99	14
Gas-Mask Testers, Misc.	3
Gas-Mask Testers, New Type	2
Gas-Mask Testers, Unit	3
Gas Detectors, Persistent (cases)	7
Gun Boxes	14
Flame Throwers	45
Flame Thrower Chests	5
Flame Thrower Nozzles	28
Flame Thrower Nozzle Chests	5
Flame Thrower Pressure Tanks	1
Pressure Regulators	9
Protective Clothing (piece)	1,300
Protective Suit, Heavy Rubber	4
Protective Covers, Horse	12
Protective Leggins, Horse	228
Smoke Candles (cases)	62
Smoke Candles Type 94 (Cases)	60
Smoke Candles, Self-Proj. (cases)	4

Chemical Warfare Equipment (Continued)	Amount
Smoke Generators (F-S)	10
Smoke Grenades (cases)	13
Smoke Pots (cases)	5

QUARTERMASTER EQUIPMENT:

Rations

Bamboo Shoots, Pickled (cases)	100
Candy & Soap (tons)	5
Canned Rations (tons)	2
Cigarettes (cartons)	250
Crackers (cases)	125
Dried Carabao (cases)	500
Energy Rations. A/C Spec. (cases)	20
Oil, Cooking (cans)	1,200
Oil Pills (boxes)	500
Potatoes, Irish (bags)	500
Rice (bags)	5,970
Rice (lbs)	46,580
Salt (bags)	236
Salt (lbs)	100
Seaweed (cases)	30
Sugar (bags)	125
Tea, Green (bags)	25
Tobacco, Plug (boxes)	20

Clothing

Belts, Leather (cases)	1
Pajamas (bales)	24
Shoes, Rubber (cases)	10
Trousers, Shirts, Asstd (cases)	201
Uniforms	10

Miscellaneous

Adding Machine	2

Miscellaneous (Continued)

Item	Amount
Ammo Pouches	156
Beds, Double-Deck	10
Bed Rolls	4
Blankets	1,435
Camouflage Nets (cases)	29
Canvas (bales)	2
Carbide Lights	5
Carabaos	25
Carriers, MG Clips	6
Cement (bags)	310
Chairs	8
Cloth (yards)	575
Desks, Field	4
Fishnet	1
Gasoline (drums)	344
Grease (cans)	1
Grease (5-gal drums)	9
Halters	11
Hopper, Rice	1
Horses	80
Horse Shoes	354
Kitchen, Field	4
Kitchen, Rolling	2
Oil Cans	216
Oil (15-gal drums)	67
Oil, Kerosene (55-gal drums)	35
Packs, Waterproof	8
Pack Carriers, W/Cinches	78
Punk (cases)	600

Miscellaneous (Continued)

Item	Amount
Rope (feet)	30,000
Saddle	1
Sewing Machine, Hand	3
Tables	2
Tent	1
Typewriters	5
Toilet Tissue (cases)	10
Ammo Carts	25
Caribao Carts	324
Field Carts	2
Barges	1
Boats, Motor	10
Boats, "Q"	141
Boats, Misc.	38
A/C, U/I	125
A/C Engines	302
A/C Tires	261
A/C Accessories (tons)	22
A/C Aux. Fuel Tanks	87
RR Locomotives	5
RR Cars	575
Refrigerators	2
Pressing Machine	1
Barrage Balloon	1
Printing Machine	1
Scales, Balance	1
Oil Lamps	26
Polish, Simonize (cases)	3
Misc. Supplies (tons)	75
Food Dumps (large)	2

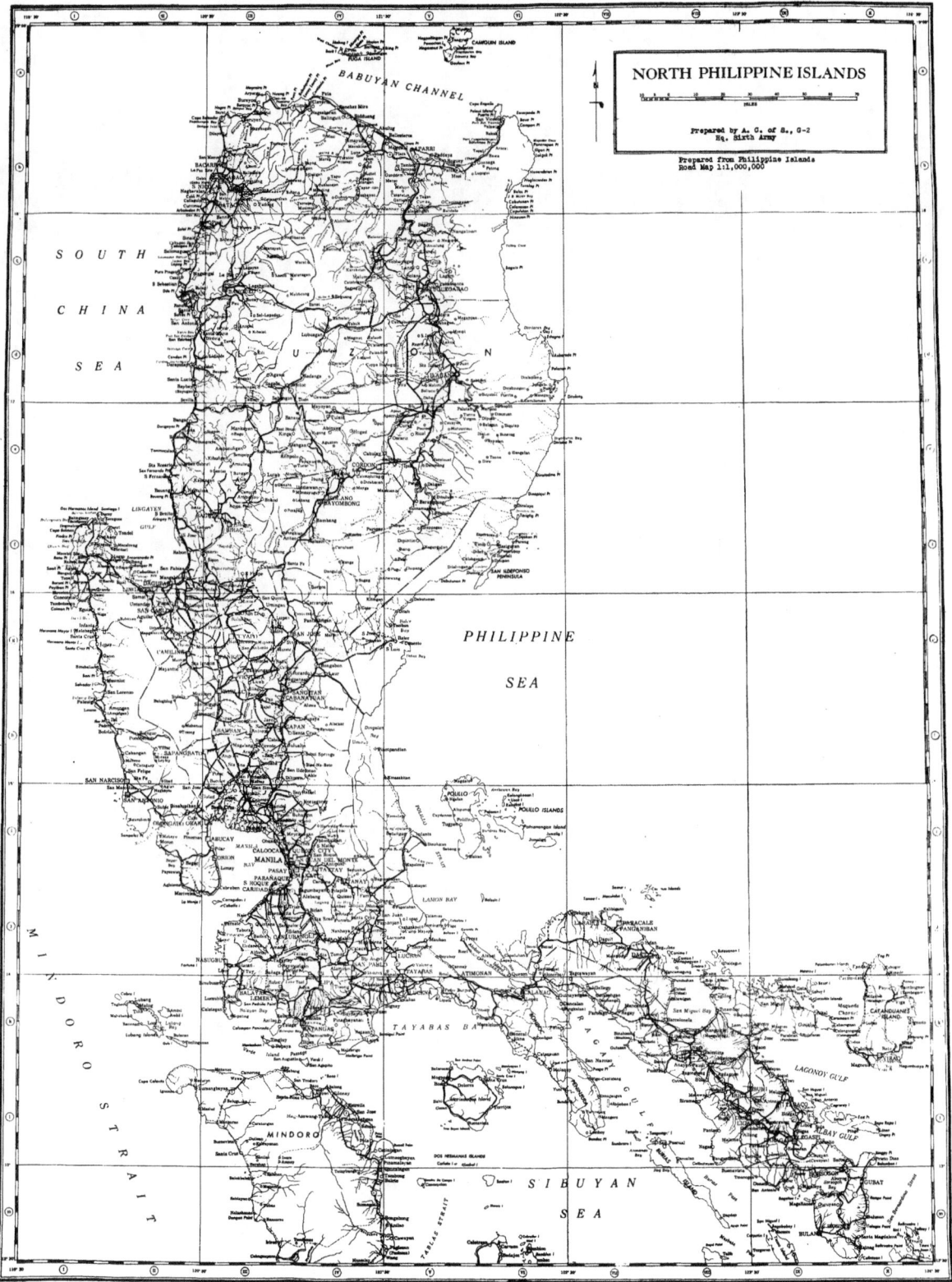

www.ingramcontent.com/pod-product-compliance
Lightning Source LLC
Chambersburg PA
CBHW082117230426
43671CB00015B/2723